ABOUT THE AUTHOR

Tom Verde is a writer and journalist. He holds a Master's Degree in Islamic Studies and Christian-Muslim Relations from Hartford Seminary. He has lived and traveled in the Middle East, North Africa, and Europe and written about religion, history, and culture for the *New York Times*, National Public Radio, Religion News Service, and *AramcoWorld* magazine.

Queens of Islam

The Muslim World's Historic Women Rulers

by Tom Verde

OLIVE BRANCH PRESS

An imprint of Interlink Publishing Group, Inc.
Northampton, Massachusetts

First published in 2025 by

Olive Branch Press
An imprint of Interlink Publishing Group, Inc.
46 Crosby Street, Northampton, MA 01060
www.interlinkbooks.com

Back cover illustration is by Spanish painter Leonar Solans

Grateful acknowledgement to *AramcoWorld* for permission to use text written by the author and previously published in the magazine in 2016 as part of the "Malika" series.

Library of Congress Cataloging-in-Publication data available
ISBN-13: 978-1-62371-794-0

Printed and bound in the United States of America

The believers, both men and women, are allies of one another.
—Sura 9:71, The Holy Qur'an

Well-behaved women seldom make history.
—Laurel Thatcher Ulrich

CONTENTS

A Note on Names, Titles, Spellings, and Sources

Khayzuran, Khayzaran, or Khaizuran? Razia or Radia? There are multiple variations on the many Arabic, Persian, Turkish, and Malay names that appear in this book, depending on the time frame of the source (medieval, Renaissance, early modern, modern) and its origins, i.e., Middle Eastern, Central Asian, European, etc. Given the dizzying variety of spellings found in both primary and secondary source materials, I have chosen to shorten cumbersome proper names and remove the diacritical marks that appear in Arabic and other non-Western languages, to make them less confusing.

Thus, Abū Ja'far Hārūn ibn Muhammad al-Rāshīd becomes Harun al Rashid and simply Harun thereafter. The same goes for the definite article "Al" that prefaces many Arabic names. I leave off the hyphen in Al-Mansur, for example, rendering it Al Mansur and Mansur on subsequent reference. The exception to this rule is when quoting sources, both primary and secondary. In these cases I have left the spellings and diacritics as they appear in the original texts. Out of respect, I also make an exception for Islam's holy book, spelling it Qur'an, which is how it is transliterated into English from Arabic, the original language of its revelation.

As for titles, these too vary, from source to source and century to century. The women profiled in this book are variably referred to as "queen," "sultana," "empress," or "princess," depending on their ranks at any given time and the type of Islamic state where they lived. Many reigned over sultanates, which are Islamic states governed by a sultan, the rough equivalent of a European king. Thus they were often referred to as "queens" by Western chroniclers.

Since I too am a Western chronicler, I tend to use "queen" as the royal designation for the women in this book, except where "sultana" (the feminine form of sultan) is the more proper and accurate title.

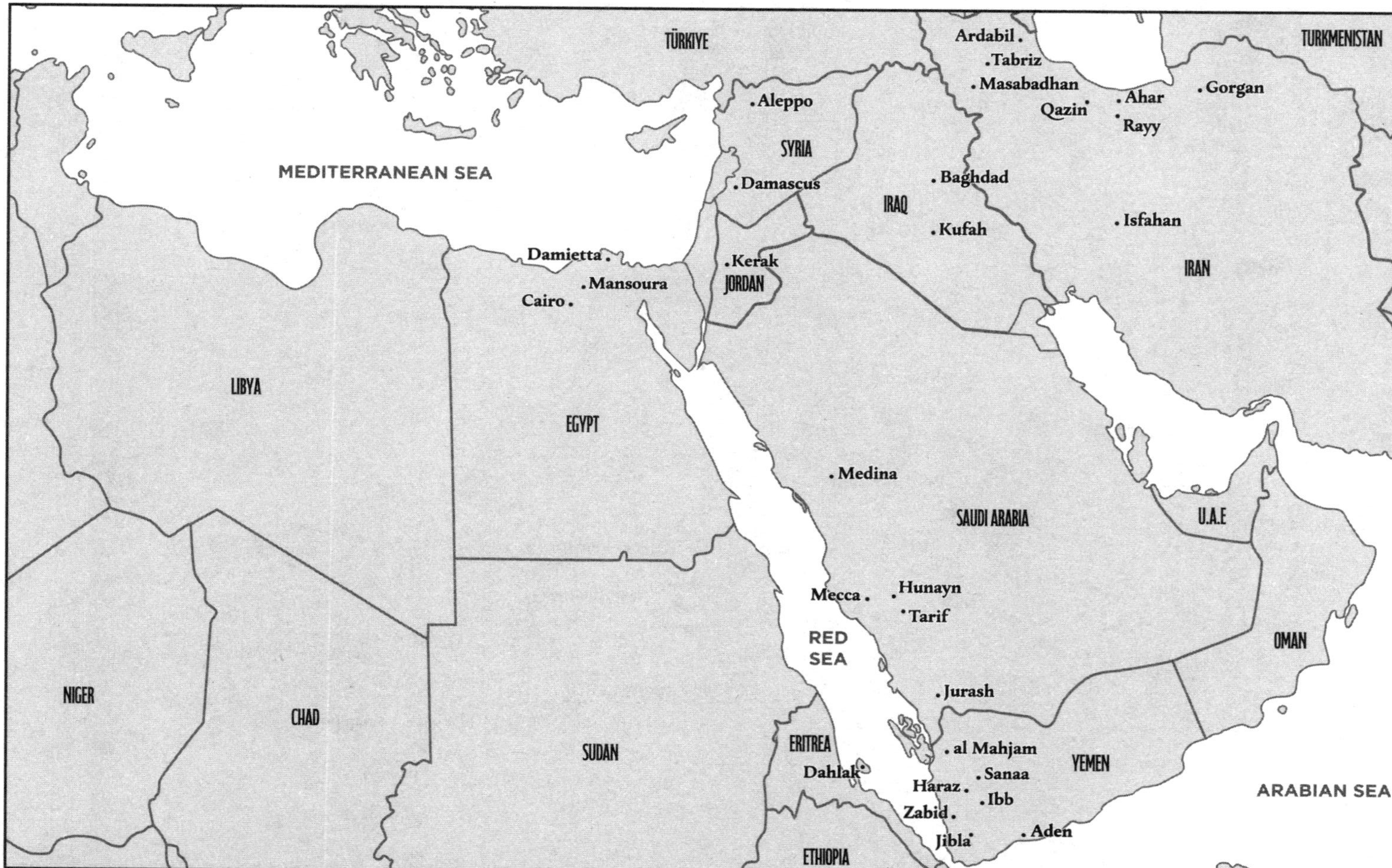

The Middle East

India & Afghanistan

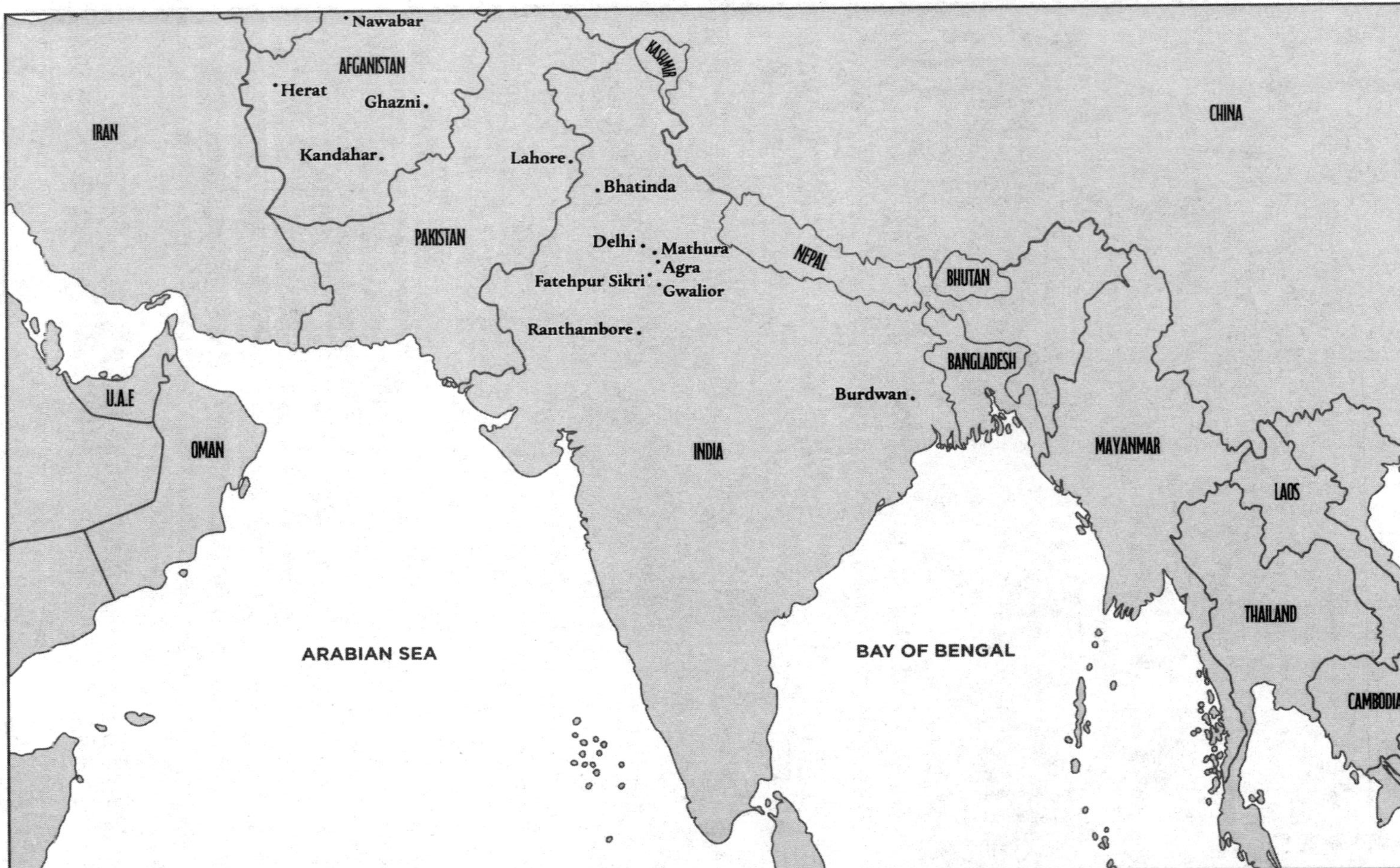

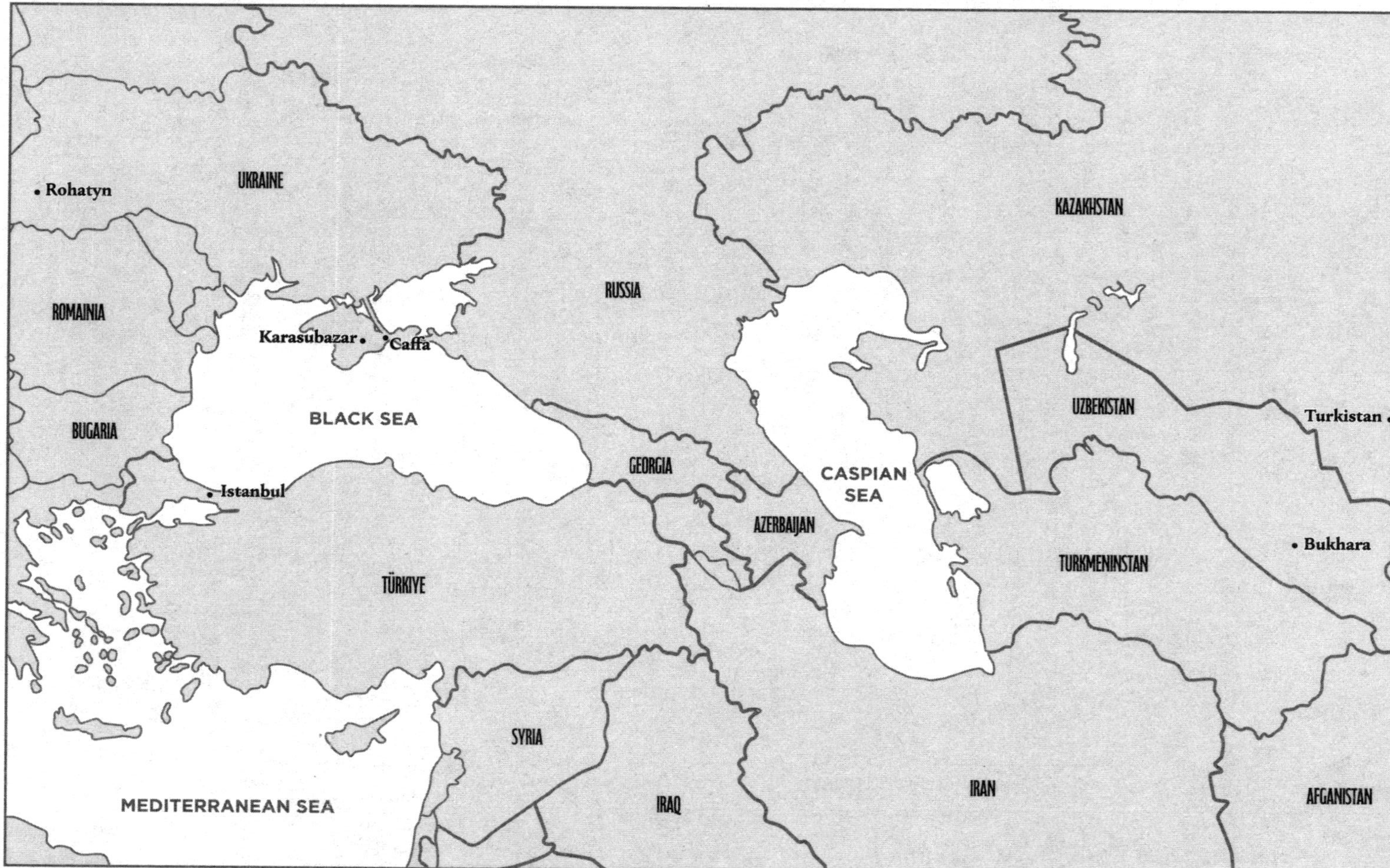

Central Asia

North and West Africa

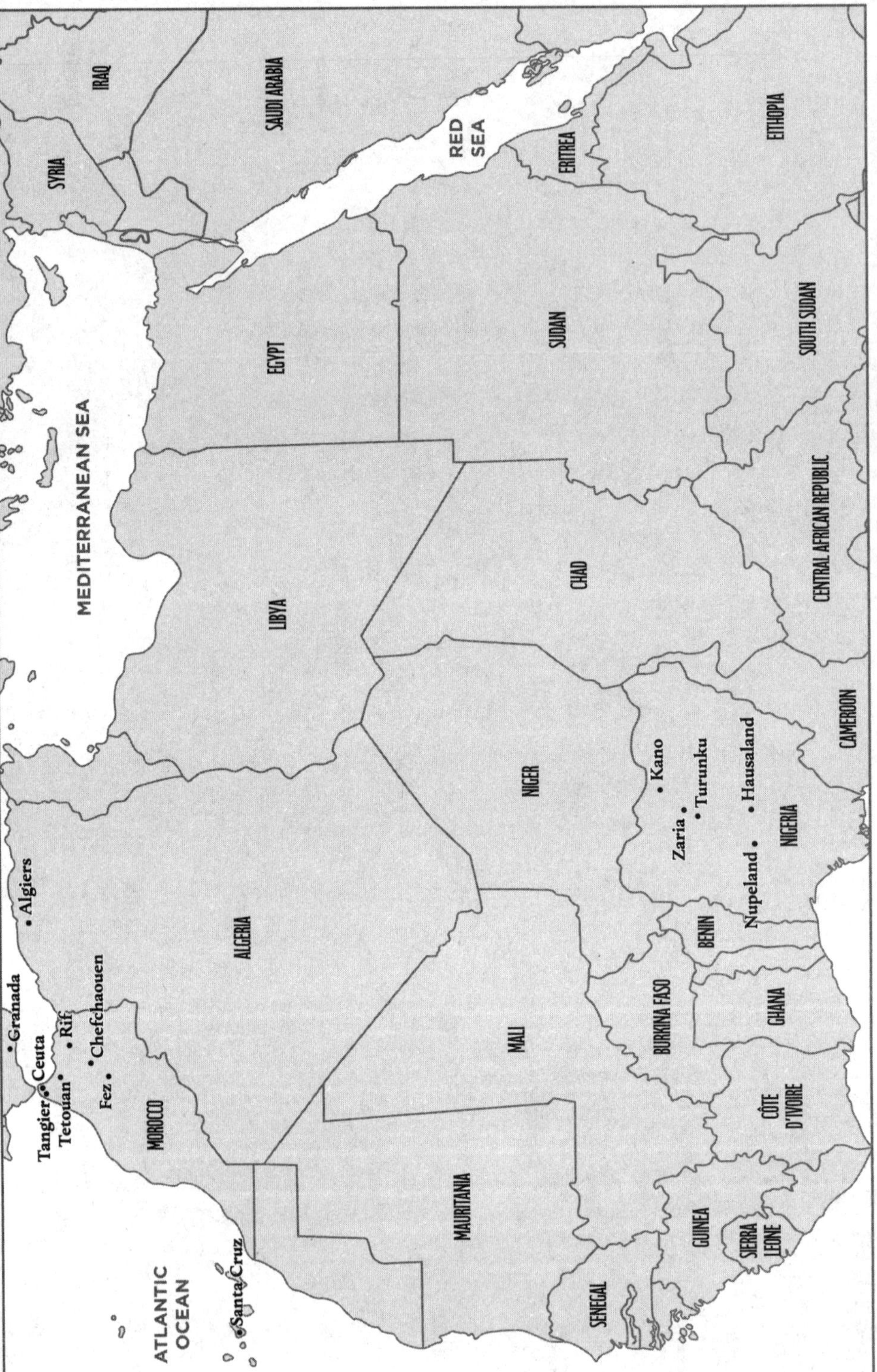

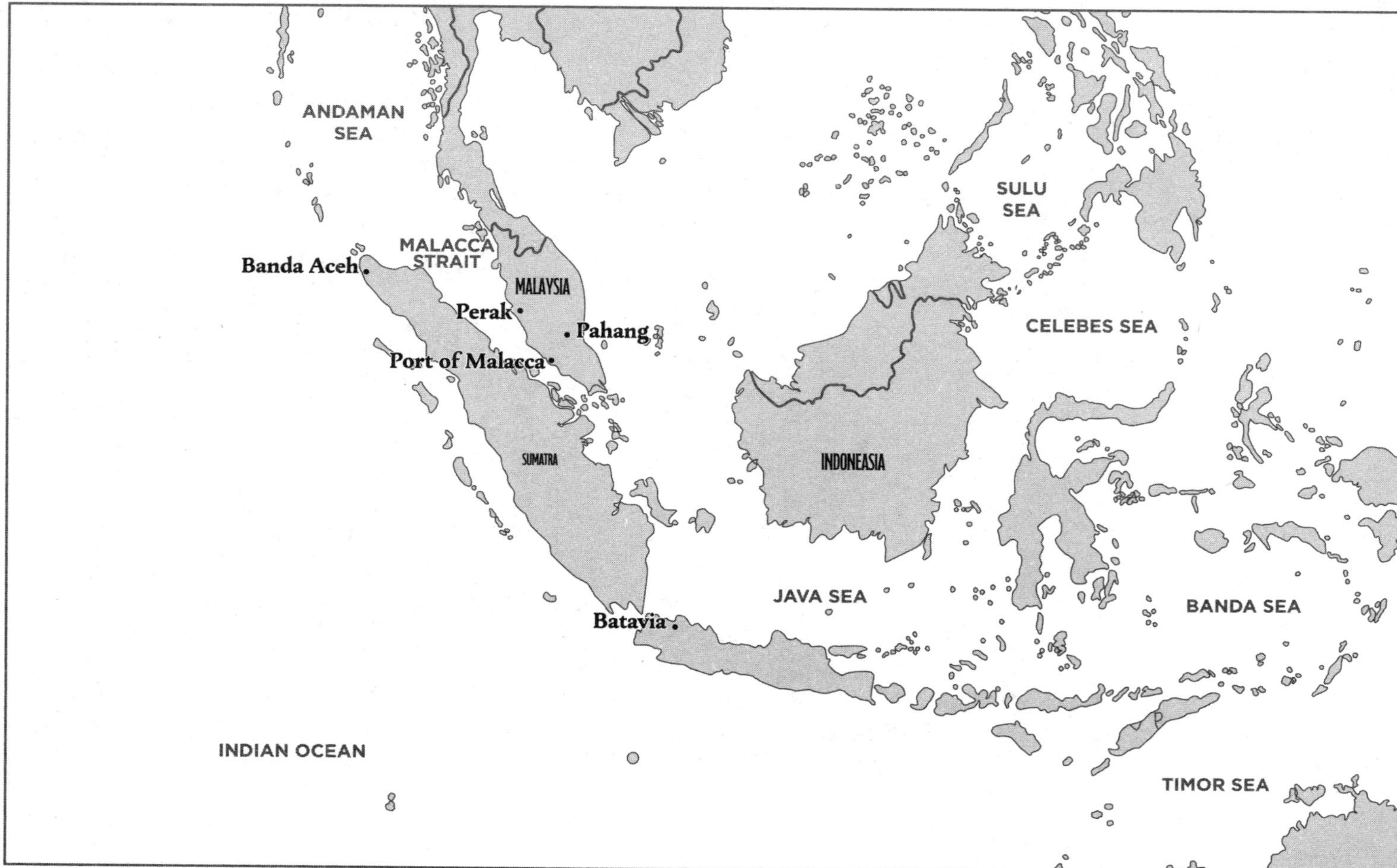

Indonesia & Malay Peninsula

Who's Who/What's What

CHAPTER 1

Abu al Saffah, "the Bloodshedder" (r. 750–754): First caliph and founder of the Abbasid Empire, centered in Baghdad.

Al Khayzuran (d. 789): Wife of Abbasid caliph Al Mahdi, mother of caliphs Harun al Rashid and Musa al Hadhi; first woman to rule over an Islamic state.

Al Mahdi (r. 775–785): Abbasid caliph, son of Al Mansur and husband of Al Khayzuran.

Al Mansur (r. 754–775): Abbasid caliph and founder of Baghdad.

Al Tabari (839–923): Persian historian of Abbasid Empire.

Barmakids: Persian administrators who rose to prominence under the Abbasids.

Fadl ibn Rabi: Administrator who served under caliphs Musa al Hadhi and Harun al Rashid.

Ghitrif: brother of Al Khayzuran.

Harun al Rashid (r. 786–809): Abbasid caliph, son of Al Mahdi and Al Khayzuran; brother of Musa al Hadhi.

Jafar bin Yahya al-Barmaki (767–803): Persian vizier of Harun al Rashid; son of Yahya.

Jafar: Son of caliph Musa al Hadhi.

jawari: Female slaves.

Musa al Hadhi (r. 785–786): Abbasid caliph, son of Al Mahdi and Al Khayzuran, brother of Harun al Rashid.

Rita: Daughter of Abu al Saffah, wife of Al Mahdi; her offspring were passed over for succession in favor of Al Khayzuran's sons.

Salsal: Sister of Al Khayzuran, mother of Zubayda.

Yahya, aka Yayha al Barmaki (d. 806): vizier to Harun al Rashid; ally and most favored advisor of Al Khayzuran.

Zubayda (765–831): Cousin and wife of Harun al Rashid.

CHAPTER 2

Ahwal (Said al Ahwal): Rebellious leader of Najahid dynasty (see Najahids).

Ali bin Muhammad al Sulayhi (r. 1047–1066): Founder of Yemen's Sulayhid dynasty; father of Arwa.

Al Hussain ibn at Tubbay: A general in the service of Arwa; commander of district of Ash Shair.

Al Mufaddal: A military commander in the service of Arwa.

Al Mukarram Ahmad (Mukarram) (r. 1067–1084): Sulayhid sultan of Yemen; son of Ali bin Muhammad al Sulayhi and Asma; husband of Arwa.

Al Mustansir (r. 1036–1094): Eighth Fatimid caliph.

Amir (also *Emir*): A monarch, aristocrat or high-ranking political or military office holder.

Arwa bint Ahmad al Sulayhi (c.1048–1138): Sulayhid Queen of Yemen; daughter in-law of Queen Asma.

Asgar (Mukarram al Asgar): Mukarram "the Younger," son of Arwa and Al Mukarram Ahmad.

Asma bint Shihab al Sulayhi (r. 1047–1067): Sulayhid Queen of Yemen; mother in-law of Queen Arwa.

dawah: Islamic missionary activity.

Ismaili: A branch of Shia Islam that regards Ismail as the rightful seventh imam in the line of succession from the Prophet Muhammad.

Najahids: Sunni Muslim dynasty that ruled parts of Yemen from 1022 to 1158. Enemies of the Sulayhids.

Najib al Dawla: Fatimid nobleman sent from Cairo to provide Arwa with military support. Made an unsuccessful attempt to overthrow her.

Najm al Din Umara (1121–1174): Historian of Fatimid Yemen.

qadi: An Islamic judge.

Saba bin Ahmad al Sulayhi: Cousin of Al Mukarram Ahmad, named by him as his successor. Arwa's second husband.

Tayyibis: A sect of Ismailism that considers Abul Qasim al Tayyib (b.1129/1130) as the legitimate twenty-first imam. With the support of Arwa, the Tayyibis spread their doctrines to India and beyond.

CHAPTER 3

Chahalgani: The "Corps of Forty," a council of Turkish slave amirs who served as an advisory cabinet to the Sultan of Delhi during the thirteenth and fourteenth centuries.

Mahomed Kasim Ferishta (c. 1570–1620): Persian historian of the Delhi Sultanate.

Rukn al Din Firuz (r. April 30, 1236 –November 19, 1236): Sultan of Delhi, son of Iltutmish and Shah Turkan, half brother of Razia.

Abdul Malik Isami (1311–1350): Delhi-born historian of the Muslim rule in India.

Minhaj al Siraj Juzjani (1193–after 1266): Principal historian of the Mamluk Sultanate of Delhi, contemporary of Sultan Razia.

Muhammad Ghori (r. 1173–1206): Afghan warlord; founder of Ghurid Dynasty in Northern India, which paved the way for the Sultante of Dehli.

Muiz ud din Bahram (r. 1240–1242): Sultan of Delhi; son of Sultan Iltutmish; half brother of Sultan Razia.

Qutubuddin: Son of Sultan Iltutmish, executed by order of Shah Turkan.

Qutubiddin Aybek (r. 1206–1210): General under Muhammad Ghori; first sultan of the Sultanate of Delhi.

Rajputs: A Hindu warrior class of aristocrats; enemies of the Delhi Sultanate.

Razia (r: 1236–1240): Sultan of Delhi; daughter of Shams ud Din Iltutmish.

Shams ud Din Iltutmish (r. 1211–1236): Third Sultan of Delhi; father of Razia.

Turkan Shah: Mother of Razia; wife of Iltutmish.

Shah Turkan (1195–1236): Stepmother of Razia; ruled as Queen mother during the brief reign of Firuz.

CHAPTER 4

Izz al Din Aybak (r: 1250–1257): First Mamluk sultan of Egypt; second husband of Shajarat.

Fakhr al Din: Commander of the Egyptian army under Shajarat.

Al Maqrizi (1364–1442): Medieval Egyptian historian.

Al Malik al Salih (r. 1240–1249): Ayyubid Sultan of Egypt; first husband of Shajarat.

Shajarat al Durr (r. 1250): First and only female sultan of Egypt.

Turanshah (r. 1249–1250): Sultan of Egypt; son of Salih.

CHAPTER 5

Hurra (r. 1515/1519–1542): Governor of Tetouan, Morocco. Aka Sayidda al Hurra (not to be confused with Yemen's Queen Arwa, who was also known by this title).

Moulay Ahmed al Hassan al Mandari: Hurra's son-in-law.

Moulay Mohammed: Hurra's half brother, governor of the Moroccan city of Chefchaouen.

Moulay Ali Ibn Rashid: Hurra's father; founder of Chefchaouen.

Ahmed al Wattasi (r. 1526–1545/1547–1549): Sultan of Morocco; husband of Hurra.

CHAPTER 6

Hafsa (1472–1534): Mother of Ottoman sultan Suleiman I.

Haseki: Title for the royal consort of the Ottoman sultan.

Hurrem Haseki Sultan/Roxelana (1504–1558): Ottoman queen. Concubine and wife of Suleiman from 1533; mother of six of his children.

Ibrahim Pasha (1495–1536): Suleiman's boyhood friend and grand vizier.

Mahidevran (1500–1581): Concubine of Suleiman, mother of his son, Mustafa.

Mehmed (1521–1565): Son of Suleiman and Roxelana.

Mihrimah (1522–1578): Only daughter of Suleiman and Roxelana; wife of Rustem.

Mustafa (1516–1553): Son of Suleiman and Mahidevran.

Ogier Ghiselin de Busbecq: Sixteenth-century Flemish writer; ambassador to the Ottoman court in 1581.

Rustem (1505–1561): Husband to Mihrimah, son-in-law of Roxelana; served as grand vizier after Ibrahim Pasha's death.

Suleiman I, "The Magnificent" (r. 1520–1566): Tenth sultan of the Ottoman Empire; husband of Roxelana.

Valide Sultan: Title of the queen mother; highest-ranking member of the harem.

CHAPTER 7

Abbas I, "The Great" (r. 1588–1629): Fifth Safavid Shah of Iran.

Haydar (1544–1576): Son of Shah Tahmasp I; brother to Ismail II and half brother to Pari Khan Khanum. Reigned for a single day as self-declared shah, May 14–15, 1576.

Iskandar Beg Munshi (1561–1634): Iranian court historian.

Ismail I (r. 1501–1524): Founder and first Shah of Safavid Iran.

Ismail II (r. 1576–1577): Third Shah of Safavid Iran; brother to Haydar and half brother to Pari Khan Khanum.

Khayr al Nisa Begum (r. 1578–1579): Wife of Shah Mohammad Khundabanda, sister-in-law of Pari Khan Khanum. Reigned briefly as queen mother after Pari, whom she had ordered killed.

Mahde Ulya: Title of the queen mother of the shah.

Mohammad Khundabanda (r. 1578–1587): Fourth shah of Iran; son of Tahmasp I; husband of Khayr al Nisa Begum.

Pari Khan Khanum (1548–1579): Persian princess; daughter of Shah Tahmasp I. Intermittent ruler of Safavid Iran after the death of her father.

Qizilbash: Turkic militant supporters of the Safavid Empire.

Safavids: Dynasty of Shia rulers who governed Iran from 1501–1736.

Shah Tahmasp I (r. 1524–1576): Son and successor of Ismail I; father of Pari Khan Khanum.

Shahzada Sultanum: Sister of Shah Tahmasp.

CHAPTER 8

Amina (1533–1610): Queen of the northern Nigerian kingdom of Zazzau under the royal name Amina Sarauniya Zazzau; reigned from 1576 to 1610.

Bakwa Turunku (r. 1536–1566): Queen of Zazzau; mother of Amina.

Muhammad Bello (r. 1781–1837): Historian and first Caliph of Sokoto, West Africa.

Nikatau: King of Zazzau; father of Amina and husband of Bakwa Turunku.

Nohir: King of Zazzau; father, or possibly father-in-law, of Bakwa Turunku; grandfather of Amina.

Karama: King of Zazzau; Amina's uncle, or possibly brother.

Zaria: Amina's sister.

CHAPTER 9

Akbar "the Great" (r. 1556–1605): Third Mughal emperor, father of Jahangir.

Ali Quli Khan Istajlu, the "Tiger Slayer" (d. 1607): Courtier and administrator in the service of Mughal Emperor Jahangir; first husband of Nur Jahan.

Asmat Begam (d. 1621): Mother of Nur Jahan; wife of Mizra Ghiyas Beg.

Alexander Dow (d. 1779): Eighteenth-century Scottish writer and military officer in the East India Company.

Jahangir (r. 1605–1627) Mughal emperor, born Prince Salim, son of Akbar the Great; husband of Nur Jahan.

Khafi Khan (c. 1664–1732): An Indo-Persian historian of the Mughal Empire.

Mizra Ghiyas Beg (1544–1622): Civil servant under Jahangir; father of Nur Jahan.

Mughals: Dynastic, Muslim rulers of India from 1526–1857.

Muhamad Hadi: Secretary and diarist of Jahangir.

Mutamad Khan: Contemporary biographer of Jahangir.

Nur Jahan (1577–1645): Born Mihr un Nissa, Mughal empress, who reigned from 1620–1627. Wife of Jahangir; daughter of Mizra Ghiyas Beg and Asmat Begam.

Johannes de Laet (1581–1649): One of the directors of the Dutch East India Company. Author of *The Empire of the Great Mogul*, a history of the Mughal Empire.

Niccolao Manucci (1638–1717): Venetian traveler and author whose "Storia do Mogor" was a firsthand account of Mughal history and life.

Khurram (r. 1638–1658): Fifth Mughal emperor, whose royal name was Shah Jahan; son of Jahangir.

CHAPTER 10

Abdul Rauf al Singkel (1615–1693): Islamic scholar and jurist; served as chief religious judge under Sultana Safiatuddin.

Iskandar Muda (r. 1607–1636): Twelfth sultan of the Sumatran kingdom of Aceh; father of Sultana Safiatuddin.

Iskandar Thani (r. 1635–1641): Thirteenth sultan of Aceh; husband of Sultana Safiatuddin.

Nuruddin al Raniri (d. 1658): Islamic scholar and jurist; served as chief religious judge under Sultana Safiatuddin.

orang kaya: Indonesian aristocratic merchant class who operated as a sort of cabinet for the sultans of Aceh.

Safiatuddin (r. 1641–1675): Sultana of Aceh, born Putri Sri Alam in 1612; ruled under the royal name Tajul Alam Safiatuddin Syah.

Preface

In 2011, I was asked by an academic journal if I might be interested in reviewing a new history of Cairo written by architectural historian Nezar Al Sayyad. As I thumbed through the pages of the richly informative book, I was intrigued by the story of Shajarat al Durr, a key figure in the city's medieval history, who Al Sayyad described as "the first and only woman to rule Egypt during Muslim times." A Muslim woman? Ruling an Islamic kingdom? In medieval times? Certainly I was aware of prominent Muslim women who held political office in Muslim-majority countries during the modern era. Perhaps the most famous was Pakistan's Prime Minister Benazir Bhutto, assassinated in 2007 by a suicide bomber with suspected ties to various Islamic extremists groups as well as disaffected factions within the Pakistani government. A subsequent news report from the BBC on the assassination described Bhutto as "the first woman to lead a Muslim country," a characterization I now know to be inaccurate.

Had Shajarat in fact been the first? Were there others? One of the delights (and curses!) of being a writer is curiosity, and before long I learned that Shajarat was just one of many dynamic, powerful women who sat on the thrones of various Muslim kingdoms, sultanates, and empires throughout history, stretching back nearly to the founding of Islam itself. Some ascended the throne in their own right, others served as regents for incapacitated husbands or male successors then too young to rule. Some proved insightful and able administrators, courageous military commanders, or both. Others differed little from their equally flawed, power-hungry male counterparts, sowing the seeds of their own downfalls. Royal families being royal families, their reigns were also rife with palace intrigue, love affairs, sex scandals, and power grabs. What their stories made clear is that Islam's attitude towards the role of women in politics and society is far from monolithic and that, historically, Islamic culture has not unilaterally condemned equality among the sexes. Instead, the record shows that throughout the faith's long history, individual women have asserted themselves, achieved positions of power, served as effective rulers, and been recognized as such by those they governed as well as the diplomats who attended their courts. Their leadership demonstrates that, prior to the modern era, there were Muslim societies that accepted and supported the authority of strong women who, by their nature, embodied feminism long before it became a sociological concept.

After writing a series of profiles of a half dozen such women for *AramcoWorld* magazine in 2016, I determined that their stories, and those of nearly a dozen more Muslim women rulers, deserved to be gathered and told. Hence the publication of this book.

Queens of Islam examines the lives of fifteen of the most remarkable female leaders of Muslim dynasties, empires, and sultanates, from Islam's earliest centuries up to early modern times. Like the Muslim world itself, the book's geographic scope is wide, ranging east from the shores of Morocco to the scattered islands of Indonesia, and south from the steppes of Ukraine to the Indian subcontinent.

By the eighteenth century, the relentless juggernaut of European colonialism began gobbling up and subjugating this vast territory, eroding the political power of Islam's aging, faded empires. There were still Muslim women who ruled after 1700, but many did so under the yoke of colonialism. Examining the roughly thousand-year arc of history from the Abbasid Empire (founded 750 CE) through the close of the seventeenth century keeps the focus on an era when Islamic states still ruled a good bit of the world, and when there were Muslim women, those in this book included, who did so as well.

Many of their names are known to scholars and specialists, to whom I am deeply indebted (see Bibliography). But academics were not the primary audience I had in mind when I began this project, though I hope it is of value to some. Rather, I sought to engage those whose response, whenever I told them I was working on a book about Muslim women rulers throughout history, was, "Really? Were there any?"

I was glad they asked. The answer to that question refutes misrepresentations of women in Muslim culture as subservient, marginalized, and repressed—as some extremists would have it—while honoring the memory of the remarkable female rulers whose lives are celebrated in this book.

CHAPTER 1

Al Khayzuran (d. 789)
Zubayda bint Jafar ibn al Mansur (d. 831)

Baghdad's Legendary Queens

On a late November day in 789, heavy rains falling from a leaden sky pelted the mudbrick walls of Baghdad, transforming its hardpacked, dusty streets into sludgy conduits of mud. It was a good day for a funeral.

Leaving his palace on the western bank of the Tigris, Harun al Rashid, twenty-three-year-old caliph of the Abbasid Empire—"Commander of the Faithful" and "God's Power on Earth"—stepped barefoot into the muck. Forgoing royal finery, he wore instead the humble garments of a mourner: a plain white robe, cinched at the waist with a patched and tattered blue shawl. Upon his shoulder rested the casket of the former female slave Al Khayzuran, Arabic for "the Reed," so-called because of her slender frame. Normally, the life of a slave would have meant little to a man of Harun's power and position. But Khayzuran was no ordinary slave: she was his mother and the most beloved wife of the late caliph Al Mahdi, his father.

Protocol of the day mandated that caliphs exercise emotional restraint at the passing of a woman, even a queen. For a Muslim ruler to serve as chief pallbearer at his mother's funeral, let alone muddy himself to his ankles before the eyes of all men, was an exceptional demonstration of public grief . . . and respect.

The funeral procession crossed the Main Bridge leading from the center of the famously round city to the Rusafah district on the eastern banks of the Tigris. The district was home to the oldest Muslim cemetery on that side of the river, a burial place already sacred to Zoroastrian Persians long before the founding of Islamic Baghdad nearly three decades earlier. Though it was also the final resting place of famed Sunni theologians, jurists, and many a subsequent Abbasid ruler, the crowded graveyard would ultimately be named for the woman being interred there that day: the Khayzuran Cemetery.

Washing the mud from his feet, Harun donned a pair of boots and stepped down into his mother's tomb to offer the requisite prayers for the dead. These duties done, he emerged from the tomb and made the first official proclamation of his reign. The first, that is, without his mother's approval.

"He summoned [one of his close aides, Fadl ibn Rabi] and said to him, 'For some time now . . . I have been intending to confer on you some administrative charge, but my mother has (hitherto) been restraining me and I have accordingly been obedient to her command,'" Harun declared publicly. "'[B]ut now take over the seal ring from Ja'far (b. Yahya al-Barmaki).'" Jafar was the son and successor of Yahya, Khayzuran's longtime ally and favored vizier (chief advisor), keeper of the royal signet ring, the official symbol of administrative power. The mud, the humility, Harun's frank admission of the extent of his mother's role in the management of the empire—all of it testified to Khayzuran's considerable power and influence as the first woman to reign as de facto ruler over an Islamic state. And it all began in a Meccan slave market some three decades earlier.

According to most medieval chroniclers, Khayzuran came from Jurash, in the mountainous Asir region between Yemen and what is now Saudi Arabia. She may have been born in Mecca (as she herself claimed, according to some sources) or perhaps Iraq. She may also have been a Berber, from North Africa. The consensus, however, is that she was at least raised, if not actually born, in Jurash, a remote stopover on the main caravan route linking the southern Arabian Peninsula to the Levant. The date of her birth is also uncertain. Given that she was no more than fifty at the time of her death, she was likely in her mid-forties when she passed, since it is speculated that she first met Harun's grandfather, Abbasid caliph Al Mansur, founder of Baghdad, while he was performing the hajj (pilgrimage to Mecca) in 758. At this time, she was likely somewhere between twelve and fifteen years old, since Mansur declared that she was at a ripe age "for childbearing."*

The occasion of the introduction was Mansur's visit to the slave market of Mecca, where Khayzuran caught the caliph's attention. She was brought there and put up for sale by her master, a member of the Banu Taqif tribe from Taif, to the southeast of the holy city. Other accounts say she was kidnapped in Yemen by slave traders who brought her to Mecca. Either scenario was likely, since the avenues to slavery during this era were varied. Some slaves were captured in battle and hauled off as human booty; others were sent as tribute from conquered regions or as gifts from hopeful allies; still others, perhaps like Khayzuran herself, were kidnapped by roving slave traders.

Under the Abbasids, the slave trade, especially the trade in female slaves (*jawari*), was an increasingly active and profitable enterprise. "Demand for slave women," as one modern scholar noted "came from the highest rulers to poor men who could not afford the dower needed to marry a free woman."

The ethnic origins of slaves were as wide as the Abbasid empire's reach, which stretched from northern India to Egypt and across much of North Africa. An eleventh-century auction catalog by Baghdadi Christian physician Ibn Butlan expounded on the topic of *jawari* diversity and—in cringeworthy sexist and racist detail, from a modern perspective—the pros and cons of each ethnic stereotype.

"Indians," Butlan wrote, possessed "great beauty" and amiability, but had a "tendency to age early." Women from Medina were "well-proportioned" and "[f]it for singing." Zanj (East Africans) were "[d]ancers by instinct" and hard workers. Armenians "[w]ould be pleasing were it not for their monstrous legs" while white-skinned Turks were "treasures for childbirth."

Yemenis, like Khayzuran, Butlan observed, blended the most desirable qualities of Berbers and Medinese (well-spoken, fine physique, good singers,

* While by modern standards, sex with girls this young would clearly be considered child abuse, it should be remembered that for much of human history, women began reproducing at a much earlier age than today. Biblical scholars speculate that one of history's most famous mothers, Mary of Nazareth, was likely fifteen or sixteen when she gave birth to Jesus, a common marriageable age for Jewish women at the time.

personal charm) with the "soft . . . femininity of the Meccans; generally with pretty faces."

There are no known physical descriptions of Khayzuran. But if Butlan's ethnographics are to be trusted, she was fit and slender (as her name, which her future husband gave her, implies; her true given name is unknown), with dark hair and a tanned complexion from a life spent, at least up until that point, mostly outdoors, tending livestock (sheep, cattle, goats, and camels) or coaxing crops of wheat, sesame, and barley from the hardscrabble soil of the Asir's steeply terraced mountainside farms. Like her figure, her hands may also have been slender and delicate and well-suited to playing an instrument. Slaves who showed aptitude were trained in music in Mecca before being offered on the auction block. Such training was an advantage, for in the Abbasid court "concubines whose readiness with verse or skill of voice and fingers charmed the hearts of caliphs." In fact, it may well have been her singing voice, rising angelically above the clamor of the slave market, that caught Mansur's ear, before her good looks drew his eye.

But Khayzuran soon demonstrated that she was more than just a proverbial "pretty face." According to tenth-century Persian historian al Tabari, she learned the Traditions, or *Sunnah* (Islamic social and legal customs and practices) in Mecca. Her instructor was no less than the renowned Syrian theologian Al Awzai (d. 774), founder of the Awzai school of Islamic jurisprudence and a contemporary of Hanifah—another famous jurist—with whom he debated in the public marketplaces of Islam's holiest city. She also gained a reputation for at least freely quoting, if not composing, verses of poetry, which she had inscribed on drinking vessels as gifts to Mahdi and Harun.

Charmed by Khayzuran's intelligence, talent, and beauty, Mansur nonetheless stopped short of buying her himself. Instead, he recommended her to his son, along with his fatherly, frank assessment of her promising childbearing potential. During his interview with the young Yemeni slave, Mansur questioned her about her origins and her family. "Born at Mecca and brought up at Jurash," was reportedly her reply. She added that she had "none but Allah" for kin, though this was a lie, as she would later reveal.

Regardless of her background, for the time being she had one job to do: bear Mahdi children, preferably sons. In 764, she lived up to her obligation by giving birth to a boy, Musa al Hadhi, followed by Harun two years later.

Other children included a third son, Isa, about whom little is known, and a daughter Banuqah (or Banujah), meaning "little lady," upon whom Mahdi doted.

Both Musa and Harun were born in Rayy, near modern Tehran, where Mahdi, not yet caliph at the time, was serving as viceroy for his father. It was sometime after Harun's birth that the young prince brought Khayzuran with him to Baghdad.

Mansur's glittering new city was the center of the Islamic world over which the Abbasids—descendants of the Prophet's uncle, al Abbas, from whom they took their dynastic name—had only recently asserted their authority. The dynasty rose to power in 750 after obliterating their predecessors, the Damascus-based Umayyads, at the Battle of the Great Zab River in northern Iraq. The rout was thorough, led by Mansur's aptly titled brother, Abu "al Saffah" ("the Bloodshedder"), who saw to it that every surviving Umayyad royal was tracked down and executed. The last Umayyad caliph, Marwan II, met his grisly end in Egypt where he was captured, killed, and had his tongue fed to a cat.

(Only one member of the clan, Abd al Rahman I, managed to escape the Bloodshedder's systematic wrath. After fleeing to the Iberian Peninsula, he established Spain's Islamic kingdom, al Andalus, which survived another seven hundred years. As for the gruesome fate of Marwan's tongue, the custom may date to ancient Egypt and its tradition of cat worship. Those who blasphemed, bore false witness, or criticized the state or the state religion would have their tongues cut out and fed to stray cats in the area. The punishment is thought to be an origin of the phrase "Cat got your tongue?")

In contrast to the Umayyads, who treated non-Arab Muslims as second-class citizens and excluded all but pure-blooded Arabs from positions of power within the government, the Abbasids were far more politically and culturally ecumenical in their approach to running their empire. This included the embrace of Persian administrators (like Yahya) as well as the Persian taste for luxury, on full display in Mansur's magnificent new capital, which he dubbed *Madinat al Salaam* (the City of Peace), erected on the ruins of a Biblical settlement and Persian market town on a bend in the Tigris River.

"Have you seen in any corner of the world/a tranquil abode like Baghdad?!" inquired the ninth-century poet Umara ibn Aqil, and with good reason.

The expansive city spread across both sides of the river and was "covered with parks, gardens, villas and beautiful promenades, and plentifully supplied with rich bazaars, and finely built mosques and baths" wrote the Abbasid-era geographer, Yaqut al Hamawi. In the heart of the metropolis, enclosed by a circular wall about a mile and a half in circumference, stood the main mosque and caliph's palace, featuring gardens "adorned with exquisite taste with plants, flowers, and trees, reservoirs and fountains."

Its houses, ibn Aqil rhapsodized, "overlook[ed] courtyards with open doors,/made beautiful with decorations and ornaments" while the passageways and reception halls of the palaces and mansions of the royal family and court dignitaries were adorned with jewel-studded carpets, columns inlaid with gold and ivory, and gilded verses from the Qur'an. Beyond the courtyards and grand reception rooms, private living quarters were "tastefully furnished with luxurious divans, costly tables, unique Chinese vases and gold and silver ornaments."

These and other luxury goods—diamonds, spices, furs, ivory, and more—flowed into the city's bustling marketplaces from India, China, and the Far East, via the Persian Gulf and Arabian Sea.

"This is the Tigris," Mansur boasted. "[T]here is no obstacle between us and China; everything on the sea can come to us on it."

Overland, camel caravans bearing merchandise from the mountains of Iran to the north and from North Africa, Arabia, Syria, and Europe to the west all converged in the heart of the city thanks to its strategic location along the famed Silk Route. "It was the place," observed the ninth-century Arab geographer and historian Yakubi, "where all the world's wealth was gathered and all the blessings of the universe existed." With a population of half a million people, Baghdad was larger than Constantinople or any other Middle Eastern city, the world's largest metropolis outside of China.

"The least province in my empire, under the least of my servants," Harun once bragged to his rival, the Byzantine emperor, "yields a larger revenue than the whole of thy empire." This was the fabled city of *One Thousand and One Nights*, the famed collection of Middle Eastern folktales ("Aladdin and the Magic Lamp," "Ali Baba and the Forty Thieves," etc.) in which Harun prominently featured. Though much of the magnificent medieval city was long ago crushed to dust by centuries of invasion and destruction, under the Abbasids it represented "the pinnacle of Islamic strength and splendor" during a period known to historians as the Golden Age of Islam. It was an era also renowned for its intellectual achievements. Under the Abbasids, classical Greek works of Plato, Euclid, Aristotle, and Ptolemy as well as Persian and Sanskrit treatises on philosophy, geometry, astronomy, mathematics, medicine, and science were collected and cataloged in the royal library established by Mansur and translated into Arabic by teams of scholars working in Baghdad's famed Bayt al Hikma (House of Wisdom), a translation center/think tank founded by Harun. The translations ultimately made their way to Western Europe, where they were rediscovered by medieval Jewish and Christian scholars who in turn translated them into Hebrew and Latin. These and future generations owed a debt to Abbasid scholars for essentially preserving what became the bedrock canon of Western learning.

Like that of many women in premodern, political Islam, Khayzuran's path to power during this heady age of wealth, wonder and intellectualism—so unlike anything she had known before—was via the harem, a much misunderstood and misrepresented institution.

"Harem" derives from the Arabic word for "forbidden" or "unlawful" and ultimately came to mean an area of the house that was off limits to most males, with the exceptions of the caliph or other close male relations* (see "Harem Fantasies," p. 8).

Under the early Abbasids, the harem wasn't a single place, but collectively referred to the women in the caliph's household—both wives and concubines—many of whom had residences or apartments of their own, with their own staffs of managers, servants, and slaves. Some of these women became independently wealthy, running their own businesses via agents in their employ. Others rose to high positions at court, most notably that of *qahramana* (stewardess) who ran the caliph's household and had the power to make financial and managerial decisions as well as the freedom to move "seamlessly between the private world of the harem and the more public spheres of society."

Like Khayzuran, many women in the harem—often the more physically

* The word shares the same root as "haram," an Islamic doctrine meaning something forbidden (e.g., the consumption of pork) under Islamic tradition, law, or according to the Qur'an.

attractive and intelligent—were trained as musicians, singers, and dancers to entertain at court. Taught how to read and write, they also learned to compose poetry, studied literature, history, and religion, while some additionally pursued philosophy, arithmetic, and science.

A harem education clearly had practical advantages. A flirtatious smile might initially attract the attention of a caliph, crown prince, or wealthy courtier. But maintaining that interest required a fluent, conversational grasp of the topics that interested these men: history, astronomy, literature, and the law. As the late sociologist and feminist historian Fatima Mernissi observed, "Pretty girls who got lost in serious conversations had no chance to be noticed, and even less chance to last." Meanwhile, favorites who quickly realized this "surrounded themselves with competent teachers."

Harem Fantasies

Muslims were hardly the first to domestically segregate the sexes, a Western tradition dating as far back as the gynaeceums, i.e., "women's quarters," of ancient Greece. Yet "forbidden" fruit is often prone to overblown fantasy, and the image of the harem as a place where half-naked women languidly lounged about awaiting their turns in the sultan's bed was an Orientalist fantasy dating to the Ottoman era (see Roxelena, Chapter 6). Such fantasies were largely concocted by Western males—mostly diplomats—to whom access to the harem was denied. Had they gotten access, they would have discovered that many of the residents of the harem weren't engaged there as sex objects but support staff. These female slaves spent most of their days cooking, cleaning, sewing, and generally tending to the dull and often physically demanding chores associated with keeping the harem and the caliph's household up and running. While it is true that some women became sexual partners (concubines), this was not the only purpose of the harem, which functioned in different ways throughout Islamic history, depending on the dynasty.

Thus, the more highly cultured a woman was, or rose to become, the better her chances of survival in the competitive environment of the harem that could be as cutthroat as any corporation where favor or disfavor rested not just on physical attractiveness but on wit, charm, and cleverness. "The harem," it's been said, "was no place for a shrinking violet."

Whatever their motivation for self-improvement, the end result was that residents of the Abbasid harem were among the most highly educated individuals in the Muslim world at the time, not to mention Europe. So despite its enduring reputation as a louche and luxurious den of debauchery, the harem was in many ways closer to a finishing school or women's college than the Playboy Mansion, particularly for a woman of Khayzuran's talent, intelligence, and ambition. We get hints of this early on in her relationship with Mahdi. As a favored concubine, she enjoyed a level of trust and intimacy with him that extended beyond the bedroom and rivaled, if not superseded, that of his first wife (and cousin), Rita, high-born daughter of Saffah, the empire's founder.

Unlike his austere, wispy-bearded, and notoriously chintzy father—whose famed frugality earned him the nickname Abu Dawanik, "Father of the Farthing," i.e., the smallest coin in the kingdom—Mahdi enjoyed the rollicking high life of a prince and heir apparent, spending freely at court on lavish dinners and entertainments, featuring bards, jesters, musicians, and dancers—diversions that Khayzuran equally enjoyed. The two also shared a sense of humor and enjoyed playing practical jokes, as well as mocking Mansur's sour-faced temperament (behind his back!).

This is not to say there were never lovers' quarrels. Khayzuran was known to be demanding, and Mahdi generally assented to her requests, often out of fear of arousing his favorite concubine's fiery temper. On one occasion when he stood his ground (history doesn't provide the precise details of what the fight was about), the caliph left the harem in a fit, his costly clothes ripped to shreds by Khayzuran, who berated him as a "picker of left-overs."

"What good have I ever received at your hands?" she exclaimed, basically advising him not to let the harem door hit him on the way out. Venting his frustration to court scribe and historian Waqidi, (who recorded the incident), Mahdi pointed out the obvious answer to her question: "[I]t was I . . . who bought her from a slave-trader, and she has seen from me what she has seen (of great benefit and favor)."

In the end, the two made up, thanks to the intervention of Waqidi, who defused the situation by coddling Mahdi's male ego, assuring him that women were essentially hysterical by nature. Just consider Eve, made from one of Adam's curved ribs, Waqidi observed, citing an Islamic tradition based on the Bible story. Try and straighten the rib, and it will break. The wise husband is better off just letting it go and accepting women's inherent "crookedness."

The incident was a lesson learned for Khayzuran who, as hotheaded as she could be, recognized that there were limits to her influence, and that she was not the only woman in Mahdi's orbit. While the Qur'an permits up to four wives (so long as a husband can "deal justly," i.e., fairly and equitably with them), men could have as many concubines as they could afford and support.* The far reach of the Abbasid empire provided a steady supply of new slave girls, among them gifted singers and musicians, many of whom often captured the caliph's attention. Mahdi reportedly paid 100,000 dirhams (an exorbitant sum) for one exceptionally attractive *jawari* by the name of Maknuna. Reportedly lithe and slender (Mahdi apparently fancied a type) and famed in her home town of Medina as a talented singer, she was said to have made Khayzuran particularly jealous. "I never had such fear of another woman as I had of her," she later admitted.

At the same time, she was not about to be outmaneuvered by the batting eyelashes of charming rivals. Upon Mansur's death in 775 and Mahdi's ascension to the throne—a rare (for that time) bloodless transition—Khayzuran made one of her first strategic and unprecedented moves to secure power.

"In this year," Tabari succinctly, albeit significantly put it, "al-Mahdi manumitted his slave girl (*umm walad*)** al-Khayzuran and married her."

The manumission of slaves was an act enshrined and encouraged in the Qur'an and Islamic law. It was a win-win for slaves—whose opportunities for social advancement suddenly looked much brighter—and masters, who could anticipate "eternal rewards" for their clemency. Yet at a time when

* Since sophisticated concubines could fetch tens or even hundreds of thousands of dinars on the open market, it was mostly royals, high-ranking court officials, or wealthy merchants who could afford one if not several concubines, of Khayzuran's caliber anyway.

** A title given to a concubine after she bore her master a child.

caliphs were expected to marry fellow members of the aristocracy, elevating Khayzuran's status from slave, to concubine, to wife, to preeminent royal and undisputed ruler of the harem was "a bold break with convention."

Khayzuran soon demonstrated that she had scant regard for convention. Angling for her marriage to Mahdi—who "accommodated his wife's ambitions"—was but the first step. Once established as the most favored woman of the harem, she deftly moved beyond its barriers to "become a strong presence in the corridors of the palace and political circles." She joined Mahdi at court (albeit from behind a screen to preserve her modesty, according to Islamic custom), absorbing the workings of the affairs of state. At her own palace, she heard petitions from members of court, both men and women, as well as generals, nobles, and merchants, asking her to intercede with her husband on their collective behalf. The experience helped her cultivate critical alliances with power brokers at court who were keenly aware of how easily a word of hers in Mahdi's ear could influence political outcomes.

Chief among these bureaucrats were the Barmakids, traditional guardians of the famed Buddhist shrine and pilgrimage center of Nawabar (Nava Vihara) in Balkh, a Persian provincial capital in what is now northern Afghanistan.*

Descended from Buddhist priests, the wealthy and distinguished Barmakids converted to Islam around 705, in the face of the faith's inevitable domination of the region. First entering the service of the Umayyads, the Barmakids switched their allegiance to the Abbasids when they realized the latter would ultimately rule the Middle Eastern Muslim world. The former Buddhists steadily rose in prominence, transitioning from secretaries to the far more powerful, newly minted office of chief advisor to the caliph, a position known by its Persian name, vizier (*wazir*). Model bureaucrats, the Barmakids were "in many ways the public face of the Abbasid government."

In addition to their most trusted ministers, they also became the Abbasids' near relatives, with Khayzuran and Yahya's wife serving as wetnurses for each other's children. At the same time, Yahya became a father figure to Harun while his own son, Jafar, was the young prince's closest boyhood friend and constant companion.

* Until destroyed by the Taliban in 2001, the towering sixth-century twin Buddha statues in neighboring Bamyan were similarly venerated by Buddhist pilgrims.

A man with no patience for inefficiency, Yahya collected revenues from the empire's vast territories, directed public works, orchestrated military operations, sponsored medical and scientific research, and dutifully kept track of imperial correspondence and petitions, often laboring "into nightfall, looking into the affairs of the people and their needs." In short, he was a one-man presidential cabinet.

But it was one woman, Tabari noted, to whom he was answerable: "Al-Khayzurān was the one who had the oversight of affairs; Yahyā used to lay matters before her and do things on her advice."

Further evidence of Khayzuran's power and influence was her summoning from Yemen, around the time of Musa's and Harun's births, the family she had told Mansur she didn't have: her mother, her elder sister Salsal, younger sister Asma, and a brother, Ghitrif (or Ghatrif). It was a big step up for the clan, especially for Ghitrif: when Mahdi's emissaries initially went searching for him in Jurash, they found him working as a farmhand in threadbare clothes. Before presenting him at court, they had to take him shopping for a suitable set of robes.

Asma and Salsal, meanwhile, demonstrated that they shared their sister's taste for luxury, not to mention men. Shortly before Mahdi's marriage to Khayzuran, he sent her on the hajj, promising to wed her upon her return. Taking advantage of her sister's absence, Asma pursued Mahdi, who succumbed to her charms and married her. News traveled fast, and when Khayzuran returned she wasted little time in confronting her erstwhile fiancé, demanding an explanation for what "this affair with Asma" was all about. Mahdi lamely dissembled and basically replied, "Asma who?"

"Your wife," insisted Khayzuran, through gritted teeth.

Backed into a corner, Mahdi declared that the marriage was over and a divorce was forthcoming. Khayzuran may have been personally stung by her sister's—not to mention Mahdi's—betrayal, but there was more at stake than jealousy. While under Islamic law a man may have up to four wives, none of them may be sisters. Given Khayzuran's knowledge of the law, this precept would not have escaped her. In the end, she got her way, and her husband back. Salsal, meanwhile, chose a safer path: marriage to Mahdi's half brother, Jafar, known as "the Younger" (not the Barmakid, but the child of a Kurdish slave who Mansur took as one of his concubines). The union produced two children: a son, Ibrahim, and a daughter, whose given name was Sukainah, or Amat al Azziz (meaning "Handmaid of the Almighty"). But the name her grandfather Mansur affectionately gave her was the one that ultimately stuck: Zubayda ("Little Butterball") "on account of her plumpness."

As an adult, as we shall see, she not only lost her baby fat but stepped into Khayzuran's shoes as the most favored wife of a caliph—Harun—making her simultaneously Khayzuran's niece and daughter in-law. Meanwhile, the high-profile presence of Khayzuran's family in Abbasid government and palace life helped her "weave a power base at court."

But Khayzuran's biggest coup was to persuade Mahdi to designate both Musa (in 776) and Harun (in 782) as exclusive heirs to the caliphate above all others. This strategic move meant disinheriting the sons of his cousin and freeborn first wife, Rita, whose royal lineage would normally have meant her offspring would be first in line for the throne. This had been the case under the Umayyads, who barred the sons of slaves from becoming caliphs. Yet here, once again, Khayzuran, and the Abbasids, broke new ground.

Under Islam, children born to concubines already enjoyed rights and privileges unknown to their counterparts in Europe who, as illegitimate "bastards," were typically denied inheritance. By contrast, in Islamic society, children fathered by a free man and his concubine were not only considered free themselves but inherited shares of their fathers' estates equal to those of children born in wedlock. Until the eighth century, however, that legacy stopped short at ascension to the throne.

Khayzuran convinced Mahdi to abandon this policy in favor of a new paradigm that endured for the next ten centuries. Of the thirty-nine Abbasid caliphs who ruled between 750 and the fall of Baghdad to Mongol invaders in 1258, the majority (thirty-six) were born to *jawari*. Similarly, all the (ironically Umayyad) rulers of Muslim Spain were also the sons of slave women as were most Ottoman sultans.

Regarding Rita's reaction to this policy shift, history provides no evidence of direct tension between her and Khayzuran. The fact that the latter's sons were named as heirs while the former's were never even considered indicates Rita's "tacit recognition of the futility of challenging" her rival.

As Khayzuran's political power continued to increase, so did her personal wealth. Like other high-placed women in the Abbasid court, she had her own palace, likely in Rusafah, from which she ran a textile and an embroidery business with a factory based in Kufah. Paid agents "in the Lady's service" reported to her on daily operations, management, and profits. Whether made from her own factory's output or from any of the multitude of silks and costly materials that flowed into Baghdad via trade with both East and West, she was said to have owned eighteen thousand finely embroidered silken gowns and robes. She also acquired numerous properties in and around Baghdad, including an area that came to be named for her—Khaiyzuraniyyah, "an honour . . . not given to any other 'Abbasid concubines or free women"—as well as villages and vast estates on the outskirts of the city and as far away as Egypt and Mesopotamia. Her immense wealth made her the richest person in the Muslim world at the time, second only to the caliph himself. By the time of her death, her annual income was calculated at an astounding 160,000,000 dirhams, equivalent to roughly half the state revenue.

She was known to be generous with her wealth. On her first pilgrimage to Mecca, she had made the hajj when still a slave. Twelve years later she returned to the holy city—where she was once bought and sold—as a *malika* (a queen), with the power and the means to freely distribute alms and fund public works. These projects included the purchase of the house where it was believed the Prophet was born, which she had transformed into a mosque known as the Mosque of the Nativity. She also purchased, apparently for her personal use, the adjoining "House of Arqam," a residence that belonged to the Prophet's neighbor, Arqam bin Abil Arqam. It was here that the earliest converts to Islam secretly met to perform their *salah* (ritualistic prayers) and listen to Muhammad's lessons and Qur'anic revelations, at a time when followers of the new faith were being persecuted by the Meccan authorities. The house subsequently became known as the Dar al Khayzuran (Khayzuran's House).*

* The mosque survived until the mid-twentieth century, when Saudi authorities had it torn down in accordance with their ultra-orthodox Wahhabist Islamic doctrines, which frown upon the veneration of tombs, shrines, and sites of religiously historical significance lest such attention lead to the worship of anyone or anything beyond God. Alarmed at the demolition, the mayor of Mecca at the time, Shaykh Abbas Yusuf Qattan, gained legal control of the site and established a small library there in 1953, built on the foundations of the mosque. All that remains of Arqam's house is an entranceway named for him, the Bab Dar ul-Arqam (Gate of Arqam's House), one of the 262 gates that lead to the Masjid al-Haram, the Great Mosque of Mecca that surrounds the Kaaba.

Because access to lodging, drinking water, and spiritual comfort were all critical during the hajj—a journey that traversed harsh desert terrain—during her own pilgrimage as queen, Khayzuran also "ordered a shelter, a fountain, or a mosque to be built along the pilgrims' route" almost daily.

While her kindness and generosity were surely appreciated by hajjis (pilgrims to Mecca), Khayzuran's elevation at court led to antagonism and disapproval on the part of some of the senior Abbasid ladies. Several of them were in her palace one day, reclining with her on Armenian carpets and cushions. The highest ranking, in terms of pedigree, was Zaynab, daughter of Sulyman ibn Ali, one of Mansur's uncles, a founding member of the dynasty. Mahdi had advised Khayzuran to observe Zaynab's behavior and comportment in order to learn proper court etiquette and manners, as Zaynab "had been brought up to maintain the dignity and traditions of the royal house."

A servant entered and announced that there was a woman at the door, "handsome and good looking, but wearing tattered clothes," who was asking to be admitted to the chamber. Khayzuran told the servant to fetch the woman. Despite her shabby clothing, the woman's bearing and eloquent diction made it obvious that she was a person of high breeding and royal background. Asked who she was, she replied that she was Muzna, wife of Marwan ibn Muhammad, the last of the Umayyad caliphs (the one who met his grisly, tongueless fate in Egypt). She said that after her family's fall, she was reduced to living among the common people, in constant fear of being raped or abused, and so poor and destitute that "even those tattered garments I am wearing are borrowed."

The story moved Khayzuran to tears. Zaynab's response, however, was quite the opposite. She reminded Muzna of the time that she (Zaynab) came begging for the body of her uncle, Ibrahim, who was executed by the Umayyads when they were still in power.

"[Y]ou spoke harshly to me, ordered me to be thrown out and said: 'What have women to do with men's affairs?'" Zaynab bitterly recalled. Relishing her opportunity for vengeance, she had the tearful and despondent Muzna ejected from the room. Not wanting to publicly contradict Zaynab, Khayzuran, with a wink and a nod to one of her attendants, had the servant catch Muzna before she left. She was shown to one of the queen's private chambers, where she was given a new set of clothes and, at Khayzuran's command, "be shown kindness."

When Mahdi learned of the episode, he praised Khayzuran's leniency while condemning Zaynab's vengeful harshness. He summoned Muzna to court, calling her "cousin" and had her seated beside him in a place of honor, above that of Zaynab, among the rest of the royal princesses, whom he described as "your sisters in my palace."

He declared, "You shall have the same privileges and duties as they do," and "assigned to her the same fiefs as were assigned to the other royal women, rewarded her and provided her with servants." She maintained her status as a royal Abbasid princess during the reign of Harun. When she died, the "women folk [of the harem] were stricken with grief."

When Mahdi himself died in August of 785, under dubious circumstances (it may have been a hunting accident, or he may have been inadvertently killed by one of his concubines who was trying to eliminate a rival with a poisoned pear, which Mahdi ate by accident), there was a bit of a crisis of succession, despite the late caliph's best-laid plans to arrange a smooth transition of power.

Earlier that year, Mahdi changed his will to make Harun, instead of Musa, his heir. To what degree Khayzuran played a role in his decision is unclear. It is known that she favored Harun over her firstborn. Again, *why* is an open question. Both princes were said to be tall and handsome. Musa was fair-skinned while Harun inherited his mother's olive complexion. Of the two, Musa was the more ruggedly built, energetic, brave, and athletic—a man more comfortable astride a leather saddle than a silken cushion. Still, he had a fondness for literature and enjoyed debating the finer points of religion and philosophy with scholars. In contrast, Harun was slim and prone to the self-indulgent leisure of court as opposed to military affairs: carousing, dallying with his numerous concubines, and hosting lavish dinner parties where singing *jawari* strummed lutes or danced for the caliph all night long. Essentially wine, women, and song. Still, he did fulfil his princely duties when called upon to do so, joining his father on military campaigns, such as a foray in 780 against the Christian Byzantines, the Abbasids' perennial enemies to the west.

If there was a glaring difference between the two brothers, it was Musa's birth defect: a cleft lip which caused his mouth to naturally gape. Mahdi, in fact, assigned a special servant to attend his eldest son, constantly reminding him to close his lips. If that wasn't bad enough, the handicap earned him the cruel nickname Musa Atbiq ("Musa Shut-your-Mouth").

Whether the stigmatization grated on his nerves or he was naturally aggressive by nature, as he grew older Musa became increasingly ill-tempered, moody, and prone to violent outbursts. This behavior began to inspire doubts in Mahdi's mind about his eldest son's fitness for the throne, a view "staunchly supported" by Khayzuran. Putting distance between himself and his troublesome son, Mahdi dispatched Musa to govern the eastern portion of the empire, centered in Jurjan (modern Gorgan), an ancient city 250 miles north of Tehran, to the east of the Caspian Sea. Harun, meanwhile, was nominally granted viceroyship of the empire's western half, stretching from Anbar, Iraq, just west of Baghdad, to Tunisia. Mahdi nevertheless kept Harun close to court, grooming him to ultimately replace Musa as heir while Yahya, characteristically, shouldered most of the Harun's administrative duties.

Musa, being Musa, reacted angrily to the news that he was to be passed over and stubbornly refused to accept his father's decision. When royal messengers arrived in Jurjan with the official announcement, Musa assaulted them and scornfully sent them back to Baghdad. Roused to anger himself, Mahdi decided to head to Jurjan, with Harun at his side, to make sure that his eldest son, in no uncertain terms, got the royal memo about who was next in line. During a stopover in Masabadhan, a small town in the foothills of the Zagros Mountains, Mahdi either had the hunting accident or ate the poison pear, as we have seen. In either case, his death suddenly created the aforementioned crisis.

Faced with the decision of what to do, Harun, as always, turned to his ersatz father, Yahya, to ask his advice. Some counselors were urging the young prince to bear his father's body back to Baghdad in secret and declare himself caliph from within the safety of the palace walls. Yahya, however, convinced Harun that this would be a mistake. The army, which had more affection for the militarily-inclined Musa, might rebel and seize the opportunity to demand back pay (essentially a bribe) from the royal treasury to maintain order, the Barmakid advised. Best for Harun to bury Mahdi quickly, quietly, and locally. The late caliph was laid to rest beneath a walnut tree, with a door purloined from a local house serving as a funeral bier. Harun then sent the royal scepter, insignia, and seal to Musa along with his congratulations on his brother's ascension to the throne. Yahya further recommended giving the troops accompanying Harun bonus pay of two hundred dirhams each and sending them back home on leave to enjoy themselves. Thus paid off, Yahya predicted, the troops would be content to return to Baghdad and be with their families.

But the plan backfired when the troops, upon arriving home, learned that Mahdi had died and they had been shortchanged. A riot ensued and an ugly crowd surrounded and partially torched the home of the man ostensibly in charge of the city in Mahdi's absence, Fadl ibn Rabi (the same Rabi who Harun ultimately entrusted with the royal seal).

It was at this point that the real person in charge—Khayzuran—stepped in to defuse the rapidly escalating situation. She summoned both Yahya and Fadl to her chamber to consult with her. Both obeyed, though Yahya, ever the political player, stopped short of crossing the queen's threshold, lest it be perceived as superseding Musa's new authority as caliph. Nevertheless, both ministers agreed with Khayzuran that more money would be needed to quell the anger of the troops. The queen immediately authorized the release of two years' additional soldiers' pay from the treasury and order was soon restored.

The episode was a significant turning point in Khayzuran's life, "the first time that we see an 'Abbasid woman intervening directly in state affairs on [this] level." Now in her late thirties or early forties, with two grown sons—one on the throne and the other destined for it, thanks to her—she was in the full ripeness of her womanhood, her motherhood, and her political power. It was she who summoned high-ranking officials to her side, she who issued commands, she who remained calm in the face of civil unrest, and she who determined who would sit on the throne of one of the most powerful empires in Islamic history.

Thus positioned, she fully expected that when Musa was crowned, she would "exercise her authority over him in all his affairs without consulting him at all . . . assuming sole control over matters of ordaining and forbidding, just as she had done with his father." It was here that she miscalculated.

At first, mother and son seemed to get on well enough. Musa was "very obedient to his mother" and extended to her the same courtesies and privileges as his late father. He visited her at her palace when he could, sending her gifts if he couldn't find time to get away from the business of governing the empire, a responsibility he embraced with his characteristic energy and diligence. He also "met all her requests when people approached her with their needs." Consequently "[h]er door was never free from streams of people," including generals, court officials, and civil servants who, just as they had with Mahdi, recognized that access to Khayzuran meant access to power.

But after four months, the steady stream of petitioners lining up at Khayzuran's threshold began to irk Musa, the macho man among men, who grew tired of being publicly upstaged by his mother. When Khayzuran had her brother, Ghitrif, appointed governor of Yemen, the irritated caliph had enough of her meddling and sent her a stern warning via courier.

"Do not step beyond the boundaries of a woman's traditional modest position," his message read. "It is not dignified for women that they should involve themselves in affairs of state."

Khayzuran ignored the rebuke and went on receiving supplicants, including one Abdullah ibn Malik, Baghdad's chief of police, to whom she had promised a favor. Musa refused the request, but, with her prestige at stake, Khayzuran persisted, saying:

> "You must grant my wish."
>
> "No, I will not," [Musa] answered.
>
> She said, "I assured 'Abdullah ibn Malik his wish shall be granted."
>
> Al-Hadi was angry and said, "Damn that son of a whore! I knew it was him who made that request! By God, I shall never grant it!"
>
> She replied, "Then I'll never ask you for anything else again!"
>
> He replied, "And by God I do not care!"
>
> His anger intensified and she rose to leave, also in anger.
>
> He said, "Stop where you are! Listen carefully to what I am about to tell you or I am quit of my kinship to the Prophet. If I hear that any of my commanders, retinue or servants is standing at your door, I shall cut his head off and seize his wealth! Whoso wishes, let him obey! What are these streams of people that come to your door every day? Don't you have a spindle to occupy you, a Qur'an to remind you of God or a chamber that shelters you? Beware! Don't ever again open your mouth to request some favor for a Muslim or a non-Muslim!"

> She left in panic, hardly able to see where she was stepping and thereafter never uttered a word in his presence, sweet or sour.

A line had been drawn in the sand, a line etched even deeper by Musa's new plan to name his own son Jafar as heir to the throne in place of Harun. He consulted Yahya who advised him against disrupting the line of succession, lest future caliphs—Jafar included—have their own designated heirs simply brushed aside and chaos ensue every time a ruler died. Musa thanked the vizier, gave the matter some thought, and subsequently had Yahya tossed in jail. Meanwhile, he began a campaign to turn his generals against his mother.

Gathering them together, he engaged them in a bit of cat-and-mouse dialogue about who was the superior person, him or any of them? "Certainly you are, O Commander of the Faithful!" was their predictable response. Musa then asked them whose mother was better, his or any of theirs? Once again, the safest bet seemed to be, "Assuredly, your mother." The caliph pressed further, asking who among them would appreciate having their mother be a topic of gossip. All agreed that none would. Musa then laid his trap: "So what do you think about the men who keep coming to my mother and who subsequently make her affairs the subject of their conversations?"

Taking the hint, the generals ceased calling on Khayzuran who grew increasingly isolated and concerned for her safety, and not without reason. On one occasion, Musa sent her a rice dish with his compliments. An attendant cautioned her to have the food tested by giving some to a dog. The animal dropped dead on the spot. When Musa sent a message asking how his—hopefully late—mother liked the rice, she responded, tartly, that she enjoyed it very much.

"You can't have eaten it, because if you had, I would have been rid of you," Musa fumed.

Failing to eliminate his mother, he attempted to poison his brother, who managed to survive, albeit under lock and key, sharing a cell with Yahya. Having had enough of Musa's murderous tyranny, Khayzuran fought back, reportedly with poison herself, which she had mixed into one of her eldest son's drinks. The potion didn't kill him but drove him to a sick bed with a stomach ulcer, a condition that ran in the family.

There are stories that when Khayzuran learned of Musa's condition, she rushed to his bedside for a tearful reunion during which the dying caliph acknowledged Harun as his successor. Yet far juicier rumors circulated that after her failed attempt at poisoning her troublesome son, the determined queen mother dispatched a bevy of *jawari* to his bed chamber to smother him by sitting on his face. When informed of his death, Khayzuran simply and coldly remarked, "If Musā's dead, that leaves Harūn."

Historians have, rightly, regarded both stories with skepticism, considering their sources. The mother-son reunion version came from the pen of Masudi, in his masterpiece *Muruj al Dhahab wa Maadin al Jawhar* ("Meadows of Gold and Mines of Gems"), written in 947, at a time when the Abbasid empire was starting to decline and in need of bolstering. The image of a mother clutching the hand of her dying son to her breast, as opposed to plotting his murder, was more consistent with the reputation of the woman who mercifully restored the impoverished Umayyad princess, Muzna, to a position of honor. Meanwhile, the version of Musa's death at the hands—or rather, derrieres—of a dozen or more dancing girls, acting on the orders of the caliph's cold-hearted mother, appears in Tabari. Yet the medieval Persian author attributes the story to Yahya ibn al-Hasan, maternal uncle of Fadl ibn Rabi, Harun's vizier whose promotion Khayzuran had blocked. In this case, political payback might explain her depiction as a filicidal femme fatale.

However it occurred, Musa died on the 14th of September, 786, after a brief rule of barely fourteen months. Khayzuran released Yahya from jail and had dispatches sent throughout the empire that Harun was the new caliph. "These measures by Khayzuran had never been witnessed in Islamic history in such magnitude," noted one modern historian. "She had managed to topple a caliph and install another."

Just as he did in the past, Harun turned most of the responsibilities of governing over to Yahya and, perforce, to his mother. Together, Khayzuran and the devoted vizier ran the empire for the next three years, until Khayzuran's death, passing her sense of civic duty to her niece/daughter in-law, Zubayda, Harun's favorite wife.

As an adult, Zubayda's "charity was ample, her conduct virtuous," according to the thirteenth-century biographer Ibn Khallikan. In her chambers, it was said, a hundred slave girls tasked with memorizing the

Qur'an recited "one-tenth of it daily; so that her palace resounded with a continual humming like that of bees."

Unlike Khayzuran, she was born into the lap of luxury, but, like her mother in-law, she had extravagant tastes. According to al Zubayr's eleventh-century *Book of Gifts and Rarities*—a sort of *Lifestyles of the Rich and Famous* of its day—the cost of her wedding alone ran to fifty million dinars, at a time when the annual cost of living for an average middle-class family in Baghdad was about 240 dinars. The sumptuous event—more extravagant than "had ever been seen in Islamic times"—featured a ruby-and-pearl-encrusted waistcoat "whose value could not be assessed" for the bride and gifts of gold dinars in silver bowls and silver dinars in golden bowls for the guests.

A stylish trendsetter, Zubayda was "the first to introduce the fashion for slippers embroidered with precious stones and for candles made of ambergris—fashions which spread to the public," according to Masudi. On state occasions, it was said she "could scarcely walk under the weight of her jewellery and dresses" and had to be propped up by servants.

Yet the famously pious and compassionate queen also spent lavishly on public works. During her fifth pilgrimage to Mecca, in 805, she was distressed to see that drought had devastated the populace and reduced the sacred well of Zamzam to a mere trickle. She ordered that the well's depth be increased and spent nearly two million dinars on improvements to the water supply of Mecca and its surrounding province. These immense public works projects included the construction of an aqueduct from the spring of Hunayn, sixty miles east, as well as the famed "Spring of Zubayda" on the plain of Arafat, an important stopping point on the hajj. When her engineers cautioned her about the expense, never mind the difficulty, of the project, "she replied that she was decided to have [the work] executed, were every stroke of a [pickaxe] to cost a dinar." To ease the journey for pilgrims, she also financed the construction of the Darb Zubayda (Zubayda's Way), a nine-hundred-mile road running from Kufa, south of Baghdad, to Mecca, with water stations at regular intervals and hilltop fire beacons to guide travelers at night. Contemporary historian al Azraqi (d. 834) declared that the "people of Mecca and the pilgrims owe their very life to [Zubayda] next to Allah" and pilgrim cries of "God bless Zubayda" echoed along the route for generations. In a personally painful decision, she also put the needs of the state ahead of her own flesh and blood, ultimately endorsing her stepson, al Ma'mun (786–833) as caliph over her morally corrupt son, al Amin (b. 787), deposed in 813, the year of his death.

Zubayda died in 831, yet her reputation as a woman of power and influence lived on, not only in her public works but in literary history. As the clever and resourceful tale-spinning wife of Harun, protagonist caliph in *One Thousand and One Nights*, she is a key figure in the classic work, "a forceful and glamorous character . . . second only to Harun al-Rashid himself."

But the glitz, the glamor, and the glory were destined to fade. As the empire expanded—into Egypt, Iran, Central Asia and beyond—centralization became increasingly difficult to maintain. Smelling blood, tributary rulers in the provinces began itching for independence—among them an emerging Arab-Berber dynasty from North Africa known as the Fatimids.

CHAPTER 2

Asma bint Shihab al Sulayhi (r. 1047–1067)
Arwa bint Ahmad al Sulayhi (c. 1048–1138)

A Family Affair in Yemen

The Fatimids traced their ancestry to Fatima, the Prophet Muhammad's daughter and the wife of Ali, the Prophet's cousin and companion. Ali was the last of the Rashidun, or "rightly guided" in Arabic, the first four caliphs (successors) to lead the Muslim community (*umma*) after Muhammad's death in 632. The first three Rashidun—Abu Bakr, Umar, and Uthman—were close companions of the Prophet and related by marriage. Ali, however, who served as caliph from 656 to 661, was related by blood and therein lay the first major doctrinal dispute in the nascent religion, a division that lives on in the Muslim world to this day.

The majority of Muslims hold that Muhammad never named a successor. Rather, he intended that the caliph should be chosen from among the most qualified members of the *umma* (the worldwide Muslim community), a purposeful decision intended to preserve the democratic nature of the new faith. The worthiest candidate for caliph was someone whose conduct most closely reflected the Prophet's own behavior and customs, known in Arabic as *sunnah*. Such believers thus came to be known as Sunni Muslims and today constitute some 90 percent of the world's Muslim population, estimated to be 1.5 billion people.

There were those, however, who held that only members of the Prophet's immediate family had the spiritual and political authority to lead the Muslim community. To them, Ali was the first truly legitimate caliph. These supporters of Ali came to be known as *Shia*, from the Arabic phrase *Shiat Ali*, or "party of Ali." While over time, Shia Islam further broke down into multiple denominations, much like Protestant Christianity, its two main branches remain Twelvers and Ismailis, who embrace such shadowy doctrines as mysticism, numerology, and an understanding of the cosmos that is rooted in ancient and esoteric Neoplatonic philosophy. Twelvers meanwhile acknowledge twelve—and only twelve—descendants of Muhammad as legitimate imams (religious leaders of the *umma*), the last imam having gone into occultation, or hiding, in 874, destined to reappear at God's appointed time.

Ultimately these departures from mainstream Sunni Islam weren't just theological: they grew decidedly political as Ismailis sought to spread their religious doctrines, and their power, far and wide, a movement that engulfed regions once firmly in the hands of the predominantly Sunni Abbasids. A key year was 969, when the founders of the Fatimid dynasty and their Berber armies swept into Egypt from their stronghold in Algeria, conquering the country and establishing a new, palatial capital on the Nile, *al Kahira* (the Victorious), known to the English-speaking world as Cairo. At its height, during the tenth and eleventh centuries, the extent of Fatimid influence and its missionary efforts (*al dawah*) stretched from the Atlantic coast of North Africa to the shores of India, with governors and client kings ruling various cities and fortified provinces in the name of the caliph-imam.

Among these major areas of influence (*gazira*, in Arabic, or sectors) was Yemen in the southwestern Arabian Peninsula. At the time, the country was a patchwork of local, tribal dynasties, both Shia and Sunni, warring with one another for supremacy in the region. One of the most powerful and influential Yemeni rulers to emerge during this turbulent time was not a *malik* (king) but a *malika* (queen), Arwa bint Ahmad al Sulayhi who, uniquely in the history of medieval Islam, was both the political and religious leader of her people.

Like Zubayda, Arwa had an inspirational mother-in-law for a mentor: the noble and highly revered queen, Asma bint Shihab al Sulayhi. Asma was a woman "who wore power and pearls with the same distinction," and, much like Khayzuran, directed "all the important affairs of the realm" alongside her husband, Ali bin Muhammad al Sulayhi, founder of Yemen's Sulayhid dynasty.

Sulayhi was the son of a well-respected *qadi* (judge) from the Haraz district. This mountainous region extends inland from Yemen's sweltering Red Sea coastal plain (the *Tihama*, an Arabic expression meaning severe heat and lack of wind) to the cooler, dryer highlands of Sanaa, a distance of some 250 miles. Raised a Sunni, Sulayhi was recruited to Ismailism by Yemen's chief Ismaili Fatimid *dai* (missionary), Sulaiman bin Abdullah, an influential member of the powerful Zawahi clan. It was Sulaiman himself who instructed Sulayhi in the secretive doctrines of Ismailism during the early years of the eleventh century. Recognizing great potential in the young convert, Sulaiman named him his successor as *dai*, while at the same time cultivating Sulayhi's political ambitions. This support and mentorship ultimately positioned Sulayhi to establish a new Yemeni dynasty, the Sulayhids, whose territory extended westward from the capital city of Sanaa to Zabid in the Tihama and south to the Red Sea port of Aden. In 1047, the succession became official when Sulayhi publicly swore his allegiance to the caliph headquartered in Cairo.

Famously just and fair, Sulayhi earned the devotion and critical military support of many of the major tribes throughout southern Yemen. By 1063, most had pledged themselves to him and the Fatimid Ismaili cause and caliphate. The lower classes admired his virtuous conduct and even-handed sense of justice. As for the tribal leaders, he won their trust through negotiation and diplomacy, resorting to military force only as a last resort. To maintain order, he installed deputies in the various key cities, provinces, and forts that now fell under Sulayhid central authority.

Not all, however, welcomed the unorthodox Ismaili doctrines, never mind Sulayhi's expansionist policies. The steadfastly Sunni Najahids, descended from a line of Black, Abyssinian (Ethiopian) slaves based in Zabid, bore an abiding grudge against Sulayhi for having Najah, founding father of the dynastic tribe, poisoned by a slave girl in 1060. They remained redoubtable rivals for control of southern Yemen and a deadly threat to the stability of the Sulayhid kingdom throughout Sulayhi's lifetime and beyond, as we shall see.

In his campaign to subdue the Najahids and win over the rest of Yemen's tribe, Sulayhi's greatest ally was his wife and cousin, Asma, "one of the most famous woman of her time and one of the most powerful." According to Yemeni chronicler Najm al Din Umarah (d. 1174) in his *Tarikh al Yaman* (History of the Yemen), Asma attended state councils "with her face uncovered" and was addressed by her husband as *mawlatuna*—literally, "the woman to whom we owe allegiance" or "Our Lady"—a rare honorific, especially when used by a husband of noble rank in reference to his wife. Her exalted status was reiterated each *Jummah* (Friday prayer) when the *khutbah* (sermon) was given in her name, together with those of the king, her husband, an "indisputable criteria of sovereignty in Islam."

The daughter of one of Sulayhi's uncles, the young Asma was also an accomplished poet who reportedly "had few equals in beauty, and was unmatched in literary culture and intelligence." As queen, she was said to be "of a generous and noble disposition, liberal in the rewards she bestowed upon poets, and in the sums she granted in acts of benevolence and other deeds."

Court poets, true to the era, repaid her kindness and munificence with chivalric, flowery verse that praised her as a "fair beauty, who is generous as the rain cloud." Her official, royal title was *al sayyida al hurra*, meaning "a sovereign woman who obeys no superior authority"—in short, a "liberated woman." One gushing palace poet summarized the love and respect of his fellow Yemenis by declaring that "Asma's hath obscured the name of the loftiest among the stars," i.e., that of Bilqis, the legendary Queen of Sheba or Saba, as ancient Yemen was known. Among Yemenis, *Bilqis al Saghrira* (the little Queen of Sheba) was the most loving and reverential sobriquet one could bestow on a woman.

Added to these genteel qualities were guts and ingenuity, which were put to their greatest test by the rebellious and bloodthirsty Najahids. After Najah's death, his sons fled to the Eritrean island of Dahlak in the Red Sea, where they nursed their wounds and plotted their revenge. During that time, one of the sons, Said al Ahwal (dubbed "the squint-eyed" by the clearly pro-Sulayhid chronicler Umarah) emerged as the new tribal leader. Hellbent on avenging his father and crushing the spread of Ismaili doctrines in Yemen, Ahwal landed secretly in the Tihama in 1066 and began stirring up an insurrectionist campaign to topple the Sulayhid dynasty.

Sulayhi, fatally, ignored these threats. While performing the hajj with Asma in the fall of 1067, the Yemeni ruler's encamped caravan was attacked by a ragtag band of Najahid rebels at al Mahjam, an agricultural hamlet in the northern Tihama. Sulayhi and most of the royal party were brutally slaughtered by the marauders, many of them armed with nothing more than nail-studded palm fronds. Asma, her daughter Fatima, and other women of the royal household in the convoy were imprisoned in Zabid, then in the hands of the Najahids. In a grisly display of vengeance, Ahwal had Sulayhi's severed head carried before Asma's howdah (a luxurious, tented camel saddle). Upon reaching Zabid, the Najahid leader commanded that the head be stuck on a pike outside Asma's jail cell window, left there to ooze and foully rot in the blistering heat and humidity.

The brutal assassination and revolt threw the country into a state of chaos, as the ultimately faithless tribal leaders, without Sulayhi on hand to allay and/or subdue them, believed the writing was on the wall for the Sulayhids and joined the rebellion. The fate and survival of Yemen's Fatimid, Ismaili cause now rested with Sulayhi's son and successor, Al Mukarram Ahmad. Mukarram was famed as a "dashing warrior and eloquent orator" who shared his father's commitment to Fatimid vassalage. At this troubling point in Sulayhid history, however, his was a shaky and uncertain inheritance.

Meanwhile, back in Zabid, Asma remained dignified and brave in the face of her peril, providing moral support to her fellow female prisoners while plotting how she might free herself and her companions. In Umarah's rather dramatic account, which verges on pulp fiction, the ingenious queen eventually managed to smuggle a letter to her son in a loaf of bread that she slipped to a beggar. In the desperate letter, she claimed she was "great with child" by the villainous Ahwal and begged her son to rescue them before the rest of her ladies were similarly defiled.

Whether or not Asma had actually been raped by Ahwal remains unknown, but her stratagem worked. True to his reputation for oration and bold action, the outraged Mukarram stood before a crowd of his fellow Sulayhids and passionately exhorted them "to vindicate the honor of their tribe." His rhetoric proved persuasive, and in 1068 he set out for Zabid at the head of an army of three thousand troops, determined to literally rescue the damsels in distress.

Though outnumbered nearly seven to one, Mukarram's forces bravely stormed the city, managing to overwhelm the Najahids, who they slaughtered in great numbers. By the midday prayer time, the battle was over, with the piled-up bodies of dead Najahid warriors blocking the main gateway to the city. Meanwhile, their "squint-eyed" leader escaped with his life, slinking off to take refuge once more in Dahlak in boats he had standing by in case he lost the battle. But the victory came at a high cost to Mukarram personally. Upon reaching the dungeon where his mother was imprisoned (guided to the spot by the gruesome, fly-covered head of his father, still decaying on its pike outside the barred window) he greeted her with a salutation befitting her station: "May God safeguard and perpetuate thy renown, O our Lady."

Not recognizing her son behind the visor of his helmet, she asked his name. When he responded "Ahmad, son of Ali," she replied that those were common enough Arab names and asked him to remove his helmet so she could see his face. When he did as she requested, his mother was overcome with joy and relief, exclaiming, "Welcome, our Lord al-Mukarram!"

At this point, the unfortunate man of the hour was overcome himself with what Umarah described as "the wind," followed by a shudder and facial spasm: the symptoms of what was likely a stroke that paralyzed him from the waist down. The attack also left him with lingering head and facial spasms, not to mention considerably weakened in mind and spirit.

As tragic as the event was, for Asma there was little time for mourning. Realizing her son was permanently incapacitated, she stepped in and "conducted the affairs of [the] kingdom" thereafter. It was Asma, and not Mukarram, who, per royal prerogative, conferred revenues and castles upon her son's supporters. According to the fifteenth-century Yemeni historian Idris Imad al Din, in his *Uyun al akhbar*, or *History of an Islamic Community* (another primary source on the Sulayhids), Asma also directly corresponded with Sulayhid governors concerning sensitive military and financial affairs of state, the duties of an actively reigning monarch. Official correspondence from Cairo provided further evidence of her elevated status as Yemen's de facto ruler. In 1068, the reigning Fatimid caliph Al Mustansir sent two letters addressed to the Yemeni queen congratulating her on her safe return to Sanaa and delivery from the hands of the Najahids. It was rare during this era for a caliph to write directly to a woman, as well as a great honor. In both letters, Mustansir underscored his respect for his female vassal by invoking her virtues as "al-Hurra, the noble, the pure, the pious, the honored, guardian of the faithful, mother of the loyal princes, God protect her." In a later letter to Arwa, once she had succeeded to the throne, the Fatimid caliph praised Asma for "her loyalty" to the Fatimid cause and reiterated the trust he had in her to "play a role in political affairs."

Upon Asma's death in 1074, with Mukarram yet incapable of ruling, the duty fell to his wife, Arwa. By this time, the concept of being ruled by a woman was not unacceptable to the Yemeni tribes, nor, given the country's legendary connections to the Queen of Sheba, altogether culturally unfamiliar. In time, Yemeni chroniclers, both ancient and modern, would regard Arwa's reign as among the most prosperous and prestigious in the nation's history, whose positive impact on the Fatimid *dawah* exceeded all expectations back in Cairo.

Like many notable Islamic queens who came before and after her, Arwa was possessed of both brains and beauty in equally generous helpings. Niece to Sulayhi, she was born in his homeland, the southwestern Sulayhid stronghold of Haraz, in either 1045 or 1048. Orphaned at a young age, she was raised in the palace in Sanaa under the care of Asma, who oversaw her education in accordance with the Fatimid tradition of providing equal schooling to both men and women (see "A Fatimid Tradition of Female Education," below).

A Fatimid Tradition of Female Education

The importance of education was paramount to the Fatimids, whose Ismaili teachings as well as Islamic arts and sciences culminated in the "sessions of wisdom" (*majalis al-hikma*). These public lectures were open to both men and women, an unprecedented policy. Classes for "the wives [of the caliph] and the noble women" were held in the palace, wrote the eleventh-century historian Al Musabbihi, while Cairo's Al-Azhar Mosque was the educational setting for "the simple people and strangers in the city [with] separate sessions for women." Stemming from these innovative medieval customs, "to this day the culture and education of girls and women remains one of the major priorities of the Ismaili community," noted scholar Heinz Halm, in *The Fatimids and their Traditions of Learning*.

She was "of fair complexion, tinged with red, tall, well-proportioned, but inclined to stoutness [and] perfect in beauty" as Umarah described her. Her name, in any case (Arwa, Arabic for a female ibex), reflected her grace and beauty. She was also a gifted reciter of the Qur'an and a "well read and a skillful writer" with a mind like a trap. It was said that "nothing could surpass" her ability to read between the lines and "distinguish between the literal and the true meaning" of a text.

Both Asma and Sulayhi recognized greatness in their niece at a young age. As a girl, Arwa once told Asma about a dream she had in which she was sweeping the hallways of the palace with a broom. Asma responded that the dream was symbolic, foretelling the day yet to come when her young niece "shalt sweep away the dynasty of the [Sulayhids] and . . . appropriate their kingdom." Sulayhi, meanwhile, commanded that Arwa be treated with "respect . . . for, by Allah, she will be the preserver of our race and guardian of our crown." Recognizing her capabilities and intelligence, Sulayhi personally instructed her in the fiscal management of the kingdom, especially that of the city of Aden, her dowry upon marrying Mukarram sometime between 1065 and 1069, when she was in her late teens (possibly 17 or 18). The rich trading city's annual tribute (about 100,000 dinars, equivalent to $3,650,000 in today's money) made her personally quite wealthy.

Arwa put her skills and good fortune to practical use upon ascending the throne with the blessings of her husband after Asma's death. Mukarram unequivocally decreed that all power devolve to her, due to his physical inability to govern and the fact that the two young sons she bore him had at the time not yet come of age. Umarah, not too subtly, suggests there was yet another, less noble reason for Mukarram's abdication: the sad fact that, in his illness, he had given "himself up to the pleasures of music and wine."

Though initially reluctant (she argued that a woman who was still young enough "for the marriage-bed, could not be fit for the business of the state"), Arwa ultimately embraced her official royal title, like that of Asma's: *al sayyida al hurra*. Like her predecessor, she had the title read out during the *khutbah*, the wording of which also emphasized the legitimacy of her reign: "May Allah prolong the days of al-Hurra the perfect, the sovereign who carefully manages the affairs of the state." In addition, she had coins minted in her name bearing the inscription "Queen Arwa," another key criteria of sovereignty in medieval Muslim society.

Invested, as she was, with royal authority by her husband, and inspired by her aunt's example of what it meant to shoulder the duties of a queen, Arwa wasted little time in taking responsibility for the kingdom she inherited. One of her first official acts was an ambitious and bold one: the relocation of the capital from Sanaa to Jibla, in the mountainous, agriculturally rich southwest.

The city was fairly new at the time, founded in 1065 by Abd Allah, one of Sulayhi's brothers, though its roots were likely much older. Archaeological evidence found on nearby Jebal (Mount) Takar suggests that Jibla may have been part of a settlement established by the Himyarites, a Greco-Roman Jewish state that governed southern Yemen from around 100 BCE to 570 CE. That Jews were both active and influential in Jibla is evident in the city's name. Jiblah was a local Jewish pottery maker, apparently of some renown. Situated about five miles south-southwest of what is today the regional capital city of Ibb, the town rises dramatically some 7,200 feet from a mountainous gorge between two *wadis* (riverbeds). Its surrounding landscape, as it was in Arwa's day, is terraced, with fields of sorghum and other grains, dotted with clutches of jujube and carob trees and patches of cacti. Like most of Yemen's traditional historic architecture, its houses and public buildings are composed of stuccoed mud-brick or stone, with decorative facades offset by rustically stylized Palladian stained-glass windows. Nestled tightly together, the towering structures rise like teeth from the jagged, black basalt cliffs.

Umarah offered a characteristically colorful narrative to explain Arwa's decision, shortly after Asma's death, to relocate the capital to this remote and imposing location. Assembling the citizens of Sanaa outside the palace windows, the queen had her husband gaze out upon the people and asked him what he saw. "[N]ought . . . but the lightning flashes of drawn swords and of lance blades," was his reply. Removing to Jibla several days later, she asked him the same question. There, "his eyes fell upon men leading rams or carrying vessels filled with ghee or with honey. 'Life among these (industrious) people,' she said to Mukarram, 'is to be preferred.'"

Umarah's subtle panegyric, with its description of drawn swords and flashing lance blades, indicated simmering political unrest in Sanaa that still lingered in the wake of Sulayhi's death. The times called for a strong leader to thwart resistance to Sulayhid rule and quell rebellion. Arwa, however capable, was still new to the game of governing. But she was catching on fast. On her journey to inspect Jibla as the site of her new capital, she did so at the head of a large army (a rare action at the time for a woman) and with the dynastic treasure among the wagon carts in her entourage. These demonstrations of military and economic might were intended to remind the tribes that not only was a Sulayhid still in charge of the country, but a wealthy, powerful Sulayhid queen at that. Another incentive for the move was that it put her and her forces within striking distance (less than a hundred miles) of the Najahids who had retaken the Tihama. In addition, she was now strategically and geographically that much closer to wavering tribal allies, like Aden's Zurayids, who had recently cut back on their annual tribute, anticipating weakness from the young female ruler.

But these fair-weather allies underestimated her. Like her diplomatic uncle, Arwa believed a display of arms, rather than actual costly warfare, could still send a message—a message powerful enough to discourage rebellion and solidify allegiance to the Sulayhid cause. Such realpolitikal calculations proved that Arwa—not yet thirty years old—was beginning to think and act like a ruler. While her husband languidly reposed in the royal gardens at Jibla, she "energetically took up the responsibilities of running the State in the troubled times that synchronized with her rulership."

Her political instincts paid off, and what followed was "a period of some brilliance" under the Sulayhids that began with significant investments in infrastructure—usually a winning gambit for politicians. At Jibla, in addition to a palace she built a mosque and, later, restored the Great Mosque of Sanaa. The palace, called Dar al Izz (The House of Glory), was said to have had 354 rooms, one for every day of the Muslim calendar year (lunar year), though some dispute that claim, arguing that Arwa was too fiscally responsible to sanction such lavishness. While the palace is now in ruins, both mosques still stand today.

Embarking on a wide program of reforms, she also endorsed agricultural land development, boosting the production of Jibla's farms by commissioning the construction of terraces, irrigated by newly built aqueducts. The aqueducts also provided for working plumbing in the palace and directed water to nearby Yifrus, twenty-five miles south, as well as to the surrounding villages. At least one of the aqueducts built during her reign still brings water from the mountains to the ruins of the palace to this day.

To facilitate an increase in trade, she built roads through difficult mountain passes that connected her new capital to major cities throughout the region, including the Samara Pass, a verdant highway linking the ancient Himyarite city of Dhamar with Ibb. Journeying through Yemen in the 1930s, British colonial officer W.H. Ingrams recounted traveling along one mountain roadway built during Arwa's time and remarked on its enduring integrity and engineering genius.

"The broad pavement of well-shaped stones was stepped and followed reasonable gradients, with watering places for man and beast at intervals," Ingrams reported. "It ran up and down green turfed mountain sides and along it bloomed in her memory a riot of wild flowers . . . Perhaps no one rides up and down passes we followed without remembering, as a beduin told me, that Queen [Arwa] built them eight hundred years ago."

So revered is her legacy in and around Jibla, that to this day the name "Arwa" remains one of the most popular for local girls.

Keen on women's health issues and education, she built women's hospitals and established religious and cultural centers where she saw to it that "scholars and teachers were well paid." At these institutions, the queen stipulated, even slaves—both male and female—were to receive educations. In addition, like Asma, she was a patron of the arts, writers, and poets. In memory of her regard for learning, today's Arwa University in Sanaa is among one of several educational institutions in the country named for her.

She also lowered taxes throughout the kingdom and kept a close eye on her governors, nipping fiscal corruption in the bud by reviewing their accounts annually, a skill she learned from her father in-law. A story related by Umarah and set during during Asma's reign illustrated the need for such close oversight. Lying in his bed chamber, the queen's newly appointed governor of Zabid felt the sprinkling of dust on his face and was amazed to find that it was gold. Ripping out the ceiling, he discovered a cache of extorted tax money hidden there by his predecessor. After turning over the bulk of it to charity and the state, he went on to govern for fifteen years, during which time no one registered a grievance against him.

By favoring diplomacy over battle and paying adversaries for their fortresses rather than besieging and destroying them, Arwa was able to expand Sulayhid influence to what it is now Oman, Bahrain, and the western coast on India. In her negotiations with these annexed territories, she established numerous treaties that she, famously, never broke. Her one overt act of aggression—one that mixed vengeance with political expediency soon after she ascended to the throne—was to bring her father in-law's assassin, Ahwal, to justice. She did so by taking full advantage of one of his greatest weakness: his male pride.

She had one of her allies, Al Hussain ibn at Tubbay, commander of the nearby fortified district of Ash Shair, write to Ahwal, advising him that since Mukarram was no longer physically fit to rule, his young and inexperienced wife was in charge of the government. Appealing to Ahwal's vanity, Hussain convinced the Najahid that with Mukarram out of commission and no one in authority but a mere woman, he, Ahwal, "was now the most powerful king" in Yemen. The letter further spelled out a strategy for taking over the entire country: combine forces and seize Jibla, with Ahwal attacking from the Tihama and he, Hussain, closing in from the mountains.

Emboldened by Hussain's apparent treason, Ahwal was lured out of his Zabid stronghold by Arwa's plot and set out for Jibla with an army of thirty thousand spearmen. Arwa, meanwhile, dispatched a cavalry of three thousand Sulayhid warriors from Sanaa with orders to head south, below Jibla and Ahwal's column. Their mission was to flank the enemy army and shadow it as it made its own way south to ostensibly join forces with Hussain.

The oblivious Najahid was in fact marching directly into Arwa's trap. When he halted below the fortress of ash Shair, "the two armies," Arwa's and Hussain's "fell upon him from either side" in a classic pincer attack. All but two thousand of the Najahid forces "were put to the sword." Among the survivors was Ahwal's wife, Umm al Muarik, who had traveled with his contingent. She was taken prisoner and forced to identify the severed head of her husband from among the carnage. In a gruesome bit of poetic justice that purposefully mirrored Asma's ordeal, Arwa had the rebel's head stuck on a pike outside the window of Muarik's prison quarters in the Dar al Izz back in Jibla.

"Oh that thou hadst eyes, Lady Asma," the queen was said to have exclaimed, invoking the sufferings of her beloved aunt/mother in-law and mentor, "wherewith to see the head of the squint-eyed slave below the window" of his imprisoned widow.

Between her defeat of the Najahids—destructively stubborn impediments to the Ismaili cause—and her programs of reform, Arwa's reputation was essentially going viral back in Cairo, where Mustansir and his ministers received news of the bold and effective queen's rise to power with mixed emotions.

While there were those who were uncomfortable with the idea of a woman ruling, it was hard to argue with her success, particularly her economic, political, and religious expansion of the Fatimid *dawah*, which reached the distant, wealthy trading cities of Gujarat state. The founding of these missionary outposts there on India's northwest coast helped establish new trade routes, linking India and the Indian Ocean to Egypt and the Mediterranean via the Nile and the Red Sea port of Aden, "a place where maritime and market risks could be managed, profits maximized, and losses mitigated." Whereas Abbasid Baghdad was once the place "where all the world's wealth was gathered," Fatimid Egypt now became the focal point of a vast commercial network extending all the way from South Asia to western Europe (Muslim Spain). Touring Cairo's bazaars in the eleventh century, Persian traveler Nasir Khusraw marveled that "there were no less than twenty thousand shops" in the city, selling all manner of exotic and imported treasures such as boxes and other personal items crafted from tortoise shells, flawless crystal vessels etched by master craftsmen, and "porcelain, so fine and translucent that you can see your hand behind it when held up to the light."

Critical to the importation of these and other luxury goods was the network of overland routes built by Queen Arwa's engineers plus access to Red Sea via the bustling commercial port of Aden, which the Fatimid-era geographer Al Muqaddasi described as "the entrance-hall of China and the warehouse of the West."

At the same time, the Fatimids were facing political and economic pressure from rebellions within Egypt as well as the loss of Syria to invading Seljuq Turks. So when Mustansir sent his first official letter to Arwa in August of 1078, he devoted a good bit of ink to buttering her up as "the guardian of believers, male and female, in Yemen . . . keen to keep the orderliness of religion, until the banners of truth shine." He then urged her to continue "enforcing your justice in Yemen, so your news can spread around to the furthest of corners."

Able as she was to keenly "distinguish between the literal and the true meaning" of the written word, Arwa had little trouble grasping the subtext of Mustansir's letter. Safely distant in its "far corner of the southern Arabian Peninsula, with its steep challenging mountains, away from the Abbasid powerbase of Iraq," she realized that her kingdom was "an inviting place" for the fruitful growth of Fatimid Ismaili doctrines, not to mention the dynasty's political ambitions, especially since the Najahid rebels had now been subdued (at least for the time being). Meanwhile, expanding control of the Arabian Peninsula and nudging the Fatimid empire's borders in the direction of Baghdad (by 970 the dynasty had already gained control of Mecca and Medina) meant that she was a key player in the ultimate political triumph over the Abbasids, an imperial objective ever since the first Fatimid armies marched into Egypt.

In short, the Fatimids desperately needed her politically, economically, and religiously while both she and Mustansir understood that "the fates of [their] two states were intimately interconnected." It was international diplomacy 101, and Arwa was no longer a student but a master.

In 1084, Mukarram died, throwing the Sulayhid kingdom into something of a crisis as often happens upon the death of monarchs. In his will, Mukarram named his cousin, Saba bin Ahmad al Sulayhi, as his successor. Known for his aggressiveness in battle, his piety, and a knack for poetry, Saba was nonetheless a bit of a comical character. "In his external appearance [he] was ill-favored [and short in stature], nor did he appear to advantage in the saddle," wrote Umarah in describing, as politely as he could, an unattractive, shrimpy fellow with a proto-Napoleon complex who looked somewhat awkward astride a horse.

This was not the person Arwa had in mind to fill her husband's shoes, let alone take charge of the kingdom she had essentially governed herself for the past decade. She knew that if she was going to stay in power, she had to somehow forestall Saba's ascension to the throne. Keeping the news of Mukarram's death a secret for nearly a year helped buy her the time she needed.

It was a risky maneuver. She well understood that the period immediately following the death of a ruler was potentially a time of crisis and chaos. She witnessed this herself in the aftermath of Sulayhi's assassination, when her late husband's succession was far from certain. If news reached the tribes that Mukarram was dead, local tribal leaders, especially those less sympathetic to the Fatimid cause, might rally to support Saba or try and usurp her themselves. Meanwhile, she wrote to Cairo, alerting Mustansir of Mukarram's death and asking the Caliph to endorse her ten year-old son, al Mukarram al Asgar ("the Younger," essentially Mukarram Junior), instead of Saba, as Yemen's new king.

Quite capable of reading between the lines of a text himself, Mustansir recognized that maintaining the status quo under Arwa, albeit as regent until Asgar came of age, was far preferable to years of violent unrest and inter-tribal squabbling that might result from a tumultuous change of regime. Not only would political instability risk undermining the *dawah*, it could, just as critically, negatively impact the Fatimid bottom line.

Bearing all this in mind, Mustansir sent a letter to Arwa in July of 1085 officially appointing Asgar as Mukarram's successor and instructing the Yemeni queen "to act in her son's interest and assist him in gaining the loyalty of the members of the *da'wa* in [Yemen]." In the official, state correspondence, the caliph referred to Arwa as "the noble lady" (*al sayyida al hurra*) and "mother of the new king," praising her as "the one on whom [he] would depend to guard the da'wa, and to loyally serve Fatimid affairs."

In a subsequent declaration, issued soon thereafter, Mustansir went a startling step further: he appointed Arwa as *hujja* ("proof" or "proof of God") of the Sulayhid *dawah*, making her the highest religious authority in the kingdom, second only to the caliph-imam himself in the ranks of the Ismaili religious hierarchy. In addition to the nation's political ruler, she was now "the religious figure whose example was to be followed by the community of believers," responsible for all missionary activities in the *gazira* of Yemen and its furthest reaches. Her leadership of both the state *and* the religious establishment (in some respects, like England's monarchs, though not quite so purely symbolic) was unprecedented in Muslim history. No other woman in the Islamic world, before or since, has served in this dual capacity.

To appease Saba—who wasn't exactly pleased to learn that he had been denied what he considered his rightful inheritance, per Mukarram's will—Arwa appointed him deputy to Asgar in 1086, a job that entailed the military defense of the realm. Despite his gung-ho attitude towards warfare, Saba was not the most gifted of generals. His first foray that same year against a coalition of Zaydis and the persistently rebellious Najahids ended in crushing defeat. Meanwhile, Arwa's stepfather, Amir bin Sulayman al Zuwahi, opportunistically came crawling out of the woodwork at what he perceived to be a moment of weakness and unrest to pick a fight with Saba, while eyeing the throne for himself. The chaos Arwa was hoping to avoid was beginning to swirl around her, and she reached out once more to Mustansir for help.

The caliph responded in a special *sigil* (official correspondence) in June of 1087, addressed to "the Sulayhid and Zuwahid sultans, the Hijazi sayhs [semi-nomadic tribal leaders] and the groups of blessed believers"—in short, Yemen's entire Ismaili community. In his missive, read aloud in public squares throughout the realm, he issued a stern warning, commanding all "to abide by his wishes or face rejection as infidels, with the anger of God, the Prophet and the imams falling upon" those who refused to recognize Arwa's authority. Those "who followed her and her young son were following their imam, and those who approached her were approaching him," he emphasized, using verbs that stressed his authority (*yamur*, to order) and religious power to ban (*yuharrim* and *hurrima*, from *harama*, Arabic for "forbid"). He also took the opportunity to remind Arwa's subjects of her political and spiritual authority as well his unwavering support for her as "*al-Hurra*, the Queen, the Lady, the Righteous, the Faithful, the Powerful, the Preserver of Religion . . . the Supporter of the believers, the Cave for the followers . . . the Supporter of the Commander of the Faithful and the Protector of his Blessed Followers." He ended the declaration with an injunction to the Yemeni tribes to unite, as they did in the past, under the Sulayhid banner, and to obey both the young Asgar and his mother.

The powerful and unambiguously worded declaration broke yet another precedent, underscoring the potential severity of the situation brewing in one of the most important *gaziras* in the Fatimid Empire. Most *sigils* were communications from one ruler to another. For a caliph to directly address the general public in an official communication was practically unknown at the time. Of all of Mustansir's surviving *sigils*, this was the only one written to the local population.

The resulting calm in the wake of Mustansir's intervention didn't last, however. Sometime around 1090, both Asgar and his younger brother died. Their sad passings left Arwa in a difficult situation. Even though she had effectively reigned as sovereign since 1074, officially it was either as a surrogate to her husband or regent for her son(s)—not as sole ruler of the nation. As noted earlier, within the borders of Yemen it was generally accepted among the tribes that "the queen did not really need a husband to rule." But from a public relations perspective, in Cairo anyway, the notion of a childless widow as the sole occupant of the throne was more of a concern. The formality of a wedding, if only on paper, would satisfy grumbling clerics and high-minded officials at the Fatimid court.

Conveniently at this juncture, Saba proposed marriage to Arwa, a win-win from his perspective, as it not only placed him on the throne he'd always regarded as his anyway but also offered him the hand of "perhaps the most sought-after woman of her time."

The problem was, Arwa wasn't in the market for a husband, particularly one with Saba's reputation for ineptitude. Having ruled the kingdom unaided for more than a decade and a half, she was disinclined to share the throne with anyone and rejected Saba's offer. A stalemate ensued, followed by the predictable saber rattling and skirmishes between forces loyal to either side.

When news of the conflict reached the ears of Mustansir, the tables turned on Arwa. As supportive of "the noble lady" as he had been in the past, the caliph realized that the best way to maintain order and quell potential rebellion was to promptly sanction Saba's marriage proposal. He fired off a quick, three-line missive commanding Arwa to marry Saba, followed by a more formal letter—the contents of which amounted to the same thing—hand delivered and read aloud to her assembled "ministers . . . secretaries, and the officials of the state" by Yamin al Dawla, a high-ranking eunuch from the Fatimid court. (The choice of Dawla as envoy ensured the discretion and integrity of the encounter; as a eunuch, he would have been allowed to enter the quarters of the queen who was, at this point, a single woman.)

Dawla's address, delivered on behalf of his master, opened with the usual diplomatese, praising Arwa as "Queen Sayiddah . . . Sovereign Lady of the Kings of Yaman, the Pillar of Islam, the Treasure of the Faith," and so forth before getting down to the non-negotiable business end of the missive.

"Our Lord the Prince of the Faithful gives thee in marriage to . . . Saba, son of Ahmad," Dawla intoned before Arwa and her entourage, prefacing the statement with a grave reminder from the Holy Qur'an that, "Unto no believer, male or female, belongeth liberty of choice when God and His apostle have decreed a command, and whosoever opposeth God and His apostle wandereth signally astray." (The passage is from the Qur'an, concerning an arranged marriage made by the Prophet between one of his female relatives and a low-born freeman—a marriage that the woman and her family resisted.)

A gift of a hundred thousand dinars and fifty thousand dinars-worth of fine robes, perfumes, and other luxury items was tossed into the bargain. Still, no amount of money could compensate Arwa for what she was being commanded to surrender: her independence.

Cornered, she nonetheless remained characteristically composed in the face of this unwelcome turn of events. She didn't immediately accede to Mustansir's order, nor did she refuse it. Instead, she cleverly and astutely returned the caliph's Qur'anic volley by citing scripture herself.

"Verily a gracious letter hath been conveyed unto me," she declared, quoting—appropriately enough—the then-pagan Queen of Sheba's reply to Solomon when the great king and prophet (in the Islamic tradition) ordered her to submit to him and the "true Religion" of Islam. "And behold it saith: 'In the name of God, the Merciful, the Gracious. Resist me not but come unto me with submission.' I say not touching the command of our lord, 'O ye counsellors advise me, and nought will I determine until ye shall have spoken.'"

In the Qur'anic story, the members of Bilqis's council reply that her people are warlike and "endued with strength," ready to defend her wishes to the death, whatever they may be. But, wary of war, Bilqis soberly observes that should she resist, she would invite invasion:

> Kings, when they
> Enter a country, despoil it,
> And make the noblest
> Of its people its meanest

With Bilqis's words in mind, Arwa realized that resisting Mustansir's command could lead to costly bloodshed and devastating losses—not the least of which could include her own throne—despite the devotion of her people to "their Mistress." Like Bilqis, she there and then sought the advice of her ministers, who gently but insistently persuaded her that she had no other choice.

In the end, she agreed to the marriage, but the scripture-laden exchange between Arwa and Dawla wasn't merely theological banter. As a "savant in the sciences of the Qur'an, and its interpretation" (as the medieval historian Idris Imad al Din described her), Arwa was well aware that Bilqis's ultimate submission to Solomon represented her understanding that he was no ordinary king, but a prophet and God's representative on earth. By emulating Bilqis before Dawla and the court, Arwa was publicly declaring her submission to God's will, via His imam Mustansir, "Prince of the Faithful," and spiritual father of the Fatimid empire.

Saba, on the other hand, while a "Pillar of the Khalifate [and] Prince of the Amirs," did not rise to this level of authority, at least in Arwa's estimation, as she soon made abundantly clear. Upon her new husband's arrival in Jibla, she kept him waiting outside the city walls for a month, sending out food for him and his troops while keeping the gates to the town—and the wedding chamber—resoundingly bolted. Increasingly angry, not to mention embarrassed, Saba sent the queen a secret request to let him at least be seen entering the palace and her bedroom, so the public would think the marriage was consummated. Arwa consented and on their staged wedding night she sent a slave girl who resembled her to the bed chamber in her place. (Other accounts say Arwa herself spent the night in the room, disguised as a slave.) Prudish as well as puny, Saba "sat without ever raising his eyes upon" whomever was in the room that night, let alone lay a finger on her. Come dawn, he said his prayers and left the bed chamber for good, withdrawing his proposal. There is some evidence that he may well have known of Arwa's ruse. Before departing, he remarked to the slave girl (or Arwa herself, which would have been even more romantically poignant, if he knew who she was), "Tell our lady that she is a precious pearl, to be worn only by whoever is worthy of her."

In 1094, Mustansir died, having sat on the throne for fifty-eight years, the longest reign of any Fatimid caliph. In contrast to the stability of his long rule—facilitated in large part by his powerful (some say manipulative) vizier, Badr al Jamali—a bloody battle erupted over his succession. As primogeniture was not an established Ismaili custom, Jamali took the opportunity to install Mustansir's youngest (and thus most impressionable) son, al Mustali, as caliph. The move bypassed the late caliph's first born, Nizar, who fled to Alexandria and raised an army in support of his own claims to the throne.

While they never quite reached Cairo, Nizar's forces caused enough damage along the way to devastate the nearby countryside.

Though hundreds of miles away, the crisis reverberated in Yemen, where Arwa received a communication from Mustali's mother, the queen, seeking the Sulayhid court's support—a "rare epistle between two queens" during that era. In her letter, the queen mother described the unrest gripping Egypt, closing with a reminder of how critical the Sulayhid kingdom was to the overall stability of the Ismaili *dawah*. Mustali himself followed up his mother's letter with a similar plea to Yemen's "noble lady."

Reading the tea leaves as she usually did, Arwa coolly reckoned that the safe money was on Mustali, given Jamali's track record of managing the caliphate and clinging to power. It was a wise bet. Within a year, Nizar was captured, imprisoned, and eventually executed. But his cause didn't end with his death. The dispute over the legitimate heir spiraled into schism that forever divided the Ismaili community into Mustali and Nizari branches, with even further divisions yet to come. Arwa remained loyal to the Mustali caliphate and that of his son, Al Amir, who succeeded to the throne in 1101.

At the same time, she began to discreetly distance herself from Cairo, sensing that the Fatimid empire's foundations were beginning to crack. Between the dynastic infighting, the religious factionalism, and new external threats from the armies of the First Crusade that arrived in northern Syria in 1097 and began hacking away at Fatimid territory, the empire was under siege from all directions. Now in her early fifties, Arwa was experienced at deftly managing relations with shaky allies. She dutifully sent her annual tribute to Cairo and received the occasional gift in response. But she sensed relations were waning.

Meanwhile, she had to cope with her own domestic brush fires. In 1097, Saba died. While Arwa had no interest in another husband, the job of military commander was now open and she appointed a loyal servant, Al Mufaddal, to take Saba's place. As a youth, Mufaddal had been a page in Mukarram's service and was well known to Arwa, acting as a personal courier between her and her husband. In adulthood, he took his father's place as governor of Takar, the fortified, mountaintop palace south of Ibb, where the Sulayhids stored the bulk of their treasure and which served as Arwa's summertime palace.

In his new role as Arwa's top general, Mufaddal served her well, repressing various uprisings, including those of the reliably rebellious Najahids. He also restored Sulayhid authority over the critical port of Aden, where the ruling Zurayid tribal chiefs grumblingly agreed to resume paying their annual tribute, albeit at the reduced rate of 50,000 dinars, half of the original amount.

"In all things reliance was placed upon his judgement and upon his sword," Umarah observed, while "the Queen came to no decision without his advice."

Arwa articulated her faith in her beloved general during an audience at the Takar fortress. Mufaddal asked that she relocate the state treasury to Jibla and relinquish her authority over the fortress solely to him. But such was her trust in him—a trust approaching nearly that of a spouse—that she saw no need to remove a single dinar from the castle. "The citadel is yours," she assured him. "You are the man of the Sulayhid house, and there are no restrictions between you and me, due to your eminence."

In the end, his eminence—or at least his sense of propriety—may have done the faithful general in. While he was on a diplomatic mission to the Tihama in 1110, a half dozen Sunni scholars raised an army of twenty thousand like-minded Sunni rebels together with six thousand Khawlan tribesmen from the north, who banded together to capture Takar. Mufaddal was forced to race back to set siege to his own castle. As the siege dragged on, the Khawlan reinforcements began to lose interest and started to desert. Undaunted, one of the Sunni leaders, Ibrahim ibn Zeydan, vowed never to give up until Mufaddal was dead.

But first, he would humiliate his foe.

The rebel Sunni jurist dragged the women of Mufaddal's harem from their chambers dressed in their most intimate finery and had them dance, publicly, on the castle battlements, tapping their tambourines. Upon witnessing the dishonorable spectacle, Mufaddal, it was said, returned to his tent and died from shock and embarrassment.*

Umarah reported that he may have taken his own life by sucking poison from a secret compartment of a ring that was found in his mouth.

* Given the double standards of the time, it wouldn't have occurred to Umara to mention that it was the women who probably were most embarrassed and humiliated by the incident.

In either event, Arwa lost her most reliable general and was on the verge of losing a critical Sulayhid stronghold as well. Taking matters into her own hands, she led a large company from Jibla to Takar—another rare instance of a Muslim queen marching at the head of an army—and, per her usual tactics, negotiated a surrender by paying off the rebels. Ibrahim personally walked away with 20,000 dinars while a new deputy was appointed who was agreeable to all parties.

Casting about for a replacement for Mufaddal, she settled on Asad, one of his cousins. But the new commander lacked his predecessor's military acumen, and several key Sulayhid citadels were captured by rebels, including Takar (briefly), before Asad was killed in battle in 1120. Meanwhile, the tribute from Aden began withering to a trickle before coming to a complete stop once more.

Worried about her kingdom's security, Arwa wrote to Cairo asking the caliph to send an advisor whose presence might send a message to any rebellious subjects that she could still summon the power of an empire should she so wish. Amir dispatched a brassy, egotistical nobleman, Najib al Dawla, who Arwa appointed as her new military commander. At first, Najib succeeded in restoring some castles to Sulayhid authority. But he failed to subdue rebellious factions in major cities such as Aden, Zabid, and Sanaa. In 1123, Cairo sent reinforcements—four hundred Armenian archers and seven hundred knights—yet their foreign presence only irked the local Yemeni troops, who remained loyal to Arwa.

By 1125, Najib began blaming his failures on Arwa, the aging queen, whose mind, he declared, "had become weakened." He planned to arrest and imprison her but Arwa, learning of his treachery, swiftly responded by sending troops to lay siege to his fortress at Janad near Taizz, in the south. As the queen's troops hammered away at the castle walls, Najib's army managed to resist the attacks, though not without costly losses. While both sides flexed their male, testosterone-driven muscles, Arwa, ever the pragmatist, devised a less destructive way to secure the castle: the dissemination of fake news.

She arranged to have ten thousand Egyptian dinars (coins that would have come from Cairo) distributed to her troops while at the same time had spies spread the rumor that the source of the windfall was Najib himself. Feeling outraged and betrayed by the news that Najib was subsidizing the enemy, his army deserted him, leaving the castle gates unguarded for Arwa's troops to march right through. With helmet in hand and shuffling his feet, Najib stood before the queen, humiliated, abandoned, and apologetic. Looking down at him from her throne, she said, bitingly, "Perceivest thou, the artifice accomplished by her of whom thou hast said her mind was weakened?"

Upon hearing report after report of Najib's failures, Amir finally recalled him in 1129. Arwa, meanwhile had him arrested and sent back to Cairo in a wooden cage, a public symbol of his downgraded, once-upon-a-time golden boy status. An accident at sea spared the state the trouble of an execution. On its way to Egypt, the ship sank transporting the prisoner along with an envoy from Arwa bearing expensive gifts for the caliph. Najib and Arwa's envoy both drowned. Rumors were whispered that the queen herself paid the captain to scupper the ship, but it seems unlikely that she would intentionally drown her own secretary, not to mention have her costly gifts end up at the bottom of the Red Sea.

The following year there were celebrations in Cairo: a son, Abul Qasim al Tayyib, was born to Amir. Arwa, still a loyal, albeit increasingly uneasy Fatimid subject, pledged her support to the infant child as the designated heir to the imamate/caliphate. But the celebrations were short-lived. On October 7, 1130, Nizari assassins stabbed Amir to death during a public procession through the streets of Cairo. What happened to Tayyib at this point remains a mystery. Some accounts say he was whisked away from the palace, never be to seen or heard from again. A grimmer version of the story is that he was murdered in his crib on the orders of Amir's cousin, Al Hafiz, who just happened to be next in line to the throne. Others offered theological explanations: the infant Tayyib had gone into concealment (*sitr*) and thus remains hidden unto this day.

Whatever the fate of the poor infant, the result was yet another Ismaili schism, between those who accepted Hafiz as caliph (Hafizis) and the Tayyibis, who clung to the belief that Tayyib was the legitimate imam and would one day return.

Loyal to the line of succession established under Mustansir's vizier, Jamali, Arwa, and her Yemeni subjects dedicated themselves to the Tayyibi *dawah*, thus finally severing the kingdom from the Fatimids for good. The divorce was a long time coming, and in the end Arwa didn't need the support nor the headaches associated with dealing with Cairo, where the factionalism made the empire a more troublesome ally than it was worth.

Predictably, her domestic rivals—the Zurayids of Aden and some of the Hamdanid clan in Sanaa—declared their allegiance to the Hafizis. Yet Yemen's Tayyibis triumphed in the end. Upon the eventual collapse of the Fatimid dynasty in 1171, Hafizi Ismailism disappeared. Meanwhile, the Tayyibi branch of the faith survived not only in Yemen but in Western India, where the Gujarat Ismaili community established during Arwa's reign survives to this day, under the name of Dawoodi Bohras. From there, the sect spread to Pakistan, East Africa, and other parts of the Middle East.

"That the minoritarian Musta'li-Tayyibi community of the Ismai'lis exists at all today is indeed mainly due to the foresight and leadership of Sayyida Hurra," observed scholar Farhad Daftary, co-director of London's Institute of Ismaili Studies. Scholars like Daftary also acknowledge indebtedness to the Tayyibi Ismailis for the preservation of the bulk of Ismaili texts produced during the Fatimid period, a circumstance that also "may be attributed largely to Sayyida's foresight."

Arwa spent her final years beholden to none but her loyal subjects to whom she remained, like Asma before her, their beloved *Bilqis al-Sughra*, "Little Queen of Sheba." If there were any lingering doubts about the legitimacy of a woman simultaneously occupying the throne and leading the faithful, contemporary poet and scholar Al Khattab ibn Hasan devised a neat theological solution to the controversy.

"[T]he human body is nothing except a cloth or a cover for humanity. We find that many who appeared to us in female covering were of the highest and most noble position," he wrote, citing as examples Maryam, mother of Jesus, Khadija, wife of the Prophet Muhammad, and Fatima, wife of Ali. The womanly form, in other words, is just an outer cover; true nobility resides within, and it is one's duty "to obey them as all who believe should obey, without questioning the gender of those who carry the message."

Arwa died in 1138, at around the age of ninety-two. She was laid to rest in Jibla, in the mosque that bears her name, also known as the Hurrat al Malikah mosque (mosque of the Noble Queen), one of the oldest Islamic religious structures in the country. Her long, inspiring life, as Khattab wrote, "brought light to a place of darkness" and her shrine remains a pilgrimage site to this day, despite several unsuccessful attempts by Sunni fanatics to destroy it.

In her will, Arwa left a rich treasure (golden tiaras, sapphires, rubies, pearls, and other precious stones and jewelry) to endow the Tayyibi cause. She also added a codicil bearing witness to Fatima, "the radiant and the pure," honoring her as the fifth among the *ashab*, or "People of the House," who were the Prophet's closest family members. Multiple meanings have been read into Arwa's intention behind this addition to her will, ranging from a reiteration of the Sulayhid's Ismaili Fatimid legacy to her respect for and possibly identification with one of the earliest women is Islamic history to embrace and support the faith.

While Tayyibi Ismailism lived on, the Sulayhid dynasty died with Yemen's "noble lady." Within a century however, a new Islamic empire emerged some three thousand miles to the east, in northern India, governed by the daughter of a slave.

CHAPTER 3

Sultan Razia (r. 1236–1240)

India's Queen of Justice

The searing, northern Indian sun beat down upon worshipers as they emerged from the Qubbat al Islam Mosque in Delhi, on a November afternoon in 1236. It was a Friday *Jummah*, an occasion when the riotously decorated mosque—a triumph of Indo-Muslim architecture dating to the twelfth century—would be filled to capacity with Delhi's citizens. As they thronged into the courtyard, filtering past the cloister's ornately carved columns, repurposed from older Hindu and Jain temples, the clear, high sound of a woman's voice stopped them in their tracks.

The voice was resolute and impassioned—an urgent plea to the city's residents to rally. It echoed from the terrace of the Sultan's residence, the *Dalwat Khana*, or White Palace, overlooking the courtyard. Gazing up at the platform, the crowd saw a solitary figure draped in a red cloak standing there. They recognized her. It was the Razia, daughter of Shams ud Din Iltutmish, late ruler of the vast and powerful Sultanate of Dehli. If any missed her words, the symbolism of her red garment was clear enough: an oppressed person seeking justice, per a public policy instituted by her father who died seven months earlier.

At stake was not only her own life, but the fate of the sultanate itself, now in the hands of her inept and morally bankrupt half brother, Rukn al Din Firuz. His rights to the throne, which Iltutmish, in writing and before witnesses, had legally bequeathed to Razia, were dubious. He had already looked the other way at—if not been outright complicit in—the murder of one rival, his younger half brother, Qutubuddin, "a youth of great worth and promise," in the words of one contemporary chronicler. With others critical of the young, degenerate sultan's reign disappearing like characters in an Agatha Christie play, Razia rightly feared that she was next.

"My brother killed his brother and now he is trying to kill me as well," she cried to the people below, who were beginning to listen. In contrast to Firuz's shortcomings, she recounted the many virtues of her beloved father: his religious devotion, his respect for learning and education, his military victories, and his dedication to justice for all his subjects, day or night. Outside the palace gate, he had a cast-iron bell hung from a chain strung between two marble lions. Petitioners seeking a hearing in the middle of the night could ring the bell and have their cases looked into "there and then" by the sultan himself. During the day, per Iltutmish's decree, anyone seeking justice should wear a red colored cloak, as opposed to the solid white clothing most Indians wore at the time. In this way, whenever the Sultan "held a public audience or rode out [from the palace] and saw someone wearing a colored robe he looked into his petition and rendered him his due from his oppressor."

At a little more than thirty years of age, with everything to gain, but more critically everything to lose, Razia knew her only choice was to bring her case directly to the citizens of Delhi, banking on the glaring political symbolism of the scarlet robe enveloping her body like a shield.

It was a shrewd calculation. While Firuz was popular in the hinterlands, his sister had always been more beloved by the citizens of Delhi. "[S]tirred up to excitement," the crowd began to vigorously shout its support for Razia, who ultimately won the day and the throne. Yet in spite of the many lessons she learned about effective governance from her father, her reign was beset with challenges. Nonetheless, she consistently stood her ground as the first female Muslim ruler in India and the only female ruler of the Sultanate of Delhi, an Islamic empire that endured for three centuries, founded by a Central Asian slave-general from Turkestan.

Stretching, at times, across much of the Indian subcontinent, the Sultanate of Delhi emerged in the aftermath of a series of hit-and-run raids on northern India by Turkic (Central Asian) Muslim armies more interested in plunder than putting down roots. India's fate changed, however, in 1192, when Muhammad Ghori, an itinerant Afghan war lord, carved out a more permanent Islamic presence in the region after crushing Hindu resistance at the Battle of Tarain, about seventy miles north of Delhi. The decisive battle put an end to seven hundred years of Hindu rule in northern India, paving the way for one of Ghori's up-and-coming Mamluk* slaves and military commanders, Qutubiddin Aybek, to formally establish the sultanate in 1206.

A bit of a good cop, bad cop rolled into one, Aybek had a reputation for bestowing gifts "by hundreds of thousands" while famously slaughtering an equal number of enemies. Kidnapped by slave traders as a boy in Turkestan and raised in Persia, Aybek was trained to fight in the elite Mamluk military (the Marine Corps of the Muslim Middle Ages). As an adult, he was widely admired for his "manly bearing" and proficiency with bow and arrow. Unfortunately, he was less adept with a mallet: In 1210 the revered founding father of the Delhi Sultanate literally went down swinging, succumbing to injuries sustained while playing polo.

His successor, Aram Shah, lasted even less time on the job (about eight months). This figured. Aram was a hapless Sultan, enthroned by Delhi's nobles for no other reason than that he was "readily available," even though there were more qualified maliks (Turkic chieftains) in the far corners of the sultanate. Among them was Iltutmish, another rising Mamluk star. It helped that he was also Aybek's own son in-law, married to the Sultan's youngest daughter, Turkan Shah.

Iltutmish was the son of a tribal leader of the Qara Khitai Ilbaris, a nomadic people from the Central Asian steppes, with ethnic roots in Mongolia, Northeast China (Manchuria), and eastern Russia. As a youth, he was "endowed with comeliness, intelligence, and goodness of disposition." A bit too good, perhaps. Like the Biblical story of Joseph, his jealous elder

* Mamluks were a non-Arab, ethnically diverse class of slaves from Central Asia, southern Russia, the Caucasus, and eastern Europe who were captured when young, converted to Islam, and then trained to provide military and administrative services to Arab and Ottoman Islamic dynasties during the Middle Ages and the Renaissance. After their training, they were freed—since technically Muslims were not permitted to enslave other Muslims—and many rose through the ranks to become generals, viziers, and even sultans. For more on the Mamluks, see Chapter 4 and Chapter 6.

brothers sold him as a slave to a traveling merchant from Bukhara. There he was bought by a local religious authority who gave him a good education and may have instilled in him his deep devotion to Islam, for which he later became renowned. Sold and resold several times over the years, he eventually ended up in the ancient, commercial city of Ghazni in southeastern Afghanistan. There, he was purchased by Aybek, who took note of the handsome youth's bearing and charismatic personality. The Delhi potentate so admired Iltutmish that he treated him like a son, keeping him at his side during several military campaigns, where the gifted Ilbari slave "displayed great valor" while dispatching his master's enemies "to the lowest depths of Hell."

Various prestigious government appointments followed, drawing the attention of Ghori himself, who liberated Iltutmish, sending him a document of manumission and lavish robes as symbols of his freedom. It was an unheard of honor, since neither Aybek nor any of the other Mamluk amirs (high-ranking army officers) and noblemen had been freed; now Ghori had liberated the slave of one of his own slaves.

With Aybek's death and the amirs' confidence in Aram waning, Iltutmish reckoned the moment had come for him to seize power. An oath of loyalty from the head *qadi* and a delegation of the ulema (scholars of Islamic doctrine and jurisprudence) offering him the sultanship along with their allegiance added legitimacy to his claim to the throne which he secured by easily defeating Aram in battle, on the plain of Jud near Delhi, in 1211.

A restless ruler, Iltutmish spent a good part of his twenty-five years as Sultan in the saddle, stamping out Hindu rebellions and subjugating Muslim vassals. In the process he expanded the sultanate's borders, from the outskirts of Tibet in the north to the shores of the Bay of Bengal in the south. He also managed to diplomatically stave off the advancing armies of Mongol emperor Genghis Khan (no easy task) and attract an approving nod from the Abbasid caliph in Baghdad who, in 1229, officially recognized India's so-called slave dynasty.

When he did manage to sit still, the enlightened sultan commissioned the building of forts, endowed religious institutions (including expansions to the Qubbat al Islam Mosque complex, one of India's largest), standardized the currency, and supported the arts, favoring poets in particular. In short, he paved the way for his heir to seamlessly inherit a stable, prosperous, and highly cultured kingdom, if it hadn't been for one thing. After the untimely death in 1229 of the Sultan's eldest son, Nasir al Din Mahmud, the next male in line was Firuz, who everyone (including Iltutmish) seemed to agree was, literally, a royal screwup.

"[H]is inclinations were wholly towards buffoonery, sensuality, and diversions," reported Minhaj al Siraj Juzjani (b. 1193), author of the *Tabaqat i Nasiri*, a contemporary history of the Delhi Sultanate. Among the playboy prince's favorite "diversions" was crashing through the bazaar "in a state of intoxication, seated on the back of an elephant" while hurling red-gold *tankahs* (numismatic ancestors of the rupee) in his destructive wake at the victims of his obnoxious behavior.

Juzjani also characterized Firuz as "entirely enslaved by dissipation and debauchery," hinting (in what would today be regarded as a trans- and/or homophobic condemnation) that he may have been gay or trans, preferring the company of "impersonators, effeminate men and eunuchs"—shorthand for professional male cross-dressers and dancers who were regarded in Indian society at the time as "neither men nor women" but a "third gender" known as *hijras*.

Since Firuz's younger brother, Muiz ud din Bahram, was also regarded as unfit for the throne, it was clear to Iltutmish that neither of his elder male offspring was up to the task of inheriting, let alone governing, the sultanate. He was, however, confident that Razia, his first born—in whom he had already recognized "indications of sovereignty and high spirit"—would make an exceptional ruler. Like her brothers, she had been taught the arts of war and statecraft. The only difference was, in her case, the lessons sank in.

"[I]n her father's lifetime [she] employed herself frequently in the affaïrs of government; a disposition which he rather encouraged in her than otherwise, so that during the campaign in which he was engaged in the siege of Gualiar [modern Gwalior, a rival city south of Delhi], he appointed her regent during his absence," wrote the sixteenth-century Persian historian Mahomed Kasim Ferishta.

Razia must have proven herself exceptionally worthy, for upon Iltutmish's return from the Gwailor campaign in 1232, the sultan promptly declared that his daughter, and not his sons, would succeed him. Pushing back on the decision (albeit in courtly and obsequious tones), Iltutmish's nobles—a cliquey corps of elite Turkic chiefs known as the *chahalgani* ("the Forty")* who served at court and as provincial governors—joined the ulema in questioning the Sultan's decision: "Inasmuch as he has grown-up sons who are eligible for the sovereignty, what scheme and what object has the Sultan of Islam in view in making a daughter sovereign and heir apparent? Be pleased to remove this difficulty from our minds."

Iltutmish's response was frank enough. He told his nobles that "his sons [give] themselves up to wine and every other excess" and that governing would be "too weighty for their shoulders." If there was anyone in the family who was fit for the job it was his daughter who he concluded "was better than twenty such sons."

Given the patriarchy of the era, it is not surprising that the *chahalgani* leaned more favorably towards an eldest son as opposed to a daughter as a successor, however qualified. Yet at the same time, the notion of a woman on the throne was neither shocking nor culturally unfamiliar to any of these men.

Among the ancient and medieval nomadic tribal peoples of Central Asia—including Iltutmish's native clan, the Ilbaris—women typically enjoyed what we might today regard as equal rights, largely for reasons of practicality, as historian Adam Ali observed.

"Nomadic tribes lived in harsh environments with limited resources," Ali wrote. "They therefore had considerably smaller populations than . . . sedentary peoples, and had to utilize all the members of their societies to produce food, resources, and even to wage war and could not afford to confine or seclude their women or to relegate them to sidelines as was the case in other societies."

Since Iltutmish was born into a world where women were hunters, rode horses, practiced archery, and fought alongside men, it followed that the idea of a female ruler was equally acceptable and not regarded—as some misguided Muslim extremists (e.g., Boko Haram or the Taliban) do today—as an unthinkable violation of Islamic law and tradition.** In contrast, as the late

* A number not to be taken literally but figuratively, meaning "many" in much the same way as it is used biblically e.g., forty days and forty nights.

** Given the physical demands of these roles, it should come as no surprise that the Ilbari also rejected the custom of female foot-binding, which was growing in popularity among their neighbors to the East: the Han of China's Song Dynasty.

Bangladeshi historian A.B.M. Habibullah observed, "[f]rom the 10th century onwards, that is from the beginning of the Turkish ascendancy over the Islamic world, no accepted constitutional principle, much less any rigid rule, could . . . be cited against a female sovereign." During the twelfth century, the Khitai people (Iltutmish's tribe) were ruled by a woman who followed in her father's footsteps—just one of several such instances of Turkic female rule in the region, both before and after its conversion to Islam. Thus, in Iltutmish's estimation, "a daughter succeeding her father was no unusual occurrence," nor was it a "departure from current political ideas."

Cultural, not to mention political, norms notwithstanding, Iltutmish made sure to put the matter in writing in several media. Soon after the Gwalior campaign, he had his secretary of state draw up a decree, officially nominating Razia as his heir apparent. He also issued a commemorative coin (a silver *tankah*) with his daughter's name inscribed alongside his own. (Some historians believe that, just before his death, Iltutmish reconsidered and nominated Firuz as his heir instead. They regard Firuz's investiture as governor of several provinces, including Lahore—a territory once held by the previous heir apparent, his elder brother Nasir—as evidence that Iltutmish was grooming his eldest surviving son for the throne. They also point to a passage in Juzjani that describes how "the people had their eyes upon" Firuz after Iltutmish brought him back to Delhi from Lahore in his retinue after the Gwailor campaign, a public display of endorsement. Peter Jackson, a historian of medieval Indian politics, also questions the story of the decree confirming Razia as heir, arguing that because Juzjani was not in Delhi at the time, he could not have witnessed the event nor could he have seen the document Jackson speculates was likely a later, "apocryphal" addition to the narrative at the behest of Razia's supporters. Yet Juzjani's English translator, H.G. Raverty, stated plainly that "the people may have had their eyes on [Firuz], but [Iltutmish] had already named his talented daughter [Razia] as his successor." Plus Juzjani composed his text more than twenty years after the events he describes, under the patronage of a subsequent sultan, Nasiruddin Mahmud Shah,* and not Razia or her supporters. Therefore he would have no motive nor be under any pressure to make up stories about a fictitious

* Hence the book's title, *Tabaqat-i Nasiri*, or "The Nasirean Tables," i.e., chronological biographies.

royal decree to appease Razia or legitimize her succession and reign.) None of these official measures, however, prevented Firuz from shoving his stepsister aside and seizing the throne for himself upon their father's death in April of 1236. Or, more precisely, he had his mother do it for him.

A classic wicked stepmother right out of central casting, Firuz's mother, Shah Turkan (not to be confused with Razia's mother Turkan Shah), was chief concubine in Iltutmish's harem. She was all business, no nonsense, and showed no mercy to rivals, either in the harem or the throne room. Fully aware of the court's misgivings about a woman succeeding as sultan, she started sucking up to the *chahalgani*, even before Iltutmish's death, bribing them with rich gifts in exchange for their tacit support of her decadent son.

Her networking paid off. On the very night Iltutmish died, a tight circle of provincial members of the *chahalgani* and military officers who happened to be in Delhi held a secret meeting behind closed doors to plot Firuz's enthronement—a clear violation of Iltutmish's decree naming Razia as heir. The meeting lasted until dawn when the conspirators formed a delegation to deliver the news of their decision, not to the people of Delhi but to the harem, where Shah Turkan awaited confirmation of the coup she had orchestrated.

A "monster of cruelty," as Ferishta described her, Shah Turkan celebrated her victory by systematically bumping off anyone who had ever threatened or upstaged her. She tortured and/or murdered women in the harem whom Iltutmish had favored and ensured that his youngest son by another concubine—the admired and promising ten year-old Qutubuddin—posed no threat to Firuz by having the unfortunate child blinded and killed. She then set her sights on Razia, arranging for a deep pit to be dug on the path where her stepdaughter frequently went horseback riding. The plot was discovered, however, and Razia was spared.

Meanwhile, Iltutmish's misgivings about his inept son came true in less time than it took to uncork a wine bottle.

"Every morning, he threw open the [state] treasury and spent money indiscreetly," court poet Abdul Malik Isami remarked in his history of the Muslim conquest of India, written a century later. "In mirth, he frittered away wealth and spent many months of the year in frivolity." A daily program of showering gold on "dancing women, comedians, and musicians" and drunkenly riding elephants through the marketplace didn't leave much time for the affairs of state, which Firuz surrendered entirely to his mother.

The *chahalgani* soon realized they had made a huge mistake entrusting the sultanate to a "stripling of unripe judgement . . . who drinks wine day and night," not to mention letting it fall into the manipulative hands of a vengeful woman whose approach to taking care of business was just a few corpses shy of Michael Corleone's.

The nobles, and the people, had had enough. Various maliks throughout the sultanate banded together to form a rebellion. Displaying a little backbone for the first time in his life, Firuz retaliated by leading an army against the uprising. The outnumbered troops hadn't marched more than a few miles from Delhi, however, before the Sultan's own officers, seeing the writing on the wall, deserted him and joined the rebels.

Taking advantage of the ensuing chaos, Razia chose this moment to ascend the palace terrace in her red robe and make her appeal to the citizens of Delhi for justice. Given the track records of both Firuz and his mother, it didn't take much convincing for the people to rally behind her, nor for the local authorities to seize and imprison Shah Turkan for her many atrocities. Learning of his mother's imprisonment and Razia's revolt, Firuz limped back to Delhi at the head of a small band of supporters. They were quickly overwhelmed by Razia's forces and Firuz himself was captured, imprisoned, and put to death—together with his mother, in all likelihood—in November of 1236, after a reign of barely seven months.

With one crisis over, the *chahalgani* now faced another: who would rule? Whereas Razia had earlier pled her case to the people, she now brought it directly to the nobles. In Isami's telling of the episode, she squarely reminded them of her status as her father's chosen successor:

> Here I am, daughter of His Majesty; the royal crown befits my head. It is I whom the king had chosen as his heir-apparent; to me he had entrusted his seal.* Since you went beyond the king's orders and set the crown on the head of another person, you finally came to grief. Now you regret

* Here she is likely referring to her appointment as surrogate during Iltutmish's Gwailor campaign.

> having done so . . . Since none of His Majesty's sons* in this capital is fit for kingship, you better give up all discussions henceforth and set the crown on my head—myself, daughter of His Majesty—for a few years, by way of trial; you would be relieved of all anxieties about the State. Should I acquit myself as ruler better than [a] man, you might keep me on the throne. Should you yourselves see things otherwise, you may remove the crown from my head and give it to whomsoever you please and pay your homage accordingly.

Obviously Isami was not an eyewitness to this speech, but its frankness and inclusion in his history suggest that it may have accurately reflected Razia's position, in addition to offering insights into her character. On the one hand, she made it clear that her right to the throne was unquestioned, while adding an "I told you so" or two, just to rub it in. But then she suggests a deal: if I don't live up to expectations, you can fire me—a rare proposal from a medieval monarch. If Isami's objective was to glorify Razia (as he does a few paragraphs later by quoting admirers who compared her to Venus, goddess of love and beauty, the only surviving, physical description of her, if one could call it that), it is unlikely that he would have characterized her right to the throne as anything but absolute. By offering the *chahalgani* the option to depose her if she didn't prove herself worthy, Razia displayed both confidence and humility. It is also interesting to note that in addition to the cultural acceptance of a woman as ruler, no Muslim jurist in the court—including Juzjani, who also happened to be a *qadi*—raised any legal objection to elevating Razia to the throne, because there was none to be found.

Still, the episode underscored the growing influence of the *chahalgani*, who could bestow—and take away, if it came to that—the Sultan's power. Governing the state while keeping them in check was a delicate balancing act, as Razia would ultimately learn. Yet, for the time being, the *chahalgani's* response to her proposal (again, as recorded by Isami) was both in keeping with Iltutmish's wishes and the cultural norms of the Turkic tribes.

* By whom she meant Bahram, Nasiruddin Mahmud Shah, and several other half siblings who were either as unqualified as Firuz or too young to succeed.

> A daughter is better than an ill-bred son. Many a woman has fared as vanquisher of men in battle; many a man has owed his position to a woman; if this daughter of the king were raised to the throne in this capital, she would prove better than the sons of kings.

They made it official on November 19, 1236, when Delhi's nobles seated Razia on a golden throne and "bent their heads towards her, fully resolved to carry out her orders." Nevertheless, there were still grumblers among the provincial maliks who refused to accept a female sultan. A coalition of these rebels, led by Iltutmish's former vizier, marched on Delhi from all sides, besieging the city. It wasn't until Razia herself inspiringly emerged from behind the safety of the city walls and joined her troops encamped on the banks of the nearby Yamuna river that the rebellion disintegrated. The first test of her reign was over. She proved herself more than worthy of her father's confidence in her.

With the crisis behind her, "all things returned to their usual rules and customs," Juzjani recorded. "Sultan [Razia] was a great monarch," he observed, employing the masculine form of her title, which she insisted on, as opposed to the feminized, "sultana,"* which translates as "consort" or "assistant sultan."

"She was wise, just, and generous, a benefactor to her kingdom, a dispenser of justice, the protector of her subjects, and the leader of her armies . . . endowed with all the qualities befitting a king," the chronicler gushed. Still, deferring to his male readership, he felt compelled to add the coda: "[B]ut she was not born of the right sex, and so in the estimation of men, all these virtues were worthless."

Dismissing such attitudes, Razia got right to work governing the kingdom her father left her.

At first, her reforms were civic and cultural, as opposed to political, and thus not prone to raise too many eyebrows among the *chahalgani.* Like her father, she was a patron of the arts and education, having been well educated herself, with a reputation for reciting the Qur'an with perfect pronunciation. She established schools, public libraries, research centers, and academies

* Coins minted in 1236, the first year of her rule, featured Iltutmish's name alongside hers, together with the word *nusrat* (now a common Arab name for boys meaning "victory" or "assistant.") By 1237–1238, she felt secure enough in her position to have coins minted in her name alone, under the title "Razia Sultan."

where the writings of Islamic theologians and philosophers were studied alongside the works of earlier, great philosophers. Juzjani himself benefitted from these initiatives, being appointed director of Delhi's prestigious Nasiriya College, one of the city's major institutes for the study of *tafsir* (interpretation of the Qur'an), *hadith* (traditions and sayings of the Prophet), and *fiqh* (Islamic jurisprudence).

The curricula of these schools and colleges also included courses in Hindu sciences, astronomy, philosophy, and literature. It was Razia's firm belief—in keeping with the Prophet's famous injunction that it is "the duty of every Muslim to seek knowledge,"—that truth was truth, no matter what its source. Its pursuit by Hindu scholars, she espoused, was just as legitimate as that of Islamic philosophers and scientists.

The schools that she and her father established throughout the sultanate were well endowed, offering scholarships to students who couldn't afford tuition. Just as today's prestigious universities and colleges attract the best talent, these centers of higher learning drew prominent professors and scholars from all across India and beyond, in the fields of theology, history, and the law.

Indeed, "[i]ntellectuals and creative people from many regions of the Muslim world migrated to India at this time, for the Delhi Sultanate was one of the most powerful Muslim kingdoms of the age, and most of the sultans were generous patrons of scholars and writers." This included Razia, who extended her patronage to noted poets, painters, and calligraphers who flocked to the capital, a cosmopolitan city of some three hundred thousand people. The population was made up of Muslim aristocrats and military commanders (Turks, Persians, Afghans); clergy and men of letters; wealthy Hindu merchants whose lavish homes outshone those of their Muslim competitors; and common folk including artisans, craftspeople, masons, shopkeepers, and menial clerks. At the bottom rungs of society, making up the majority of the overall population, were subsistence-level laborers and servants.

Teeming and vibrant, the city had such a reputation for sophistication and splendor that by Juzjani's day it was known simply as *hazrat*: "majesty." When Ibn Battuta visited Delhi a century later, he remarked that it was "a vast and magnificent city, uniting beauty with strength. It is surrounded by a wall whose equal is not known in any country in the world, and is the largest city in India, nay rather the largest of all the cities of Islam in the East." Arab historian al Umari, a contemporary of Ibn Battuta, never visited Delhi himself, but interviewed returning travelers who reported that the city was indeed "extensive in length and breadth and has a circumference of forty miles." That was about three times as large as central Paris, albeit a quarter of the size of today's Delhi, modern India's biggest city.

Packed within its two-toned defensive walls, composed of stone foundations with upper courses of layered baked brick, were one thousand madrasas, al Umari recorded, "out of which most are for the Hanafites and some are for the Shafites.* Besides, there are also seventy hospitals (*Darul Shafa*) where both Muslims and non-Muslims obtain the best possible treatment. Of huge buildings, extensive bazaars, and splendid hammams [bathhouses] in Delhi, the number is beyond calculation."

Providing water for those hammams, as well as public drinking, was a large, terraced reservoir, named for Iltutmish, situated just outside the city walls. Two miles in length and a mile wide, it also provided irrigation for three gardens, each twelve miles long, surrounding the city on three sides. Stone pavilions with benches alongside the reservoir's terracing offered visitors a place to sit and enjoy the shade. Domed pavilions also provided opportunities for rest and contemplation in the city's nearby cemeteries, which were planted with jasmine trees and rose bushes in a lush climate where "there are always flowers in bloom at every season of the year," as Ibn Battuta reported.

The atmosphere within the city's walls was more chaotic. Along its congested streets, customers could haggle for such fineries as perfumes, flowers, and jewelry, alongside a wide selection of household goods and staples including twenty-one different varieties of rice, all sorts of grains, sugar, imported wine, both fresh and dried fruits and vegetables, plus exotic foodstuffs including dozens of varieties of sweets. Manufactured goods included worsted and cotton fabrics, bamboo mats, gloves, armor, and weapons, all produced in crammed and clattering workshops. As the fourteenth-century Indian court poet Amir Khusrau remarked, anything and everything was available in Delhi's souks (marketplaces), even *Shir-i-murgh*, the "milk of birds."**

* Two different schools of Islamic jurisprudence.

** By which he meant a rich, savory delicacy made with milk and some sort of fowl, probably chicken. Birds, of course, do not produce milk.

This wide-ranging inventory also included human flesh. Brothels did a brisk business, as did the slave market. Assessing the city's lively trade in slaves, both male and female, historian Ziauddin Barani (a contemporary of Amir Khusrau) remarked, disparagingly, on the industry's corrupting influence on society:

> [W]ell-known reprobates and old, wicked procuresses had trained up young girls with beauty, slimness, grace and allure, bold . . . and shameless . . . to sing melodiously, to strike the rubab,* to recite *ghazals*** and to engage in repartees and play nord*** and chess. These courtesans, every one of whom was a danger to cities and kingdoms, were brought up with expensive care. Even before their breasts could ripen to womenhood, they were taught riding, polo-playing and wielding the lance with thousands of accomplishments and graces. Every alluring art and trick that induced the Muslim ascetic to put on the Brahman's thread**** and drag the mystic to the tavern was taught to them. Indian boys of graceful stature and girls of remarkable looks were taught to sing in Persian and then dressed in robes of brocade; they were trained in courtesies, customs, and manners of the court. The ears of handsome boys were pierced for pearl earrings; beautiful young slave girls were decked like brides. And (along with them) there were expert musicians and reciters of the praises of the Sultan in Hindi, Persian, in prose and verse; and also jokers and buffoons (*bhands*), who with one joke, could incite the sorrow-hearted to hilarious laughter, and the joyous hearted to such fits that they could not hold their sides from laughing. All these in the hope of the Sultan's favour came from far-off places. And the spirit distillers of Koil (Aligarh) and Meerut brought flagons of scented spirits that were 2 or 3 years old.

As one modern historian summarized the scene, "[h]ere was a co-mingling of nationalities, creeds, languages and extremes of luxuries and asceticism,

* A lute-like instrument, known throughout Afghanistan, Pakistan, and India.

** Love poems.

*** A Persian board game and possible forerunner of backgammon.

**** Meaning to abandon Islam for Hinduism.

all helping to form a colorful tapestry of beneficence and brutality, high thinking and low living, great learning and equally great ignorance, colour, rhythm, silence and clamour, grandeur and poverty, bravery and cowardice, orthodoxy and rationalism."

The focal point of it all was the Qubbat al Islam mosque complex and the neighboring Sultan's palace, gleaming in the sun, where Razia reigned in *purdah* (from a Hindi word for "curtain"), i.e., sitting behind a screen with her face veiled, attended by armed, female guards. *Purdah* was her one concession to the *chahalgani's* expectations for how a proper Muslim woman, no matter how equal (or in her case, superior) in social status, should comport herself.

Like her father, she maintained diplomatic relations with the Mongols. Also like him, she expanded the Sultanate's political boundaries, "from the territory of Lakhanawatī [west Bengal, India's easternmost tip] to Dīwal and Damrīla [lower Sind, the western corner of south-central Asia, in modern Pakistan]." Within this vast swath of the Indian subcontinent, "all the Maliks and Amirs manifested their obedience and submission."

When any of her nobles did get out of line, she acted swiftly, leading all military campaigns herself. When Malik Kabir Khan, governor of Lahore, rebelled in 1238 (possibly 1239), she pursued him across the Punjab until he ran into Mongol troops on the opposite banks of the Chenab River in northwestern India. With the Mongols being the rock and Razia's forces the hard place, Kabir was forced to turn back and submit to his sultan's authority.

Yet there were military losses as well, primarily to Indian Rajputs, an aristocratic class of Hindu warriors who persistently scanned the remote borders of the Sultanate, looking for weak spots. In 1238, both Gwalior and the fortress of Ranthambore, in the southern province of Rajasthan, two hundred miles south of Delhi, fell to Rajput forces. Politically, these were humiliating losses for Razia. Gwalior had been subdued by her father, while Rathambore, an ancient fortress, had been under Muslim control since Muhammad Ghori secured portions of Rajasthan half a century earlier, after the Battle of Tarain. In the wake of these defeats, some members of the *chahalgani*, out of earshot of the throne room, began to mutter regrets over their support for Razia.

But she was still deeply beloved by the people and the clerics, especially for her defense of the orthodox Sunni faith, which literally came under attack a year into her reign. By this time, the Tayyibi Ismailis, dispatched as missionaries to western India a century earlier by Yemen's Queen Arwa, were now firmly entrenched in Indian society as far east as Delhi, where they continued to attract converts and grow more powerful, not to mention bold. During Iltutmish's reign, they even made an unsuccessful attempt on the Sultan's life. Added to these were various other Shia denominations throughout the Sultanate, roundly denounced by the Sunni majority. Stoking the furor of these so-called heretics was one "Nur the Turk," a religious rabble-rouser who publicly condemned the ulema, accusing them of antagonism towards Shias and of fostering the belief that faith alone, without good works, was sufficient in Islam.

On March 6, 1237 (a Friday), a thousand or so armed followers of Nur violently descended upon Delhi. Half entered the city via the gateway to the Qubbat al Islam mosque, along the southern edge of the complex, while the other half crashed through the cloth merchant bazaar, headed for the newly established Muizzi College, founded by Razia, which they mistook for the mosque. Brandishing swords, shields, bows and arrows, and other weapons, the frenzied attackers indiscriminately began hacking away at worshippers and any who stood in their path. In the melee, Juzjani reported, "[m]any of the faithful were slain by the sword and many were trampled to death by the crowd." Hearing the chaos, a handful of local knight-warriors and their soldiers charged into the fray on horseback, slaughtering the rebels while worshippers who fled to the rooftop of the mosque for safety pelted the rioters on their heads with bricks and stones. Razia wasted little time responding to the uprising. Living up to her royal designation on her coins—*Jalalat al Dunya wa al Din* (Protector of the World and Religion)—she publicly reasserted her support for the ulema, making it clear that the Delhi Sultanate was a Sunni kingdom and violent opposition to the state religion would not be tolerated.

At the same time, she remained broad-minded when it came to the multinational, multilingual (Hindustani, Persian, Arabic, et al.), religiously diverse nature of the state she governed, where a Sunni Muslim majority not only ruled over Shias but Hindus as well, who were free to openly practice their faith. While some Hindus managed to rise in status and rank as merchants and military commanders, many lived closer to the bottom of the socioeconomic ladder. Recognizing their burdens, Razia attempted to eliminate the *jizya*, a tax on *dhimmis*, non-Muslim inhabitants of the Sultanate, but the *chahalgani* wouldn't hear of it. Nonetheless, she did manage to reduce and abolish some taxes on the general public, always a winning gambit for a politician.

But Razia's motives extended beyond politics. She genuinely cared about her subjects. As she put it, "Everywhere people are my supporters/because their welfare is my concern."

Indeed, as one modern historian summarized Razia's character, "What the multiple narratives of . . . this formidable young queen all agree on is her charismatic personality, her sense of justice and equity, and her sensitivity to the lives of the masses—both Hindu and Muslims—who supported her and stood by her throughout her reign."

In her desire to be closer to her people, sometime during the third year of her reign, she made a radical change in her style of governing as well as her appearance. Cutting her hair, she "laid aside [her] female dress and issued from [her] seclusion, and donned the tunic, and assumed the head-dress [of a man], and appeared among the people," sitting with them in the souks and listening to their grievances. Gone were the screen, the veil, the female guards. Dressed in male attire, she engaged directly with her people as her father had, personally dispensing justice and tending to state affairs "in the manner of a king." Relieved of the restrictive trappings of *purdah*, she even "became jovial," Isami reported.

Meanwhile, the *chahalgani* were anything but. This was not what they had bargained for when they elevated Razia to the throne. While stepping out of *purdah* was troubling enough, what really pushed the Forty over the edge was when Razia began threatening them where they felt it most: their job security.

The Delhi Sultanate had always been "a purely Turkish throne supported by Turkish nobles." And a certain class of nobles at that: rich, aristocratic, and disdainful of other races—an old-boy network of privileged families whose close connections to the reign of Iltutmish were such that they were also known as "Shamsi" maliks, after Iltutmish's first name. The curmudgeonly Barani might well have been their spokesman. In his fourteenth-century political manifesto, *Fatawa-i-Jahandari* ("Rulings on Temporal Government"), he argued against educating the lower classes because "plenty of disorders arise owing to the skill of the low born in knowledge," by which he meant that with the proper education the lower classes could oust the incumbent upper classes from their positions of power. He also objected to conversion to Islam, claiming that only those born Muslim had the spiritual credentials necessary to practice the faith.

Razia ascribed to none of these principles, and this began to make the *chahalgani* nervous. While some Hindus had risen to the rank of military commander during her reign, when she attempted to appoint an Indian Muslim convert to a prestigious position at court, the *chahalgani* pushed back. When she bestowed governorships on younger, non-Turkish servants in the court (falconers and cupbearers and the like) they disapproved.

The final straw was Razia's appointment of an Ethiopian slave, Jamal al Din Yaqut, to the post of Lord of the Stables (*Amir i akhur*, or Amir of horses, i.e., the Sultan's equerry). The position was a prestigious one, viewed as a career-making stepping stone to higher things at court because whoever held the post was in daily, ear-whispering distance of the Sultan. It was this proximity that began to inspire jealousy among the *chahalgani*, exacerbated after Razia then elevated Yaqut to the highest court position of *Amir al umara* (Amir of amirs). The envious courtiers began spying on their Sultan, digging for dirt with which to soil her reputation and remove her from the throne. Lacking anything concrete, they ultimately fell back on one of the oldest tricks in the smear campaign handbook: a sex scandal.

"A very great degree of familiarity was observed to exist between [Yaqut] and the Queen," wrote Ferishta. "[S]o much so, that when she rode he always lifted her on her horse by raising her up under the arms. This intimacy, the great favour which he had suddenly attained, and his rapid elevation to the first rank in the realm might naturally have excited envy had it happened to any individual; but it became the more mortifying when the favourite was merely an [Ethiopian] slave."

Helping the sultan into the saddle was actually part of the amir of horses' job description. But for a slave to lay hands on an unmarried, not to mention unveiled, presumably virgin queen was another matter . . . if it ever even happened. Modern historians have dismissed Ferishta's account (first suggested by Ibn Battuta, who wrote merely that Razia "was suspected of relations with a slave of hers") as scandal-mongering rubbish. They have pointed out that the record shows that Yaqut was actually named (albeit never confirmed) as a candidate for the post of *Amir i akhur* by Iltutmish. Plus on state occasions Razia always rode out from the palace on an elephant, not a horse, though it's conceivable that Yaqut could have helped her onto the elephant as well, per the duties of the position.

Whether or not Razia had an affair with Yaqut, we'll never know. What ultimately mattered, according to Peter Jackson, was that she "sought to develop a power-base of her own and neglected the Turkish slave elite which she and Firuz had inherited from their father. Her dependence on Yaqut and his promotion to the rank of intendant of the imperial stables must be seen in this context."

Now the *chahalgani's* rhetoric pivoted nastily and hypocritically 180 degrees, from "a daughter is better than an ill-bred son" to "[c]onfidence should not be placed in women," as Ismai recorded.

> To wear the crown and fill the throne of kings does not befit a woman; this is the role exclusively meant for the experienced type of man. A woman cannot acquit herself well as a ruler, for she is essentially deficit in intellect. It is better for a woman to occupy herself with the *charka* ["spinning wheel"] since attainment of high position on her part would make her intoxicated. It would befit a woman to associate herself with cotton while sorrow should be her companion and the sound of a loom should serve her as music. Wisdom did not make *kuhlah* [a crown-helmet worn by sultans into battle] to be the woman's headgear since it was meant to be worn by man. A woman who aspires after pleasure and is at the same time ambitious, can hardly be free from the sway of passion. It is better for a woman to observe *purdah* always and accustom herself to hard work, day and night . . . Since we have committed the initial mistake of agreeing to such a ridiculous idea, it would amount to another mistake on our part, if we persist in leaving the royal seal in her hands.

Still, the *chahalgani* had a problem. Razia was still beloved by the citizens of Delhi, and overthrowing her there would be tricky. So in the spring of 1240, they convinced one of her own appointees, Malik Altunia, governor of the provincial city of Bhatinda in the Punjab, to stir up a little rebellion and lure Razia from the city at the head of an army.

Taking advantage of her absence, the *chahalgani* murdered Yaqut and set Firuz's equally inept younger brother, Bahram, on the throne. Meanwhile, the Bhatinda campaign did not go well: Razia was captured and imprisoned by Altunia. Then, in one of those twists of fate you'd have to be a soap-opera writer to concoct, Altunia fell in love with his prisoner, married her, and pledged to reinstate her as sultan.

In some versions of the story, the two had grown up together in the palace and Altunia had loved her since childhood. Meanwhile, some view their marriage as further evidence of Razia's innocence in the Yaqut affair: were Altunia not convinced of her chastity, it is unlikely that he would have married her. They also speculate that, rather than a Valentine, Razia simply viewed her marriage certificate as a get-out-of-jail-free card. In Juzjani's telling of the story, Altunia's motives were no less self-serving. By allying himself with Razia, he planned to "take possession of the kingdom."

Whatever their individual incentives, the newlyweds marched upon Delhi that fall, but their army was no match for the conjoined forces of Bahram and the *chahalgani*. Deserted by their troops during a humiliating retreat, the royal couple was captured and put to death by Bahram in December of 1240.

Ibn Battuta, recounting an embellished version of Razia's demise, reported that the defeated, retreating sultan stumbled into a farmer's field, hungry and exhausted, begging for food. After eating a crust of bread the farmer gave her, she fell asleep beneath a tree. The farmer then noticed jewels glinting in the embroidery beneath her outer garment. "Realizing from this that she was a woman, he killed her, stripped her . . . and buried her in his field, then taking some of her garments he went to the market to sell them," Ibn Battuta wrote. The farmer's plan backfired when the local chief of police suspected the man of essentially fencing stolen goods, beat a confession out of him, and recovered Razia's body, which was "washed, wrapped in grave clothes, and buried again at the same place [where] a dome was built over it." (The actual location of Razia's grave remains uncertain, with Delhi, Kaithal, and Tonk, in Rajasthan state, all claiming the honor.) In other versions of the story, Razia and Altunia were found sleeping beneath a tree by bandits who robbed and killed them.

However she died, her reign, per Juzjani's calculations, "extended over a period of three years, six months, and six days."

True to form, Razia's stepbrother, Bahram—whose "reign was full of murder, treachery and intrigue"—was deposed for incompetency after two years on the throne. The sultanate was finally swallowed up two centuries later by the Turco-Mongol conqueror Timur (Tamerlane, d. 1405).

The legacies of Razia's reign were an expanded and prosperous state and a culture where the arts and education flourished. She also endorsed an inclusive society, where people of various races and religions were tolerated, an ideal that is only just being realized in India after centuries of conflict.

Though she enjoyed popular support, it was the treachery of a handful of jealous and resentful male military elites whose power she challenged that led to her downfall. She nonetheless stands as the first in a long line of women political leaders in India—Muslim, Christian, and Hindu—among the most famous being Indira Gandhi (1917–1984), who served twice as the nation's prime minister. Today, Razia is regarded as a beloved Indian folk hero, the subject of poems, a play, a novel, plus numerous documentaries, big-budget, highly romanticized movies (highlighting her love interests), and more than one epic television miniseries.

While Razia's story is now the stuff of legends, she was not the only Muslim queen who rose to power with the support of a Mamluk military elite. Around the same time that she was reigning over one of the Islamic world's most powerful empires, another courageous and clever Muslim queen was using all the means at her disposal to save her own empire from destruction and catastrophe on the sunbaked banks of the Nile.

Marriage and Queens

Why did Razia wait so long to marry, well into her thirties, which for a woman at that time was quite late in life? Some have speculated that she chose not to because she knew that by marrying she would have surrendered her independence and risked being sidelined by a husband whose motivation for wedding her might have been assuming sole control over the state, as Altunia hoped (if Juzjani is to be believed). A husband would also be free to take other wives, under Islamic law, and maintain a harem, which would have then introduced rivals for Razia's power and position. While monarchs, male and female, have usually been expected to marry and reproduce, if only to secure the dynastic lineage, there is no evidence that the *chahalgani* encouraged Razia to take a husband. Still, unmarried queens have often been regarded as a problem for the state, with England's sixteenth-century Queen Elizabeth I, Sweden's seventeenth-century Queen Christina, and Russia's eighteenth-century Empress Elizabeth all coming under pressure to wed, though none did. And royal or not, in western and non-western cultures alike, women who chose not to marry have faced unfair scrutiny. Those past a certain age have historically been referred to as "old maids" or "spinsters," meaning a single woman who had no other purpose in life beyond spinning thread. In English society from the seventeenth century into the early 1900s, "spinster" was the actual legal designation for all unmarried women, from a viscount's daughter downward. By contrast, unmarried men are "bachelors," a word derived from *bachelier*, an Old French term for a young squire in training for knighthood. The term's association with training and education under a master also provided the likely root for "baccalaureate," or "bachelor's degree," indicating the first level of certification in the university system. The patriarchy lives on: whereas aging single women have been "spinsters," single men, no matter how old, remain bachelors. Meanwhile, adding insult to injury, women who graduate from four year colleges still do so with "bachelor" degrees.

CHAPTER 4

Sultana Shajarat al Durr (r. 1250–1257)

The Cunning Queen Who Halted a Crusade

Egypt was in trouble.

Forces of King Louis of France, leader of the Seventh Crusade, launched in 1248, were bearing down on the Nile Delta port city of Damietta, gateway to Egypt for Christian armies since the ninth century.

Meanwhile, encamped with his own army at Mansoura, on the east bank of the Nile, about sixty miles northeast of Cairo, Egypt's sultan, Al Malik al Salih, lay dying from tuberculosis and an infected wound in his leg.

Watching and waiting by his side was the one person whose cool resolve, cleverness, and courage stood between Louis and the fall of the sultanate: Salih's wife, Shajarat al Durr.

With the enemy breathing down her neck, she realized that the only way to stave off the impending conquest of her country by foreign invaders was to keep her husband alive . . . even after he was dead.

Summoning the sultan's most trusted counselors to his bedside, she swore them to secrecy and shared with them her plan.

Egypt's most famous queen, of course, was Cleopatra, whose guile and political acumen, not to mention legendary seductive beauty, have made her a darling of historians, novelists, playwrights, operettists, and movie makers. Yet Queen Shajarat al Durr, who reigned in Cairo from 1250 to 1257, shared all of Cleopatra's virtues, while likewise being many things to many people. To Western historians of the Crusades, she was an incidental figure. To medieval Muslim chroniclers of those same wars, she was a respected ruler, "unmatched in beauty among women and in determination among men," who shrewdly negotiated an end to the Seventh Crusade. Modern historians of medieval Egypt differ in their assessment of this engaging women—Muslim Egypt's sole female ruler and the only queen to sit upon its throne since her more famous predecessor. Some regard her as a petty pawn, while others argue that she was a key figure in the establishment of an upstart dynasty that ruled Egypt for the next three centuries. While much has been written about Shajarat's career, little is known about her early background, including her given name. "Shajarat al Durr" is Arabic for "Tree of Pearls," a nickname inspired by the queen's fondness for pearls, strings of which she wore draped about her ears, on her fingers, and embroidered into her silken head scarves.

The date of her birth has also been lost to history, though it was probably late in the first quarter of the thirteenth century, perhaps a bit later. Some legends say she came from royal stock, but most historians, both modern and medieval, claim she was a common Kipchak Turk, from the Armenian highlands. The Kipchaks were a nomadic Turkic clan who migrated from the steppes of southern Russia around the middle of the eleventh century. They were a handsome people, known to Western medieval chroniclers as "the Blonde Ones," owing to their light-colored hair and skin. While it is uncertain if Shajarat was blonde, if genetics had anything to do with it, she was probably fair-skinned and may well have had light hair and blue eyes. Most contemporary writers, such as thirteenth-century Syriac historian Bar Hebraeus reported she was "renowned for her beauty."

Yet blonde and beautiful did not necessarily add up to bimbo, especially among the Kipchaks, whose women were both highly capable and highly revered: "I have witnessed in this country a remarkable thing, namely the respect in which women are held by them, indeed they are higher in dignity than the men," noted Ibn Battuta, while passing through Kipchak territory in the fourteenth century. The famed traveler also recorded that "the womenfolk of the Turks do not veil themselves" and traded equally with men in the marketplace.

Perhaps most tellingly, when considering Shajarat's destiny, women in government were accorded similarly equal, if not elevated, status. Witnessing a royal Kipchak reception, Ibn Battuta observed that when the queen approached the pavilion, the sultan stood and personally escorted her to her throne before resuming his own seat.

"All of this is done in full view of those present, without any use of veils," reported the astounded traveler, in whose home country of Morocco such reverence would have been unimaginable yet would ultimately play a key role in Shajarat's ascension to the throne.

Still, noble or not, many Kipchaks ended up in the service of Egypt's sultans as members of an elite corps of slaves known as Mamluks (see "The Irrepressible, Indispensable Mamluks," p. 76). Shajarat's first husband, Salih, was the first to import large numbers of Mamluks to Egypt. Kurdish by birth, Salih was the last of the major Ayyubid rulers, whose dynasty was founded in the late twelfth century by the famed Salah ad Din Yusuf ibn Ayyub (Saladin). They were a quarrelsome lot, with family members squabbling over Egypt and Syria as well as swaths of Libya, eastern Turkey, northern Iraq, and the Arabian Peninsula. Salih was not yet sultan when he acquired Shajarat in 1239. Some say she was a gift from the harem of Abbasid caliph, al Mustasim. But more reliable, near-contemporary chroniclers claim that Salih purchased Shajarat in the slave markets of the Levant.

Skilled at court politics, the beautiful Kipchak slave soon became her master's favorite concubine. "The sultan . . . loved her so desperately that he carried her with him to his wars, and never quitted her," wrote the Mamluk-era historian Al Maqrizi. When he was imprisoned by his cousin at Kerak (in modern Jordan) following a routine Ayyubid family feud in 1239, Salih chose Shajarat plus a lone, faithful amir as his sole companions. The following year, she further endeared herself to the Ayyubid prince by bearing him a son, Khalil, who sadly died in infancy. Some sources say Khalil was born at Kerak, others say Egypt. In either case, all agree that after the birth Salih freed Shajarat and married her.

Released from Kerak in 1240, the couple headed for Cairo, where Salih usurped his half brother, Al Adil II, and laid claim to Egypt's throne with the help of around a thousand newly purchased Kipchak/Mamluk warrior slaves. As these raw recruits were a bit too rowdy for the urbane streets of Cairo,

The Irrepressible, Indispensable Mamluks

The Mamluks (meaning, "those who are owned") were light-skinned slaves of various ethnic backgrounds from the Asian steppes. The males were admired for their horsemanship and fighting skills, while the women—like Shajarat—were prized for their beauty. Captured as adolescents by slave traders and sold to the sultans, the girls entered the harem while the boys were trained in what were essentially military academies. Distinct from menial household slaves, they were schooled in court etiquette, the sciences, and martial arts. Mamluks were typically Christian or pagan by birth and were raised in the Islamic faith—an important stipulation since a born Muslim could not, in principle, be enslaved. Freed upon the completion of their training, they then dedicated themselves to the service of the sultan who liberated them, as well as to the defense of Islam against its enemies, be they Mongol hordes from the east or armies of Crusaders from the west. Meanwhile, as free men, they rose through the ranks of government to become powerful viziers and military commanders in their own right. Ultimately, "the Mamluks became such a dominating and powerful force that no ruler could hold the throne of Egypt without their support."

Salih isolated them in a fortified barracks on the Nile's Rawda Island. Their outpost on the river (*Bahr an Nil*, in Arabic) may have inspired their name: Bahri (or Bahiriyah) Mamluks. Alternatively, the term might have derived from their distant place of origin, across the sea (*bahr*).

With his hired muscle, plus Shajarat, by his side, Salih got down to the business of governing in true Ayyubid fashion—by eliminating rivals and seizing their territory. This included packing his boozy, belligerent son, Turanshah—the child of his first wife—off to the far reaches of northern Syria and (allegedly) having Adil strangled in his jail cell. He then set his sights on expanding sole authority over Damascus, Aleppo, and beyond.

But before long, the sultan had more than just pesky relatives to contend with. While campaigning in Syria in the spring of 1249, he learned that the armies of the Seventh Crusade, led by Louis IX of France, were headed for Egypt, where Shajarat was enthroned as regent. Louis figured with Salih distracted in Syria, he could take Egypt and use it as a base from which to regain the greater prize, Jerusalem. Yet neither Louis nor his Crusaders were prepared for "the most cunning woman of her age," as one Syrian contemporary described Shajarat, nor for just how formidable and resourceful she could be.

Shajarat was in Cairo when she received news from her husband that Louis was bearing down on the Nile Delta city of Damietta with a force of 1,800 ships and 50,000 troops. The sultan asked her to gather an army to meet the Crusaders and prepare for the defense of Cairo. Shajarat beefed up Cairo's defenses and dispatched an army to Damietta under the command of Salih's seasoned general/amir, Fakhr al Din. But there was additional, dire news: the sultan was sick, suffering from tuberculosis and a festering leg wound. Traveling by stretcher, he would have to endure a long and labored journey back to Egypt.

Louis landed at Damietta on June 6, 1249. Fakhr was there with his troops, but after a brief skirmish, "God struck terror into their hearts," and they, along with the entire population, abandoned the city "under cover of night," as Arab jurist Ibn Wasil reported in his thirteenth-century history of Ayyubid Egypt. The "shameful" retreat, spat Ibn Wasil, allowed the Crusaders to simply walk in and capture an empty city along with all its arms, ammunition, and provisions.

Meanwhile, the Muslim forces regrouped at Mansoura, where Salih was joined at his bedside by Shajarat. The outlook was bleak: Damietta had fallen, Salih grew weaker each day, and both he and Shajarat knew he was dying. The annual flooding of the Nile was keeping the Crusaders at bay temporarily, but their advance on Mansoura was inevitable.

Through it all, Shajarat nursed her husband at his bedside. But by late autumn, the doctors who were also "at his pillow day and night . . . despaired of his life," wrote Ibn Wasil. After slipping into a coma, the sultan died on the night of November 22/23, cradled in Shajarat's arms. Uttering the prescribed Qur'anic verses over her husband's body, the grieving yet determined queen wiped the dark streaks of kohl-blackened tears from her cheeks and rose to her feet, knowing what she must do.

Because Salih had not named a successor, Shajarat realized she had to recall his only legitimate male heir, the estranged Turanshah, if only to maintain dynastic order. But his return to Egypt from Syria would take months. In the meantime, the queen feared that news of Salih's death would cause unrest among the already demoralized Muslim troops. They were still smarting from the humiliation at Damietta, even as the Crusaders began to advance towards Mansoura, now that the Nile waters were starting to subside.

So she devised a plan "in order that the Franks should not get information on the sultan's death, and thereupon be able to advance against the Muslims while there was still no-one to hold them together," as Ibn Wasil recorded. She summoned Fakhr together with Salih's head eunuch, Jamal al Din—a sort of administrative chief of staff, in charge of the Bahri Mamluks—"to inform them of the death of the sultan, and to request their assistance in supporting the weight of government at such a critical period," wrote Maqrizi. "All three resolved to keep the sultan's death a secret, and to act in his name as if he were alive."

The deception required elaborate measures, and Shajarat knew she needed to act quickly. After sending for Turanshah, she appointed Fakhr as commander in chief of the army and viceroy until Turanshah's return. These and all other "official" orders from the sultan were in fact signed by Jamal, who as chief administrator had learned to forge his master's signature. (Others say Shajarat had Salih sign batches of blank documents before he died.)

Then there were appearances to keep up. Though court officials were denied access, a doctor, who was also let in on the secret, was seen visiting the sultan's chamber daily. Regular meals, featuring Salih's favorite dishes, were brought to the door and tasted, while Shajarat had singers and musicians perform outside the chambers ostensibly to soothe the ailing sultan. There was also the matter of the body, which she had washed, embalmed, and placed in a coffin by servants. These unwitting co-conspirators were either sworn to secrecy or imprisoned—maybe even strangled—after performing their duties, to ensure their silence.

Arranging for a boat and disguised in black robes, she accompanied the coffin, under cover of night, up the Nile to Rawda Island, where she hid the corpse. She then issued orders—also forged—for construction to begin on

Salih's mausoleum adjacent to his madrasa, at the northwest corner of what eventually became the Khan el Khalili, the city's major souk. The building of the sultan's tomb during his lifetime aroused no suspicion, especially in a country where pharaohs themselves directed construction of their grand pyramid tombs.

Shajarat's stratagem worked. For nearly three months she secretly directed the affairs of the sultanate and successfully repelled the Crusaders, even as she suffered the loss of her right-hand military commander, Fakhr. (Literally caught with his pants down, the Mamluk general leapt out of his bath during a surprise Crusader attack and fought to his death in nothing but a towel.)

Turanshah arrived in late February, just in time for the capture of Louis himself and the retreat of his army. Yet, true to form, the new sultan began making critical missteps as soon as Shajarat publicly acknowledged her husband's death and stepped aside to make way for his wastrel son's succession. Turanshah's blunders, Maqrizi recorded, included alienating the Bahri Mamluk powerbase and replacing key members of the court with imported yes-men.

"He had no confidence but in a certain number of favourites, whom he had brought with him from [Syria], and whom he had invested with the principal offices of the state, in [place] of the ancient ministers of his father. Above all, he shewed a decided hatred to the Mamlukes, although they had contributed so greatly to the last victory," Maqrizi wrote. Not one for subtlety, the young train wreck of a sultan displayed his resentment of the Bahris during frequent drunken bouts when "jars full of wine would be brought to him as if it were water," according to contemporary historian Ibn Abd al Zahir. Calling out the names of his father's veteran amirs and Mamluks one by one, he lopped off the heads of lit candles with his sword, shouting, "So shall I deal with the Bahris!" with each swipe.

But the final straw was a financial one. Having spent his last dinar on his "debaucheries . . . he forced the sultana [Shajarat al-Durr] to render him an account of the riches of his father," Maqrizi reported. Then he really crossed the line, demanding that she hand over her jewels and trademark pearls. "The sultana, in alarm, implored the protection of the Mamlukes," who were only too glad to come to her defense, considering "the services she had done the state in very difficult times" and the obvious fact that Turanshah "was a prince universally detested."

Acting upon Shajarat's plea, on May 2, 1250, one of Salih's amirs, sword in hand, burst in upon Turanshah when he was carousing with his cronies and took a swipe at the sultan's head. Turanshah managed to deflect the assassin's sword with his hand, losing a few fingers in the process. Running screaming from the tent, he took refuge in a wooden tower on the banks of the Nile, but the "conspirators followed him, and, finding he had closed the door, set fire to it," reported Maqrizi. Pleading for his life as the flames climbed higher, he promised to abdicate and return to Syria, then tried to escape by leaping into the Nile. His cloak got caught on the way down, however, and he hung there, like a piñata, while the Bahris took potshots at him with arrows before he finally fell into the river and drowned. "Thus iron, fire, and water contributed to put an end to his life," Maqrizi concluded.

Whether or not Shajarat specifically ordered Turanshah's assassination is uncertain. Either way, the dramatic turn of events left the Bahri's and Egypt without a sultan. Yet it didn't take long for them to decide who should fill the position.

"When [Turanshah] was killed the amirs and the Bahrites assembled near the Sultan's palace and agreed that the functions of Sultan and ruler [of Egypt] should be assumed by Shajarat al-Durr," Ibn Wasil recorded. "The Sultan's decrees were to be issued at her command and . . . [f]rom that time she became titular head of the whole state; a royal stamp was issued in her name with the formula 'mother of Khalil,' and the *khutbah* (Friday sermon) was pronounced in her name as Sultana of Cairo and all Egypt."

The Bahris' choice made sense on several levels. First, Shajarat's regnal title—*Walidat Khalil al Salihiya*—emphasized her legitimacy as the wife of her late husband and mother (*walidat*) of their dead son. Added to this, in both the *khutbah* prayer and her coinage, were the sobriquets *al-Musta'simiyya* (a nod of loyalty to Baghdad's Abbasid ruler, Al Mustasim) and *Malikat al-Muslimin* (Queen of the Muslims). The enthronement of a woman was also a cultural fit for the Mamluks, who, to recall Ibn Battuta's observations, were quite accepting of female monarchs and women of power in general. And last but not least, she was up to the job, "endowed . . . with great intelligence" and an exceptional capacity for "understanding the affairs of the kingdom," as one modern Syrian biographer has noted.

Shajarat demonstrated her political savvy via one of her first acts of governance: a treaty with the Crusaders. The terms included the return of Damietta and the release of Louis, whose ransom (one million gold dinars) she negotiated, appropriately enough, with her French counterpart, Queen Margaret of Provence. Thus the Seventh Crusade effectively came to a peaceful, diplomatic close—despite testosterone-driven objections from hawkish generals and harrumphing clerics on both sides of the battlefield—thanks to the level-headed politesse of two queens, one Christian and one Muslim.

Still, there were those outside the close circle of Bahri Mamluks who were uneasy with the idea of a woman on the throne, particularly clerics who looked to a (questionable) *hadith* (saying) of the Prophet Muhammad: "Woe to any nation that has a woman as a leader." Distant Syrian amirs, vying for power of their own, also refused to pay homage. The most stinging objection came from the spiritual leader of the Muslim world and the man who may have once owned Shajarat: the Abbasid caliph, Mustasim.

"If you are left with no man fit to rule but this woman, then it is our obligation to send you one of ours to take the sultanate," was his scornful reply to the Bahri's request for his blessing. Not entirely independent from Abbasid rule, the Bahris knew they needed to play ball with Baghdad if they were to ultimately succeed in Egypt.

So, after eighty days of sole rulership, Shajarat was married off to a minor Mamluk *atabeg* (military commander), Izz al Din Aybak. To add a touch of Ayyubid legitimacy (and to appease Baghdad and the Syrian amirs), Salih's cousin, the ineffectual six-year-old toddler Al Nasir Salah ad Din Yusuf, was named as co-sultan.

The marriage was entirely one of convenience. Shajarat may well have personally selected Aybak because he was known to be a lightweight. "She dominated him, and he had nothing to say," observed one contemporary. Even though Islam permitted Aybak up to four wives, Shajarat insisted upon no rivals, either in the throne room or the bedchamber, and demanded that Aybak divorce his first wife, Umm Ali. The queen permitted him to play at soldiering, sending him off on this campaign and that one. But "the real power" of the sultanate remained firmly in her hands, as Zahir noted. Indeed, it was her signature on all the royal decrees, and it was she who dispensed justice and issued commands (albeit from behind a silken curtain) from the *masatabah*, a raised bench in the Citadel's majestic "Hall of the Columns." One of her first official acts, after marrying Aybak, was the proper burial of Salih in the mausoleum she commissioned. Aybak led the procession, along with several prominent Bahris, dressed in white robes, their hair cropped short in mourning. (Along with the coffin, they placed some of the sultan's clothes and weapons in the tomb, a rare exception to medieval Muslim funerary practice that may have reflected the local, time-honored Egyptian custom of grave goods. While its façade is now largely hidden by shops, Salih's tomb still stands, and its minaret remains the last Ayyubid mosque tower in Cairo.) She then commissioned a tomb for herself nearby (also still standing), together with a madrasa of her own. In fact, "she was the first to introduce the tradition of attaching funerary structures for the rulers to their religious foundations." The custom endured throughout the Mamluk period.

Culturally, she instituted a nightly entertainment/military ceremony at the Citadel called the *nawbah* of the princess. Based on similar Arabo-Andalusian musical ceremonies, it featured an amir in dress uniform performing acrobatic feats by torchlight to the rhythm of the music. She also established the tradition of the *mahmal*, a richly decorated tent-like litter placed on the back of a camel, in which she traveled to Mecca during the hajj. The Egyptian custom of parading an empty *mahmal* through streets of Cairo and sending it to Mecca during *Dhu al Hijjah* (Month of the Pilgrimage) survived into the twentieth century, while returning Egyptian pilgrims often painted *mahmals* on their doorways in honor of their journey and in memory of Shajarat.

By 1254, Aybak began to tire of his role as second-banana sultan. He exiled young Yusuf to Nicaea, squashed a Bahri rebellion or two, and fought bitterly with Shajarat over her role as ruler and for access to Salih's treasure, which she kept hidden. A court astrologer warned Aybak that he would die at the hand of a female, and, in 1257, he ultimately sealed his fate by betraying "not the queen, but the woman."

Seeking to boost his status through a marriage alliance with a new wife, Aybak sent emissaries to various Turkish/Ayyubid princes, asking for their daughters' hands. This did not sit well with Shajarat, who would brook no rivals, especially a younger, prettier one, now that she was approaching middle age. ("The co-wife is bitter, even if she were honey in a jar," went one folk-saying of the day.)

Not one to take things lying down, Shajarat wrote to An Nasir Yusuf, Ayyubid governor of Syria, offering him the throne once she murdered Aybak, thus uniting Egypt and Syria once and for all. Yusuf declined, fearing that any woman who would propose such a thing could not be trusted, and sent word to Aybak of the plot. Furious (and perhaps nervously recalling the astrologer's warning), Aybak moved out of the palace and took up residence in a pavilion by the polo fields of al Louk, west of the city. There he vented his frustrations with ball and mallet while contemplating ways to rid himself of his conniving wife.

A few days later, on April 10, 1257, he received a message from the queen, suggesting they kiss and make up. He arrived at the palace, fresh from a match, and decided to bathe before his reunion with Shajarat. In one account of what happened next, Shajarat dispatched her eunuchs, armed with swords, to kill Aybak as he was entering the bath. Hearing his pitiable cries for help, the queen had a change of heart and emerged from the shadows, imploring the killers to spare her husband. They rightly pointed out that if they stopped half way through "he will kill both you and us," and got on with the job.

A steamier version of the story appeared in the pages of the medieval Egyptian folklore epic *Sirat al Zahir Baibars* ("Life of Al Zahir Baibars"). In this account, Shajarat joined Aybak in the tub, where she proceeded to seductively bathe him personally. "Taking advantage of this moment of détente and intimacy," she playfully scolded him for desiring a younger woman. "'Do I no longer please you?' she murmured, to soften his heart." Having learned nothing about marriage, apparently, after two wives, Aybak replied "'She is young, while you are not.'" Trembling with rage, Shajarat "rubbed soap in her husband's eyes, while whispering conciliatory words to allay his suspicion, and then suddenly seized a dagger and stabbed him in the side." As Aybak thrashed about, the bathwater, pink with blood, overflowed from the tub and ran out the door, tipping off one of his sons who burst into the room and caught the queen, half naked, still gripping the blood-stained dagger.

"However highly romanticized," a modern scholar has pointed out, "this version is of genuine historical interest inasmuch as it is in all probability a faithful reflection of what was being said in the streets of Cairo in April 1257, just after the tragedy." The act was so infamously "monstrous" that it was talked about in Europe.

Whatever the actual circumstances, the deed sealed Shajarat's fate. Trying to escape suspicion, she claimed that Aybak had died in his sleep, but nobody was buying her story. Even the Bahri Mamluks refused to protect her this time, and she was arrested and imprisoned in the Red Tower of the Citadel, while Aybak's murderers ended up being crucified at its gate. She passed several days behind bars, grinding her jewels and beloved pearls to dust with a mortar and pestle, so that no other woman could wear them. Meanwhile, Aybak's fifteen-year-old son, al Mansur Ali—son of the jilted Umm Ali—succeeded as sultan and offered Shajarat up to the justice of his mother. Delighting in her revenge, Umm Ali had her former rival stripped and then beaten to death by her handmaidens with wooden bath clogs. (The "sweetness" of Umm Ali's revenge is reflected in a popular, Middle Eastern custard named for her, vast amounts of which she is said to have distributed to the poor in celebration of Shajarat's death. Coincidentally or no, a shop near Salih's tomb is said to sell the city's best umm ali.)

Shajarat's battered body, as fifteenth-century historian Ibn Iyas reported, was then "dragged by the feet and thrown from the top of [the Citadel] naked, with nothing but a garment around the waist." There she lay in the moat, gnawed by dogs, like the Biblical Jezebel, for three days until "one of the rabble descended into the moat under cover of night and cut off the sash of her garment because it was of red silk with a circle of pearls and because it smelled of musk." Eventually, her remains were collected and interred in the tomb she commissioned for herself. It remains one of Cairo's most exquisite, with a prayer niche decorated in Byzantine glass mosaics—the oldest such mosaic work in the city—executed by artisans brought in from Constantinople. The niche's centerpiece is a "tree of life" design in gold and other dark colors, festooned with Shajarat's telltale pearls.

Despite her ignominious end, Shajarat al Durr remains one of Egypt's most popular historical/folk figures. Her story has been fictionalized on Egyptian television, while the first Egyptian journal to focus on woman's rights, founded in 1901, was named after her. As for her political legacy, she stood at "the central point between two epochs of Egyptian history [Ayyubid and Mamluk] which gives her historic role its character and significance." Yet her dramatic life story also underscores "how completely women were involved in affairs of state even in the early sultanate," it has been noted. With "outstanding talents . . . realized through crisis, and frustrated by law, tradition, and brute force," Shajarat's story remains today "a woman's story from first to last."

CHAPTER 5

Sayidda al Hurra (1485?–1561)

Morocco's "Pirate" Queen

In the summer of 1541, Moroccan Sultan Ahmed al Wattasi set out from his capital of Fez on his way to a wedding: his own.

His bride-to-be awaited him in the Mediterranean coastal city of Tetouan, around 170 miles north. Situated near the mouth of the Martil River, the fortified city was one of Morocco's major entrepôts, with trade goods (gold, ivory, peacock feathers, and slaves) from the interior and beyond flowing through its heavily trafficked port.

Protectively wedged into the foothills of the snowcapped Rif Mountains, Tetouan was also a tactical base for staging raids on the equally strategic port of Ceuta, less than a day's journey up the coast. Just seventeen miles from the Iberian Peninsula, across the Strait of Gibraltar, Ceuta sat squarely in the maritime chokepoint linking the Mediterranean to the Atlantic. The economic and military advantages of its geography attracted a host of occupiers throughout the centuries: Phoenicians, Romans, Vandals, Visigoths, and, with the coming of Islam in the seventh century, a succession of Berber (indigenous North African) Muslim dynasties, all of whom capitalized on the port's tactical location. By the early fifteenth century, Ceuta was in the hands of one of Morocco's most persistent and formidable rivals at the time, the Portuguese.

But Sultan Ahmed, a Berber ruler, wasn't quite so much worried about the Portuguese at this point. His bigger concern were his co-religionists, the Saadis, an aggressive Arab dynasty from southern Morocco whose leaders sought to claim all of Morocco for themselves. Though Sultan in name, Ahmed's actual power didn't extend very far beyond Fez, and he knew it. If he was going to hang onto his kingdom, he needed the military and political support of Morocco's powerful, semiautonomous city-states, of which Tetouan was among the most critical. And so earlier that year, he sent a proposal to the city's governor: a proposal of marriage. She accepted, on one condition: that he come to her, and not the other way around. It was the only time in history that a Moroccan sultan married outside the capital.

Who was this woman, who ruled a major North African city-state and could bend a sultan to her will?

Some sources say her name was Fatima, others Aisha. To contemporary chroniclers, both Muslim and Christian, she was Sayidda al Hurra,* i.e., a free and/or noble lady, a title of respect. To the monarchs of the Iberian Peninsula, she was not only governor of Tetouan but a renowned, and feared, pirate queen who raided their shores and merchant ships, ransoming captives and seizing booty. Others believe her name was in fact a shorthand version of her title, Hurra, as this was how she was identified on her marriage certificate to Sultan Ahmed.

Whatever her actual name, to modern Moroccan historians, such as Hasna Lebbady, author of *Feminist Traditions in Andalusi-Moroccan Oral Narratives*, she was one of many "eloquent, strong and witty Andalusian-Moroccan" heroines who populate the nation's history and folklore.

Hurra's fate, like that of many political rulers, was determined by the crises of her day. Hers began with the expulsion of her family, along with members of her community, from their beloved kingdom of Granada in Andalusia (Muslim Spain) by the forces of King Ferdinand of Aragon and Queen Isabella of Castile, following the city's fall in 1492. The event signaled the end of Muslim rule in the Iberian Peninsula after seven centuries of struggle between the Moors (Spanish/North African Muslims) and the Christian kingdoms of Spain and Portugal—a series of campaigns known as the *Reconquista*.

* Not to be confused with Yemen's Queen Arwa, who was also known by this title.

These were turbulent times. The Spanish crown was jockeying for New World dominance against a whole host of Old World rivals such as England, France, and the Netherlands, while engaging with all three in a series of bloody conflicts on European soil. Meanwhile, Ottoman encroachment and hostility in the Mediterranean were ongoing threats. Fear of collusion (not entirely unfounded) between the Ottomans and Spain's Muslims made the latter a target of rising nationalist suspicions and bigotry. Their ultimate expulsion from Spain was the convulsive result of long-simmering tensions.

But first came the betrayals. Initially, after the fall of Granada to Ferdinand and Isabella, Spain's Muslims were promised that they could continue to live their way of life and practice their religion *para siempre jamas*, i.e., "forever and ever." Yet within a decade they were driven from their ancestral homes and forced to convert to Christianity. These hasty conversions included baptisms en masse in churches that were once mosques, with little or no theological introduction to the Christian faith. Adding horrifying insult to injury, in 1499, Archbishop Francisco Ximénez de Cisneros of Toledo, seeking to wipe the cultural slate clean, had thousands of copies of the Qur'an and other Arabic-language manuscripts publicly burned in the streets. By 1526, all uses of Arabic, in both speech and writing, were outlawed. That same year Spain's Muslims were offered a choice: baptism or exile.

In order to survive, those who stayed outwardly embraced their status as *nuevos christianos* ("new Christians") aka Moriscos—a pejorative term indicating their Moorish ethnicity and their degraded social status—while secretly continuing to practice Islam. These so-called "crypto Muslims" became a particular target of the Inquisition, inaugurated under Ferdinand and Isabella. To quell rebellions, the Crown relocated tens of thousands of Moriscos to various corners of Spain such as La Mancha, New Castile, or Extremadura. During one forced winter march in punishing rain and snow, with children clinging to their mothers, the commander of the operation, Don John of Austria, while favoring the deportations, nonetheless described the scene as "the saddest sight in the world."

Meanwhile, fearmongers—not unlike today's nationalist extremists—fanned rumors that the influx of this "pestilential horde" into local communities threatened to overwhelm Spain's *cristiano viejo* ("old Christian") majority population and contaminate its purely Christian, pre-Islamic

Spanish bloodlines, or *limpieza de sangre* (blood purity).

For those who chose exile, life was less harsh, though no less bitter.

"[T]he Almighty not being pleased to grant victory to their cause, [the Muslims] were everywhere overpowered and slain, until they were ultimately expelled from the territory of Andalus," mourned Algerian-born historian Al Maqqari, writing around a century after Granada's fall. The "many thousands of the unfortunate emigrants," consisting of Andalusian Muslims and Jews, were absorbed by major North African, Islamic urban centers, such as Fez, Oran and Tunis. Still others, Maqqari observed, "peopled the desert towns and districts of the country [including] Tetwán (Tetouan), Salé, and the plains of Metidja, near Algiers."

Among these refugees was the *qaid* (tribal chief) Moulay Ali Ibn Rashid, his wife, Lalla (Lady) Zohra Fernandez (a Christian convert to Islam), his son, Moulay Ibrahim, and daughter, Hurra, who was born sometime between 1485 and 1495 in Andalusia. The Rashids were a noble clan claiming descent from the Prophet Muhammad via Idrisi I, eighth-century founder of Morocco's first Islamic dynasty. Soon after their exile from Spain, Hurra's family settled in the Rif Mountains southeast of Tangier, where Ali founded and became emir of the city-state of Chefchaouen. (Some sources say Chefchaouen was founded about a decade earlier by a Rashid cousin, Abdul Hasan ibn Muhammad, whom Ali succeeded.) As a refugee himself, Ali opened Chefchaouen's gates to waves of fellow Andalusi immigrants fleeing the Inquisition and the fall of Granada. The young Hurra would have been a witness to this upheaval, and while some speculate that her later harassment of the Spanish was inspired by vengeance, her motivations were probably more political than personal.

As a girl, Hurra received a first-class education, surpassing those of the men at court. She excelled in languages, including Castilian and Portuguese, as well as theology. Among her teachers was the famed Moroccan scholar Abdallah al Ghazwani (d. 1529), whose father, the equally celebrated sheikh Oudjal, supposedly once put his hand to Hurra's head and declared, "This girl will rise high in rank."

Whether by divinely inspired edict or political practicality, Hurra took her first steps towards fulfilling Oudjal's prediction in 1510 by marrying into Tetouan's ruling family, the Al Mandaris.

Roughly thirty-five miles north of Chefchaouen, Tetouan was a frequent target of Portuguese aggression, both retributive and preventative. Fearing its proximity to its newly captured base of Ceuta, the Portuguese attacked the city around 1400 and left it in rubble.

"For 80 years it remained abandoned, until a Granadan captain decided to restore the city," reported the sixteenth-century historian Al Hasan Muhammad al Wazzan (known to Europeans as Leo Africanus), a fellow Andalusian transplant from Granada. The captain was Ali al Mandari, one of Granada's last military defenders and, by tradition, modern Tetouan's founding father. "He was given the authority to restore the city and collect taxes" Hasan wrote. "He rebuilt the city walls, erected a fort and . . . waged many a war with the Portuguese, often attacking Ceuta, Ksar and Tangiers." Wistfully recalling their lost homeland back in Spain, Tetouan's displaced residents culturally and architecturally sought to recreate its splendors in the new environment, a lasting legacy to this day.

There is disagreement over whether Hurra married the much older Abu al Hassan al Mandari or another member of the family, probably Sidi al-Mandri II, Abu's grandson (or nephew), who succeeded him. In either case, her education, strength of character, and presence of mind, established her as a political leader, independent of male supervision, instruction, or approval.

"She was trusted by her male relatives, and this seemed to be a feature of Andalusian-Moroccan women in general," Lebbady said. "She knew what needed to be done under different circumstances and these are the kinds of qualities that would have made her a leader."

The Mandari marriage alliance was a wise move. With Hurra serving as co-regent of Tetouan, and the concurrent appointment of her brother Moulay Ibrahim as vizier to Sultan Ahmed, the Rashids were now major players in the effort to militarily and economically unify Morocco against the powers of Spain and Portugal.

The need for unity was genuine.

In the late fifteenth century, Portuguese explorers Bartolomeu Dias and Vasco de Gama became the first Europeans to circumnavigate the southern tip of Africa and reach the Indian Ocean by sea. The voyages established a direct maritime route to Arabia, India, and Asia, sources of incalculable wealth from the trade in spices, silks, porcelain and other luxury goods.

Portugal's gambit ultimately cut into the profits of North African merchants who, for centuries, acted as middlemen between Europe and the East. The Portuguese also established colonies along the African coast, linking them to the interior. At the same time, the Spanish, gazing hungrily across the Strait of Gibraltar and warily at Ottoman expansion in the Mediterranean, clung stubbornly to their own outposts along the North African coast: Tripoli, Algiers, Santa Cruz, and others. Meanwhile, south of Fez, Sultan Ahmed was busy fending off the rebellious Saadi tribesmen. The rival Muslim clan had military support from the English to fight their common enemies: Spain, Portugal, and Ahmed, who actually sought an alliance with the Portuguese for help. The Mediterranean, once known as a Roman lake, had become an international and internecine stew.

With the death of her husband, sometime between 1515 and 1519, Hurra became Tetouan's sole ruler under the formal title Sayidda al Hurra, *Hakimat Titwan* (Governor of Tetouan). Europeans wondered if Sayidda al Hurra was her actual name since it appears in contemporary Spanish records as *Sida el-Horra.* What seems likely, however, is that, unaware of her given name, they confused it with her title. Nonetheless, as Sayidda al Hurra, she effectively governed Tetouan for the next quarter-century or so, during which time the city "reached an unheard of level of prosperity." Some of this prosperity derived from trade with Europe, with women's dresses being particularly sought after by Tetouan's merchants to sell in the Moroccan interior. At the same time, the city's coffers swelled with gold and other treasures looted from passing Iberian ships.

Adding to Tetouan's wealth was its feminine culture, transplanted to Morocco by Andalusi refugees. Under Hurra and for subsequent generations, women in Tetouan enjoyed high levels of education and autonomy, enabling them to play important and highly visible roles in society, as Lebaddy recounted.

> Like the women in al-Andalus, the Andalusi Tetouani women, those descendants of different waves of Andalusi immigrants who eventually constituted the bourgeoise of Tetouan . . . became calligraphers, teachers, midwives, and doctors, some of whom were famous for the *jbīra* (setting of broken bones) that they mastered. Some of them also had a substantial

amount of wealth at their disposal enabling them to wield considerable political power as well as to leave endowments for various charitable and religious purposes.

Beloved by her people, Hurra nonetheless earned a reputation as a "pirate queen" among her European rivals, stemming from her association with Oruc Reis, the famed privateer known to the West as Barbarossa. Born in Lesbos around 1474, Barbarossa, and his older brother, Hayreddin, were among the most notorious of the so-called Barbary corsairs (pirates). Based at times in various ports throughout the Mediterranean (Tunis, Algiers, et al.) as nominal servants of the Ottoman sultan, they were notorious for their exploits, including raids on Spanish colonies, ongoing battles with the Knights Hospitallers, and even a daring attack on the (much larger) flagship of Pope Julius II in 1504. A fearsome figure, Oruc sported a prosthetic arm made of silver. Despite the handicap, he fought "like a lion to the last" according to eyewitnesses. Yet he had a softer side: between 1504 and 1510, he ferried Muslim refugees from Spain to North Africa. The effort earned him the affectionate nickname *Baba Oruc* (Father Oruc), which, to the European ear, sounded like "Barbarossa," Italian for "Redbeard."

Whatever the actual color of his whiskers, Oruc's politics and sympathies attracted Hurra's attention and admiration. Joining forces, and fleets, the two ruled the waters of the eastern and western Mediterranean, raiding towns, robbing ships, and selling Christian captives into slavery. Spanish sources from 1540 tell of attacks on Gibraltar and the loss of "much booty and the taking a number of prisoners" for whom Hurra negotiated ransom. The Portuguese, meanwhile, "prayed for God to allow them to see her hanged" from a ship's mast. Sebastien de Vargas, Portuguese envoy to the court of Fez at the time, seethingly characterized her as "a very aggressive and bad-tempered woman about everything."

But whether Hurra and Oruc were actually "pirates" really depended upon which end of the ship's cannon you were facing.

"Piracy was rampant in the sixteenth century and by no means limited to the southern coast of the Mediterranean," said Lebbady. "English pirates used to intercept the Spanish galleys coming back from the Americas, and what they took as booty was a major source of income for the government of

Queen Elizabeth I."

In contrast, during Hurra's time, Morocco did not have a navy, Lebbady said, and depended on "privateers," as she called them, to defend the coast.

"Many of these privateers were Andalusis who settled in places like Sale and Tetouan. There would have been many such privateers under the command of Hurra, helping her to fend off the aggressive Iberians who were colonizing Morocco and at times enslaving most of the populations. So she was doing the same thing to the Iberians as they we doing to the Moroccans. I wouldn't call her a pirate. To refer to her as pirate is to put the blame on those who were defending their land from aggressive colonial powers."

In truth, Hurra probably never set foot on the deck of a privateer ship herself and only directed their raids from her palace in Tetouan, one of the few Moroccan ports not under Iberian control. She played a "diplomatic game" with the Spanish and Portuguese on both land and sea that was skillful, cunning, and invariably geared towards gaining the upper hand for the city, even if that meant striking trade deals with the Portuguese one day and attacking them the next. As her power grew, so did her reputation. News of her wedding to Sultan Ahmed in 1541 traveled as far as Madrid, where it troubled Philip II and was viewed by some as the Muslim equivalent of the dynamic union between Ferdinand and Isabella. The comparison was apt. The fact that Ahmed returned to Fez alone shortly after the wedding demonstrated that this was a political marriage of convenience and nothing more: a mutual bargain that benefitted both the Sultan and Hurra.

For Ahmed's part, the partnership helped to strengthen his position in the north, especially along the coast where Saadi forces themselves had fended off the Portuguese, thus gaining the sympathy of locals for their cause. If he was going to sustain control of the kingdom, Tetouan was an important toehold. As for Hurra, it expanded her authority and her power. Should she need to call on the Sultan for help, she knew she now had even greater influence at court since the death of her brother, the vizier, sometime earlier. Meanwhile, her half brother, Moulay Mohammed, governor of Chefchaouen, had ambitions to overthrow her and install himself as Tetouan's ruler while Don Alphonso, Portuguese governor of Ceuta, was a constant irritant and threat.

Ahmed's prompt return to Fez after the wedding also revealed much about Hurra's character and political savvy. With these various threats looming, she was not about to abandon her grip on the city, nor did she wish to risk ending up as just another wife in Ahmed's harem, if he chose to take other wives, which was feasible. At the time of the marriage, she was nearing fifty while Ahmed was at least ten years younger.

But despite her efforts, her power was not to last. As often happens, political intrigue led to her downfall. Her on-again, off-again diplomatic relations and spats with the Portuguese government in Ceuta prompted its governor to cut off commercial ties with Tetouan, causing local merchants to grumble that Hurra's temper and pride were bad for business. Meanwhile, her son-in-law, Moulay Ahmed al Hassan al Mandari (Abu al Hassan's grandson), anticipating the downfall of the Wattasids, allied with the Saadis. He arrived in Tetouan in October of 1542 with a small army and usurped his mother-in-law. Accepting her fate, she retired to Chefchaouen. There she founded a *zawiya* (a religious center) where she lived out the rest of her life in piety until her death on July 14, 1561. Most sources say she was buried in Chefchaouen, while others claim her tomb is outside the gates of the nearby, larger city of Ksar el Kebir.

Against great odds and in the face of increasing encroachment of European powers, Hurra managed to maintain her city's independence while preserving the cultural pride of her fellow Moroccans and their exiled, Andalusian forebears. Some have ascribed her downfall to her fractured diplomatic relations with the Portuguese, exacerbated by her fiery temper. Yet it is often the case that when powerful women assert themselves, they are regarded as difficult (usually by men), whereas assertive men are praised for their courage. Though nearly five centuries have passed since Hurra's reign, this double standard for women in business and politics endures, with numerous studies demonstrating that when women "emphasize their competence, they're seen as cold and unlikable."

Such criticisms, and even worse, were hurled at the most favored wife of the aptly named Suleiman the Magnificent (r. 1520–1566), ruler of the Ottoman Empire, one of Islamic history's most powerful dynasties. Like Hurra, she shared a taste for power and a stubborn resistance to convention when it came to the role of women in government—a role she came to define and hand down to subsequent Ottoman queens who followed in her brave and daring footsteps.

CHAPTER 6

Hurrem Haseki Sultan (Roxelana) (1500-1558)

The Most Powerful Woman in the Ottoman Empire

In the spring of 1534, "a most extraordinary event, one absolutely unprecedented in the history of the sultans" took place in Istanbul. The occasion was the marriage of Ottoman Sultan Suleiman I ("the Magnificent") to "a slave woman from Russia called Roxalana."* In town for the occasion was a representative from the Genoese Bank of St. George. In a letter to his superiors, he reported the details of the magnificent, weeklong celebrations, which, being a man of finance, he duly noted "cost thousands of pounds."

> The ceremony took place within the Palace, and the festivities have been magnificent, beyond all record. There was a public procession of all the presents which the Sultan, and the great people of the land, have made to the said Roxalana. First came two hundred mules, heavily laden with carpets, gold and silver vases, spices, jewels, furniture, and all sorts of household goods. Each mule was accompanied by two slaves, in splendid liveries, and the presents were concealed under scarves of silver and rose-coulored tissue. Then came two hundred camels, equally heavily laden with sumptuous gifts, sent to the Empress by the great ones of

* An alternative spelling of Roxelana.

> the nation, even from very distant parts of the Empire, and, finally, there were eighty black eunuchs, and eighty white eunuchs, most splendidly dressed, who walked behind the presents, and who were intended for the service of the said Empress. Every evening, all the principal streets are gaily illuminated, and there has been much music and feasting. The houses are festooned with flowers, and there are swings erected everywhere, in which the people swing by the hour and seem very happy. In the old Hippodrome, or At-meidan, a great tribute was set up for the Sultan and his court. That portion set apart for the Empress and her women was screened by a gilded lattice, through which the ladies could see all that went on in the arena. Here Roxalana and her Court beheld a great tournament, in which both Christian and Mohammedan knights were engaged, and tumblers, and jugglers, and a procession of extraordinary animals from Asia, including two giraffes, with necks so long that they seemed to reach the sky. The Empress sent round among the crowd a number of slaves, who gave the people small presents, either of money or pieces of silk. There was a liberal distribution of bread and fruits, in one of the great courtyards of the Palace . . . There is great talk, all over this country, about this marriage, and no one can understand exactly what it means.

The unnamed author of the letter concluded his report as it began: with astonishment, not only at the enormous spectacle of the wedding, but at the background of the Empress bride, "a slave woman from Russia." For, as he pointed out, never before had an Ottoman sultan made a slave girl from the harem his legal wife. But this clever, determined, and gifted young woman with an intoxicating smile would ultimately do more than wed a sultan. Parlaying her charms into a position of power and influence like no other Ottoman queen before her, she redefined the role of the Sultan's wife, ushering in the era of the *Kadınlar Saltanatı*, the "Sultanate of Women," a succession of politically savvy queens and queen mothers who ably directed government affairs and public policy from the gilded confines of the royal harem for the next century and a half.

The Ottoman Empire was one of the largest, most powerful, and most enduring the world has known. Lasting more than six hundred years, it was founded towards the end of the thirteenth century by Osman (sometimes spelled Othman), chieftain of a nomadic Muslim Turkic tribe from what is now Turkmenistan. Sometime around 1299, Osman and his peoples migrated to Anatolia and established a *beylik* (governate) to the south of the Christian Byzantine capital of Constantinople. After a century and a half of conflict with the Byzantines, the Ottomans (named for Osman) ultimately captured Constantinople in 1453, renaming it Istanbul. Eclipsing the Byzantines as a major power in the region (rivaled by Persia), the Ottomans eventually expanded their empire across three continents, dominating southeastern Europe, the Middle East, and much of North Africa.

Overseeing it all, with the aid of his grand vizier, plus legions of provincial governors, administrators, and generals, was the sultan. When not engaged in military campaigning, he lived in magnificent splendor in Istanbul, first in the Old Palace, in the heart of the busy, ancient city, and thereafter, by Suleiman's time, in the New Palace (the Topkapi). This parklike expanse of gardens, lawns, royal residences, and government offices sat atop a promontory, site of the old Byzantine acropolis. The stunning location afforded uninterrupted views of the estuary of the Golden Horn, where the Bosporus Strait, fed by the Black Sea, meets the Sea of Marmara, gateway to the Mediterranean. Just as visitors to Istanbul may today, "[f]rom the very edge of Europe, the sultan could gaze upon the shores of Asia."

While the New Palace was the seat of government, the Old Palace was the setting for the women's quarters, the harem. Like many women who rose to power via this venerable institution, Roxelana had humble origins. According to stories circulating at the Ottoman court during the first quarter of the seventeenth century, she was born around 1504 to a poor Orthodox priest from Rohatyn, a small town near Lviv, in the western Ukrainian region of Ruthenia, then a part of Poland.

In Ukrainian folklore, her birth name was Anastasia (or Aleksandra) Lisowska, though many say this is a fabrication. To Europeans, she was known as Roxelana or Roxolana, meaning "a girl from Roxolania," the medieval Latin name for Ruthenia. The region was also known at times as Red Rus, which, together with other versions of Roxelana's name ("Rosselane" "Roxa" and "Rossa") led some, like the Genoese banker, to believe she was Russian. To the Ottomans, she was *Haseki Hurrem Sultan*, a hybrid of her official title,

Haseki Sultan ("favored wife," or "royal consort," of the Sultan) and her nickname, *Hurrem*, meaning "the Joyful" or the "Laughing One." Jealous rivals, meanwhile, would ultimately refer to her a sorceress and far worse.

From the late fifteenth century, Ruthenia was a prime hunting ground for Crimean Tatar slave traders, who swept west across the Ukraine, raiding towns and villages and capturing unfortunate victims in their tumultuous wake. Writing in his memoirs (1548–1551), Mykhailo Lytvyn—a Ukrainian diplomat to the Sublime Porte (Ottoman court) in the service of the Lithuanian government—stated that "the *krymchaky* (Crimean Tatars) engaged in only two trades: cattle-breeding and capturing Ukrainians to be sold to the Ottomans as slaves."

It is likely that Roxelana was abducted from her home and family during one such raid in 1516, along with thousands of other Ruthenians that year (estimates run as high as forty thousand or more). One contemporary observer, "amazed at the great numbers of these slaves to be seen at the slave markets . . . asked whether there were any people left in the land where these slaves are brought from." So many people from Slavic lands—extending from Russia to Eastern Europe—were taken into slavery, in fact, that the word "slave" derives from association with their ethnicity.

The single largest market for slaves at the time was Istanbul. Captured Ukranians arrived there via the Crimean port of Caffa (modern Feodosia) on the Black Sea. For Roxelana and her fellow Ruthenians, the journey there was a grueling forced march of nearly nine hundred miles across rugged country with little food or rest. Further misery awaited them when they arrived in Caffa. Observing the similar processing of slaves in nearby Karasubazar (modern Bilohirsk), Evliya Celebi, a seventeenth-century Ottoman courtier and traveler, couldn't help but express pity for the poor captives.

"There a mother is severed from her son and daughter, a son from his father and brother, and they are sold among lamentations, cries of help, weeping, and sorrow," Celebi wrote.

A Polish proverb of the day woefully summarized the experience: "O how much better to lie in one's bier, than to be a captive on the way to Tatary."

Roxelena was probably around twelve or thirteen at the time of her abduction, just old enough to fend for herself if she had to. This included keeping her virginity during the ordeal, otherwise Suleiman would never have made her one of his concubines, let alone his wife. That she resisted molestation and survived the hardships of the Crimean slave trade speak to her courage, an enduring legacy—one is tempted to believe—of the people of Ruthenia. Modern Lviv and the residents of its surrounding countryside offered safe haven for refugees fleeing Russia's current war with Ukraine, bravely deterring invasion even as the region itself came under fire.

Upon arrival in Istanbul, Roxelana ended up, like most of her fellow female captives, in the Avrat Pazari, or "the Women's Slave Market," located in today's Cerrahpasa district, the source of many a harem resident. There she was noticed by Suleiman's beloved boyhood friend, brother-in-law, and eventual grand vizier, Ibrahim Pasha, who is believed to have purchased Roxelana as a gift for Suleiman sometime before 1520. Adding historical heft to the story, Lytvyn, the Ukrainian diplomat, reported that "[t]he current wife of the Turkish sultan who loves her dearly is a woman who was captured somewhere in our lands" and that "[t]he Ottoman bazaars are full of these slaves who are sold and bought to be used in the households, to be resold, to be given as presents."

Once sold, Roxelana would have been taken to the imperial harem, which, like that of the Abbasids, was a highly organized, hierarchical, practically self-governing institution with functions that went far beyond merely providing the sultan with available sexual partners.

Like everything Ottoman, the harem operated on a grand scale. The number of women in residence ran as high as eight or nine hundred at times. Its most promising residents were trained in all the domestic arts (singing, dancing, needlework, coffee-making, poetry, storytelling, book-keeping) as well the Ottoman Turkish language together with the basics of Islam, and, yes, the art of lovemaking. These skills were necessary to become proper wives, not just of the sultan but of any high-ranking Ottoman official. The majority of the women in the harem, however, were menials who did the grunt work (cooking, cleaning, serving the harem's higher-ranking residents) and were never destined for anything more glamorous or exciting than these routine chores, never mind sharing the bed of the sultan. Rounding out the household were the sultan's young children, and a quasi-military corps of Black eunuchs who dutifully guarded the premises.

Suleiman's harem, once he ascended the throne in 1520, was small compared to that of his predecessors: perhaps two- to three-hundred women, most of whom were married off to members of his court and household once they passed the age (twenty-five) of being potential sexual partners for the sultan. Still, the one permanent resident who reigned supreme was Suleiman's mother, Hafsa, the *Valide Sultan*, or "Queen Mother." Next in line was the *qadin sultan*, or "first concubine," Mahidevran, a stunning, blue-eyed, blonde-haired Circassian (some say Montenegrin), the mother of Suleiman's eldest son, Mustafa.

Rising to the surface to catch the sultan's attention among such competition required a combination of attractiveness and charm. Roxelana may have been pretty, though the reports are mixed. Of her many surviving portraits, none were done from life. Biographers have thus relied on contemporary reports from the likes of the Venetian ambassador Pietro Bragadin, who, in 1526, described her as "young but not beautiful, although graceful and petite." Yet in his love poems, Suleiman gushed on about his beloved's "black hair . . . bow-like eyebrows, [and] languorous, perfidious eyes." Other sources claim she was fair-skinned, with light-colored hair, as depicted in a 1550 portrait attributed to Titian (most likely painted by an anonymous artist in his studio). This portrait, like all others, however, was done from the imagination and not life.

As for her charm, there is far more concrete evidence and concurrence there, and it was this gift that supposedly first caught Suleiman's attention. Because she demonstrated skill with needle and thread, her initial assignment in the harem was in the royal laundry, where her reputation as an embroiderer (samples of her work remain in Istanbul museums) was matched only by her musicianship. One story goes that Suleiman was passing by the laundry when he overheard her singing Ukrainian folk songs while accompanying herself on a guitar. Stumblingly conversant in Slavic, Suleiman "stopped to talk with her in her outlandish speech." In no time, the Ukrainian slave girl had "the Magnificent, the Lord of his age" to whom "the greatest powers of Europe bowed themselves down" (as one awestruck nineteenth-century historian described him) eating from the palm of her hand. "She laughed merrily when he said the wrong words, but he showed no anger at that . . . now that she was in his eye."

While suspiciously reeking of fairy tale, the story does confirm that

Roxelana's personality, as opposed to her sex appeal, accounted for her attractiveness and rise to power. That journey began with catching the Sultan's attention during one of his visits to the harem, perhaps with a pleasing song, an evocative dance, or an up-close, engaging smile, while serving him food or drink as he lounged on floral-patterned, silk-covered cushions in the seraglio. European reports (perhaps exaggerated) detail a more formal ceremonial custom by which Sultans selected their partners, as described by a Genoese ambassador to the court of Suleiman's father, Selim.

> When the Sultan decides to go to the Serai [harem] of the ladies, sometimes in disguise, and sometimes openly on horseback, the chief of the eunuchs arranges the girls, all beautifully dressed, in line in the courtyard; and when the Sultan has arrived and the door has been shut, he and the eunuchs move along the line of girls greeting each one politely as they pass. Then, if there is one who specially pleases him, he puts a handkerchief on her shoulder, before walking on with the eunuch to stroll in the garden amongst the ostriches and peacocks and many other birds kept there. Later, he returns to his rooms to dine and to sleep. Once in bed, he asks someone to tell the girl, to whom he gave his handkerchief, to bring it to him; a eunuch duly calls her, and she comes with the handkerchief, while the eunuch leaves the room. The next day, the Sultan commands that she be given a golden dress, an extra nine aspers* a day, and two more personal maids. Sometimes he remains in the Serai for three or four days, sleeping with whom he will, before returning to his own palace.

These extended stays were more typically the habit of Suleiman's father. Suleiman himself visited the harem less frequently. When he did, more often than not it was to visit his mother, with whom he was close, and engage with his children. As for a companion, before the birth of his son Mustafa, Suleiman usually slept only with Mahidevran on these occasions. A quick study, Roxelena soon grasped that these two powerful women—Hafsa and Mahidevran—stood between her and her growing desire to be the primary

* From around 1540–1550, one Ottoman asper equaled about $2.

female in Suleiman's life. If she were to stand out at all and curry favor with the sultan, she would have to find a way to draw his attention away from the most commanding woman in his life: his mother, and the second-most important, in terms of harem politics anyway, the beautiful Circassian *qadin*, mother of the empire's heir apparent.

Displacing them both wouldn't be easy. The sultan was deeply devoted to Hafsa, whose role as *Valide Sultan* was a formidable one, "invested with almost imperial power," as British author Lucy M.J. Garnett observed during her travels through Turkey in the late nineteenth century, gathering information for a study of Ottoman sociocultural customs and political structures.

> The . . . Padishah [Sultan] requires all the persons composing his harem, from the Bash Kadin Effendi [chief concubine or consort] down to the lowest slave, to take an oath of obedience to his mother. Thencefoward she is invariably addressed as 'The Crown of Veiled Heads,' a title with which every petition addressed to her must begin. And not only within the walls of the Serai is such deference paid to her. In her walks and drives abroad she is attended by a princely train, the Imperial Guards present arms as she passes them, and the poor who line her path prostrate themselves before her. If she has occasion to communicate her wishes to the Grand Vizier, that functionary receives the royal messenger at the door of his apartment, takes the missive from him with the most profound expressions of respect, raises it to his forehead and kisses it, as is duty bound.

The relationship of Suleiman's own grand vizier, Ibrahim, extended beyond these official courtesies. Married to Suleiman's sister, Hadije, he was also Hafsa's son-in-law and enjoyed her support and protection. Mahidevran's job security, meanwhile, hinged upon her elevated status as mother of the heir apparent and her Malibu Barbie beauty. With Hafsa, Roxelana bided her time. But with Mahidevran, she skillfully used to the *qadin*'s own jealous anger to topple her opponent.

Given Mahideveran's high-ranking position, it's unlikely that she initially took much notice of Roxelana; the Ruthenian maid was just one of hundreds of women in the harem, and not nearly as attractive as most (if contemporary reports are to be believed), including Mahideveran herself, a renowned beauty. But as Suleiman became increasingly drawn to Roxelana's charms, it was being whispered at court by the Venetian ambassadors—meticulous observers of court politics and intrigues—that the smitten sultan "no longer paid attention to the mother of his eldest son . . . but concentrated all his affection on [Roxelana]."

Fuming with jealousy, Mahideveran took matters into her own hands—literally. In a violent confrontation that took place sometime in the 1520s (reported a few decades later by ambassador Bernardo Navegero), the enraged *qadin* confronted her rival, shouting, "Traitor, sold meat [i.e., something bought in the bazaar]. You want to compete with me?" as she furiously clawed at Roxelana's hair and face with her nails. Summoned by Suleiman a few days later, the chastened and abused Ukrainian maid cleverly sent word to him that she was not presentable enough. Baffled, his desire to see her quickly turned into a demand. Upon entering his chambers, she tearfully "related to him what had happened . . . showing the sultan her face, which still bore the scratches." The enraged sultan then sent for Mahidevran who not only admitted what she did, but brassily added that "she had done less to [Roxelana] than she deserved." Her haughty lack of remorse "inflamed the sultan even more," at which point "he no longer wanted her, and all his love was given to the other . . ."

The episode reveals much about life at the palace and Roxelana's talent for navigating its wily currents. The harem was a thorny, even dangerous place where strategy was the key to survival. By not defending herself against Mahidevran's attack, Roxelana ostensibly obeyed protocol, which forbade her from striking the *qadin sultan*. But she also had the wits to turn the episode to her advantage, effectively defeating Mahidevran with her own fists.

Now that she was Suleiman's favorite (unofficially, since Mahidevran's status as the mother of Mustafa still meant she was "first concubine"), Roxelana was done playing by the rules. She began her personal reformation of the harem by defying its "one mother-one son" policy. This century-old system established that a concubine could bear only one son (and as many daughters as nature provided, leading up to the birth of a male). The purpose was to prevent a single mother from exerting her influence over too many male heirs. By the same token, royal wives—aristocratic daughters of foreign rulers—were not permitted to reproduce at all, so that rival powers or clans could not infiltrate the ruling dynasty's bloodline. The one mother-one son policy also put an end to sexual relations between the sultan and those concubines who bore him sons, which also played a role in Suleiman's rejection of Mahidevran. The custom sheds further light on the need, during an age of high infant mortality, for a harem filled with concubines, each of whom was only as good (to the state anyway) as her one and only male child.

Roxelana swept aside this practice and others, albeit with Suleiman's consent. After giving birth to a son, Mehmed, in 1521, she bore Suleiman four more sons and a daughter, Mihrimah, between 1522 and 1531. She also broke custom by remaining in Constantinople rather than accompanying Mehmed to his first royal administrative appointment in the provinces. This was another tradition that kept the concubine mothers of male heirs out of sight and out of mind. Only upon the death of the sultan would the mother of the eldest male heir be permitted to return to the capital and assume the role of *Valide Sultan*.

But then Roxelana went a significant step further. Not only did she shatter tradition by remaining in Constantinople, surrounded by her children—whose births, per Islamic custom, meant she was now protected from ever being sold or given away again—she did so by flaunting something no royal concubine had ever dared demand in the past: a dowry, "the surest pledge of a legal marriage among the Turks," as the Holy Roman Empire's ambassador to Suleiman's court, Ogier Ghiselin de Busbecq, observed.

"Having . . . become her own mistress, she refused to have anything more to do with Soleiman, who was deeply in love with her, unless he made her his lawful wife, thus violating the custom of the Ottoman Sultans. The dowry is the only thing which distinguishes a lawful wife from a concubine; for no slave has a dowry," Busbecq wrote.

That was until Roxelana came along. Her lavish wedding was the most public declaration to date that "Suleiman was deeply devoted" to her and that "she felt secure enough in his esteem to exert her will, and that the sultan was willing to bend protocol to preserve his relationship with her." As one Venetian diplomat concluded, "There has never been in the history of the Ottoman house a woman who enjoyed greater authority."

Or income. Whereas the average daily stipend for a royal concubine was between 150 and 500 silver Ottoman aspers,* Roxelana's was a whopping 2,000 (around $4,000), five times that of the *Valide Sultan*'s. Upon marrying Suleiman, her dowry income soared to 5,000 golden Venetian ducats annually (about $600,000), making her by far the richest woman in the harem. With her new income came a newly created title, *Haseki Sultan*, which roughly translates to "Queen Consort," but her exalted position had a far more personal aspect: the *haseki* was the undisputed Sultan's favorite concubine, a status that, under Roxelana, eclipsed that of the *qadin*.

As *haseki*, she not only enjoyed and formally established the hitherto unprecedented right to bear multiple sons and stay at court in Istanbul permanently, the role also permitted her a greater level of contact with the sultan than any other woman, with the possible exception of the queen mother, had in the past. The royal couple's steamy correspondence underscores this intimacy and suggests that passion, as well as political ambition, had much to do with Roxelana's rise to power.

"I am begging Allah with the loudest cry I have to be able to touch your lips, that burn me up inside," Roxolana wrote to Suleiman while he was away campaigning. "I know you are in war in Allah's Name right now . . . I wish for your success. However my greatest wish is to be reunited with you. You are the only cure for my grieving, sorrowful heart."

For his part, Suleiman, under the pen name Muhibbi ("the affectionate one"), responded in equally impassioned (some might say, sappy) verse:

> Throne of my lonely niche, my wealth, my love, my moonlight.
> My most sincere friend, my confidant, my very existence, my Sultan, my one and only love.
> The most beautiful among the beautiful . . .
> My springtime, my merry faced love, my daytime, my sweetheart, laughing leaf . . .
> My plants, my sweet, my rose, the one only who does not distress me in this world . . .
> My Istanbul, my Caraman, the earth of my Anatolia
> My Badakhshan, my Baghdad and Khorasan

* Between $300 and $1,000.

> My woman of the beautiful hair, my love of the slanted brow, my love of eyes full of mischief . . .
> I'll sing your praises always
> I, lover of the tormented heart, Muhibbi of the eyes full of tears, I am happy.

While away from the capital, in addition to love poems, Suleiman would also send Roxelana presents: furs, money, even a lock of hair from his beard. And his devotion was not only saccharine but singular. "His Majesty the Sultan loves her [Roxelana] so much that, as they say, he has refused to be with any other woman but her," observed contemporary Venetian ambassador Dominico Trevisano. "None of his predecessors had ever done that and such a thing is unheard of among the Turks who have a custom of sleeping with many wives." Nevertheless, to minimize distractions, Roxelana persuaded Suleiman to marry off the prettiest young women in the harem. The playing field was getting narrower and narrower, in the *haseki*'s favor. In 1533, she happily waved goodbye to Mahidevran when the *qadin*, according to protocol, followed Mustafa to his first official appointment, as governor of the Aegean province of Manisa. The following year, Hafsa had died, leaving Roxolana the undisputed mistress of the harem, even though Mahidevran was rightfully next in line to be *Valide Sultan*. But another rival yet remained: Ibrahim.

Born near the village of Parga, on the northwestern coast of Greece, Ibrahim was captured as a boy by slave traders and presented to Suleiman as a page when the future sultan was still a young prince. The Greek youth was charming, handsome, intelligent, musically gifted, and socially adept—and quickly became Suleiman's best friend and companion. The two remained inseparable after Suleiman ascended to the throne, spending hours in each other's company, dining together, strolling through the palace gardens, boating together, even sharing the same tent on campaigns and bedchamber when the sultan was in residence.

While the close relationship raised some eyebrows at court, what generated more buzz was Ibrahim's meteoric rise in the administration. Within three years after Suleiman became sultan, Ibrahim catapulted from the posts of grand falconer and master of the privy chamber—positions outside the administrative branch of government—to the governorship of Rumelia in the Balkans, to vizier, grand vizier, and commander in chief of all the armies of the empire. But at the same time his star was on the rise, so was Roxelana's. With the two vying for the sultan's attention, conflict was inevitable. In one of her earliest letters to Suleiman, written in 1526, Roxelana referred to a disagreement (the details of which are unknown) between herself and the man who essentially introduced the royal couple to one another: "You asked why I am angry at the Pasha. God willing, when we are able to be together again, you will hear."

With Suleiman's attention and affection increasingly drifting towards his favorite concubine, Ibrahim still had at least one powerful advocate in the harem: his mother in-law, Hafsa. Her death in 1534 left him vulnerable and without many friends at court. It was easy to see why. After a decade or so of honors, wealth, and ever-increasing power and authority, the grand vizier grew arrogant and "was much hated," as Venetian ambassador Bragadin reported in 1526. The Pasha jokingly boasted that his own wedding, to Suleiman's sister, was grander than Suleiman's own because he, Ibrahim, was the only one of the two who had entertained a sultan as a guest. Pushing the boundaries of his appointment as commander in chief of the armies, he engaged in his own military campaigns and even referred to himself as "sultan" in matters of political negotiations. His inevitable downfall was swift—and messy. On the morning of March 15, 1536, servants found him in his bed chamber, his throat cut and the walls of the room splattered with blood.

While Suleiman had ordered the execution, the word on the street was that Roxelana was its architect. Scholarly opinion is that this remains "a matter of conjecture," yet "she might have exploited the rumors against Ibrahim and influenced Suleiman's decision to remove him."

Either way, upon Ibrahim's death, Roxelana lost little time securing the vacant post of grand vizier for her son-in-law, Rustem (Mihrimah's husband). Then, a fateful fire in the Old Palace in 1541 inched her even closer to the pinnacle of power.

The Old Palace (*Eski Saray*), in the center of the city, was the sultan's official residence and the historic location of the harem. Yet the newer Topkapi Palace (*Topkapisaray*) was where the court convened. After the fire, Roxelana convinced Suleiman to relocate the harem to the New Palace—another unprecedented development—with hundreds of maidservants and lavish apartments at her disposal featuring "prayer halls, baths, gardens and other comforts," as Venetian courtier, Luigi Bassano wrote in 1537. Her quarters, reported fellow Venetian courtier Bernardo Navagero in 1553, were connected to Suleiman's through a series of secret doorways in the palace as well as an iron gate in "a small walled garden of the sultan, and then through another garden, belonging to the sultana."

This easy proximity enabled Roxelana to be at Suleiman's side nearly day and night, offering her opportunity to advise him on political matters, as his mother once had. Writing to her husband in 1537 while he was away, she informed him of plague infesting the city and warned him of potential unrest in his absence.

"[S]end news quickly, very quickly because—and I swear I am not lying—no messenger has come for the last week or two. The whole world is clamoring, all kinds of rumors are circulating. Don't think that it is just for myself that I am asking."

Other correspondence shows her taking part in diplomatic relations with the court of Poland, her homeland, when Ukraine was part of that kingdom. Writing to Polish King Sigizmund II, she negotiated for the humanitarian return of captives like herself to Ukrainian/Polish lands and the suppression of the Crimean slave trade. Her efforts were enshrined in Ukrainian folklore ("Thus with the pasha's key/She set the captives free," went one song), and she remains a national heroine, especially in her hometown of Rohatyn, where her statue towers above the central square.

Yet, like any mother, highest on Roxelana's list of priorities was the safety and welfare of her children. She had genuine cause for concern. The Ottoman law of imperial succession at the time mandated fratricide as a solution to princely squabbles over inheritance. If Mustafa succeeded to the throne, her own sons were doomed.

Mustafa's popularity was a problem for anyone wishing to eliminate him, but it also provided a solution. The "envy of all the princes," as one Ottoman historian described him, Mustafa was beloved by the people and the army. "The young Sultan is born to the saddle," was the report of emissaries to the front. "[E]ven now he can lead the standards to the Lands of War more swiftly than [Sultan Suleiman]." A bit too swiftly, it seemed. By 1553, rumors of Mustafa's desire to overthrow his father were whispered into Suleiman's ear, primarily (according to court gossip) by Rustem and Mihrimah, with a script composed by Roxelana. In a finale that sent shockwaves across Europe, Suleiman supposedly watched from behind a curtain while his eunuchs strangled Mustafa with a silken cord, as it was considered blasphemy to shed royal blood.

The domino-like downfalls of Roxelana's apparent rivals, the tectonic shifts in government policies she seemed to inspire, plus Suleiman's puppy-dog devotion, all fueled inevitable jealousies, suspicions, and rumors at court.

"[T]he entire court hate[s] her and her children likewise, but because the Grand Turk loves her very much, no one dares to speak," wrote the Venetian courtier Bassano. He and others went so far as to attribute Roxelana's power over Suleiman to magic, calling her *ziadi* (witch). Ambassador Busbecq observed that there were women in the capital who supplied Roxelana with hyena bones, believed to possess "great potency in love affairs." Although "there were two hyenas in Constantinople during my stay there," he continued, "their owners were reluctant to sell them to me, saying that they were keeping them for the Sultana . . . who is commonly reputed to retain [the Sultan's] affection by love-charms and magic arts."

While more enlightened critics have since ruled out voodoo as the key to Roxelana's success, many early modern historians continued to portray her as a ruthless schemer, an unfair estimation according to more recent revisionists.

In the first place, most of what was known about the harem outside its walls was "gossip fed to Europeans who had never even stepped inside the [palace] and whose informants told them what they wanted to hear but not what they really knew, which was mostly nothing." In addition, Roxelana's critics "tend to overlook the fact that she had to fight for her own survival and the survival of her children in the very competitive world of the imperial harem, which was populated by hundreds of beautiful women and able men and ruled by the fratricide law. [Roxelana] was thus unjustly and harshly judged by her contemporaries for surviving and doing so brilliantly."

Despite her detractors, Roxelana held her head high and carried on with her royal duties. Like Zubayd before her, she established *waqfs* (charitable endowments) and famously commissioned grand-scale building projects. Her largesse included a mosque, two madrasas, a soup kitchen, a hospital (still in use today as a women's medical center), and an elementary school—all located within Istanbul's Avrat Pazari district, site of the women's slave market where she, and many a harem resident, had been bought and sold. She also endowed soup kitchens in Jerusalem and Mecca. Again, in these and other such projects, Roxelana broke precedent. In the past, the endowments of concubine mothers were limited to the provincial cities, while normally only the sultan commissioned large building projects in the capital.

Upon Roxelana's death, of an unknown disease, on April 18, 1558, Suleiman sank into a period of deep depression. He put aside colorful garments and dressed in dark, somber cloaks. At dinner, he abandoned gold plates and ate from earthenware dishes. In his final poem to her, written on the day of her death, he called her the "springtime" of his life, and commanded that her mausoleum be decorated with intricate tiles depicting spring flowers. Even in death, Roxelana defied protocol: her tomb, adjacent to the Suleymaniye mosque, was erected beside her husband's own burial place, the first woman in Ottoman history to be so honored.

Roxelana's second son, Selim II, succeeded Suleiman upon his father's death in 1566 (Mehmed died earlier). His weak and ineffectual reign is said to have initiated the empire's long, slow decline.

But without question, Roxelana's insistence that the royal household—harem and sultan's quarters—exist under one roof at Topkapi forever transformed the power structure of the government. The consolidation of the domestic (mostly female) members of royal family and the sultan's court created an environment in which women were able to increasingly influence policy by staying put, as Roxelana had, in the capital at the sultan's side. By the end of the sixteenth century, no members of the royal household, with the exception of the sultan, ever left Istanbul. As the harem gradually took on its "new role as a principal division of the residence," with a larger staff and population of royal concubines and princes, the government itself transitioned "from a state geared to expansion and led by a warrior sultan to a territorially stable bureaucratic state ruled by a sedentary palace sultan."

In the wake of Suleiman's reign, an impressive amount of that bureaucracy was directed and overseen by women, primarily the *Valide Sultans* or the *hasekis*, during the roughly 150-year Sultanate of Women period that followed Roxelana's death.

Like her predecessor, Nurbanu Sultan (r.1566–1574), wife of Selim, practiced diplomacy by establishing her own relations with Venice and France, essentially running the government with the assistance of Selim's grand vizier, Sokollu Mehmed Pasha. This was less of a coup than a practicality: Selim cared more for the pleasures of drink and courtly entertainment (music, dancing girls) than he did for the business of governing. As the first woman to be both *Valide Sultan* and *Haseki*, Nurbanu enjoyed immense power and essentially groomed her son Murad III (r. 1574–1595) to inherit the throne. Inspired by Roxelena's philanthropic achievements, the civic-minded queen also liberally endowed schools in Istanbul for the study of the Sunnah and to teach illiterates to read. In addition she established a public bath, a Sufi lodge, and a large complex of accommodations for travelers and the homeless.

Murad's wife, Safiye Sultan, became *haseki* in 1574 and *Valide Sultan* in 1595, a position she held for nineteen years. During that time, she, like Nurbanu, maintained diplomatic relations with European powers, including England's Queen Elizabeth I, with whom she corresponded personally (see "Queenly Correspondence," p. 114). Her influence was such that petitioners and civil servants came to her directly with requests for her help in expediting government affairs. A word from her in the sultan's ear could quickly lead to the dismissals and appointments of some of the most senior level members of the government, including the grand vizier and chief Islamic jurists. As the most important member of the harem, she paid herself well; extremely well, in fact. Her stipend of 3,000 aspers per day was three times that of her husband's, the sultan, and many times that of every civil servant and military commander in the empire.

Kosem Sultan, one of the last and longest-reigning rulers of the harem, became *haseki* in 1617 and ruled as *Valide Sultan* from 1623, and Buyuk Sultan (queen grandmother) from 1648 until she died in 1651. Immensely wealthy, she was also one of the most politically influential, virtually running the government while serving as regent for two sultans, her son Murad IV (r. 1623–1640) and grandson Mehmed IV (r. 1648–1687). In addition to shaping the foreign and domestic policies of the empire, she was instrumental in overhauling the system of succession by phasing out the Ottoman custom of fratricide in favor of agnatic seniority in which the throne would go to the next eldest brother of the monarch instead of his eldest son.

Queenly Correspondence

If Roxelana ushered in the Sultanate of Women, she did so during what might be called the Age of Queens, not only in the Muslim east but in western Europe as well. Anne Boleyn, Margaret of Navarre, Elizabeth I, Catherine dé Medici, and Mary Queen of Scots were all contemporary women rulers, some of whom maintained direct, diplomatic correspondence with the *hasekis* and *Valide Sultans* of the Ottoman court.

Nurbanu wrote to both the doge of Venice and Catherine, dowager queen of France and regent for two French kings. Nurbanu's correspondence with the Venetian court was by and large businesslike, though she occasionally asked for personal favors (such as the release of Ottoman captives or financial benefits for her subjects living in the Italian city), suggesting that she had the upper hand in the relationship. Catherine's correspondence with Nurbanu demonstrated a similar acknowledgement of the Ottoman queen's influential position at the Sublime Porte. "Knowing the lofty place Your Highness holds next to His Highness the great Emperor [Sultan] your son because of your rare and excellent virtues . . . we have thought to write you to request, with the greatest possible affection, that you might use all good and appropriate offices in such a commendable work," Catherine wrote, prefacing an appeal for Nurbanu's help with the renewal of French trade capitulations, first granted in 1536.

In the correspondence between Safiye and England's Queen Elizabeth I, both queens were playing a game of posturing and politesse. Many of their letters concerned the mutual exchange of lavish gifts. In 1593, Edward Barton, English ambassador to the Ottoman court, presented to Safiye "her majesty's [Elizabeth's] picture, set with some rubies and diamonds, three great pieces of gilt plate, [and] ten garments of cloth and gold." Elizabeth personally selected her gifts to her Ottoman counterpart, including, six years later, an elegant, £600 coach and an even more elaborate clockwork musical organ. For her part, Safiye reciprocated by sending Elizabeth "a suit of princely attire being after the Turkish fashion" that featured "an upper gown of cloth of gold very rich, an under gown of cloth of silver, and a girdle of Turkey work" as well as "a robe, a sash, two large gold-embroidered bath towels, three handkerchiefs, and a ruby and pearl tiara," which was temporarily lost on its way to England, nearly resulting in an international scandal!

The exchange of such gifts between monarchs went beyond royal courtesy; they were statements of the respective wealth and power of each empires, and of the potential mutual benefits that might result from peaceful negotiations as opposed to the devastating expense of war. Like Catherine, Elizabeth sought to establish and maintain trade relations with the Ottomans. Safiye, speaking on behalf of the Sultan—and thereby on behalf of the empire itself—assured Elizabeth, in somewhat sisterly terms, as befitting a fellow monarch, that "I [Safiye] will take action in accordance with what you have written. Be of good heart in this respect." She then added, warmly, "May you too always be firm in friendship. God-willing, may [our friendship] never die."

The intimate correspondence between these Ottoman queens and their European counterparts suggests an awareness of their unique role as women in a traditionally patriarchal game of diplomacy. Furthermore, as scholar Leslie Pierce observed, the "communication among female royalty was testimony to the remarkable number of politically powerful women who flourished in the sixteenth century" and "maintained an important diplomatic channel for making and keeping peace."

Politically and ideologically, these and the other members of the "sultanate of women" were descendants of Roxelana, the laughing, loving, courageous and clever young woman from the Ukraine whose impact on the empire was lasting and irrefutable. Some historians have speculated that her independent spirit was a legacy of her homeland, where the Kievan Rus' regarded women's legal rights as equal to men's. Others say her courage was inspired by the contemporary emergence of "a new type of a Ukrainian woman that came to the fore during the Cossack liberation movement (the late sixteenth and seventeenth centuries)—a Cossack woman who defended her home and land against foreign invaders along with Cossack men." To this day, despite her fame as an Ottoman queen, she is regarded as a national heroine in Ukraine and a source of pride to its people—a heritage Turkish officials have acknowledged. In 2019, at the request of the Ukrainian embassy in Istanbul, references to Roxelana's Russian origins were removed from the visitor panel near her tomb at the Suleymaniye Mosque. With the Russian invasion of her homeland three years later, the simple, diplomatic gesture of letting people know just who this brave Ukrainian woman really was seems ever more poignant.

CHAPTER 7

Pari Khan Khanum (1548-1578)
Khayr al Nisa Begum (r.1578-1579)

The Persian Princess and Her Jealous Rival

While Ottoman queens were negotiating trade agreements with their European counterparts, they were also carrying on diplomatic relations with their rivals to the east: the Safavids of Persia, founders of modern Iran.

The Safavids rose to power in 1501 under the self-appointed Shah (King) Ismail I, a fiery, red-haired, fanatical fourteen-year-old from the Silk Road city of Ardabil, in Iran's mountainous northwestern province of Persian Azerbaijan. Ismail was a descendent of Safi ud Din, a Kurdish mystic who founded the eponymous Sufi order, the Safaviyya (hence Safavids), in Ardabil, two centuries earlier. Originally Sunnis, by Ismail's time the Safavids adopted Twelver Shiism, Iran's official state religion to this day.

Under the Twelver banner and Ismail's dynamic leadership, the Safavids subdued the whole of Iran and beyond, the first time the former empire was ruled by a Persian king since the seventh century. The bulk of Ismail's army consisted of a diverse band of Kurdish and Turkic militant zealots collectively known as the *Qizilbash*, or "Red Heads," because of the red, twelve-pleated headgear they wore—a devout symbol of their Twelver Shia faith.

At their peak, under Ismail's great grandson Abbas I (aka the Great, r. 1588–1629), the Safavids ruled an empire that stretched north to south from the Caspian Sea to the Persian Gulf, and east to west across modern-day Iran, Afghanistan, Armenia, Iraq, Syria, Uzbekistan, and parts of Turkey and Russia. The vast kingdom included key trading cities along the Silk Road, which gave the Safavids a monopoly on all luxury goods (silk, spices, carpets, tea, ivory, precious metals) flowing back and forth between India, China, the Middle East, and Europe.

Their wealth and power, plus their Shia faith, put the Safavids squarely at odds—politically, economically, and ideologically—with their staunchly Sunni, equally powerful Ottoman neighbors to the west. Yet amid tensions, trade embargos, and saber rattling on both sides of the shifting borders between the two empires, cooler heads maintained order by assuming control of government affairs.

During the mid-sixteenth century, many of those cooler heads sat on the shoulders of women who played an active and influential role in Safavid politics, as well as cultural and intellectual life. One Safavid princess in particular was among the most able of her day, Pari Khan Khanum, a skilled politician who, as interregnum ruler, managed to stabilize an empire at a time of unrest, only to be betrayed by vengeful members of her own family.

Pari Khan Khanum was born in 1548 in the provincial city of Ahar, about halfway between Ardabil and the one-time Safavid capital of Tabriz. "Pari," a cognate for the English word "fairy," may have been her given name, while Khan (Lord or Sir) and Khanum (Lady) were official titles. Though an odd construct to modern ears (roughly equivalent to Lady-Sir Pari), "Khanum" was the respectful way to address a woman of her rank, while "Khan" indicated both her royal status and heritage: Her mother, Sultan Agha Khanum, was a Circassian princess from the Northern Caucasus, along the eastern coast of the Black Sea, while her father, Shah Tahmasp I (r. 1524–1576), was the son and successor of Ismail I.

A miniature painted around 1574, believed to depict Pari in her mid-twenties, shows a composed young woman, seated cross-legged in a garden setting. She is wearing a pale, pistachio-colored dress beneath a short-sleeved, cornflower blue outer robe, richly embroidered in gold thread. On her head rests a *taj kulah*, a feathered and bejeweled Persian coronet, indicating her royal status. She calmly contemplates a delicate sprig of flowers with the barest suggestion of a Mona Lisa smile on her slightly rounded face, while a stray, twisting ringlet of dark hair escapes her headdress and hangs loosely at her temple alongside a bangled earring.

The image reflects the cultured pedigree of a young royal who grew up in a society renowned for its elegant art, literature, poetry, and architecture—legacies of its rich and refined, Persian past. In Isfahan, Tabriz, and Tahmasp's capital of Qazvin, lavish, azure-tiled mosques, shrines, colleges, public baths, and palaces, awash in flowery, vegetal motifs, reflected the urban splendor of Safavid public life. In its royal workshops, exceptionally skilled miniaturists, scribes, calligraphers, illuminators, paper burnishers, and gold sprinklers produced magnificent illuminated manuscripts, culminating in the "Shahnameh [Book of Kings] of Shah Tahmasp," an exquisitely illustrated edition of Persia's national epic and a powerful symbol of Safavid artistry, wealth, and sophistication.

It was also a period of Iranian history, centuries before grim-faced mullahs dictated otherwise, when women were regarded as equals and "the active role of females of the Safavid house in the political and cultural life of sixteenth-century Iran" was both "customary and legitimate."

Respect for women in Iranian society was yet another legacy of its ancient past. From the reign of Cyrus the Great (sixth c. BCE) on through the Sassanian era (seventh c. CE), females served in the military, owned land, conducted business, traveled independently, and, in the case of royals, convened their own council meetings on policy. Such councils were recognized as influential seats of power: service at a royal woman's court was a strategic stepping stone for ambitious administrators and state dignitaries seeking higher office.

Life for women was much the same among the nomadic peoples of the Central Asian steppes from whom the Safavids descended (see "A Tradition of Equality," p. 120). So rather than the exception, the empowerment of women in premodern Iranian society was the norm: a "synthesis between Turko-Mongol nomadic steppe-traditions and Irano-Islamic ones." Well educated, financially independent, and politically and socially active, high-ranking Safavid women rode in hunting parties and military expeditions alongside men, maintained their own courts, served as counselors to the throne, patrons of the arts and charitable foundations, and, however briefly, as heads of state when the need arose. Thus, they not only shared political power with men and played

A Tradition of Equality

In addition to its Persian roots, the respect for women among the Safavids was a cultural inheritance from their nomadic Central Asian ancestors, just as it was for Shajarat and Razia, whose respective forebears, Kipchak Turks and Ilbari tribesmen, as we have seen, similarly held women in high esteem. The Safavids, like the Ottomans themselves, descended from the Oghuz, a confederation of Turkic nomads from the steppes of Central Asia and Mongolia who embraced Islam in the tenth century. The prominence of women in Oghuz society, as both political leaders and warriors, is evident in the pages of the tenth-century epic narrative *The Book of Dede Korkut*.

This collection of folktales, recounting the heroic age of the Oghuz Turks, celebrates their core value, manliness, "a trait that both men and women could possess." Among the book's famous heroines is Lady Chichek, who is "[p]urer than the moon, lovelier than the sun" but is equally renowned as a first-class rider, hunter, archer, and wrestler. When a chieftain's son comes calling with a marriage proposal, she challenges him to outride, outshoot, and outwrestle her before agreeing to the wedding.

In another tale, the towering, fearsome Lady Burla the Tall, leading a pack of "forty slender-waisted," mounted maiden warriors, storms into battle alongside her Oghuz chief husband, scattering the enemy and toppling their standard with a blow of her sword. Similarly, the hot-tempered Princess Saljan makes mincemeat of the opposition, smashing through enemy lines "from one end to the other." Clearly, Oghuz women, as the *Dede Korkut*'s English translator summarized, "do not sit passively in their tents," nor do their husbands expect them to. When the father of Lady Chichek's suitor asks his son to describe to him the best sort of wife for an Oghuz warrior, the son replies: "father, find me a girl who will rise before I get to my feet, who will be on horseback before I mount my well-trained horse, who before I reach my enemy will bring me some [of their] heads; that's the sort of girl to find for me, father."

Given these and other accounts of women holding their own in battle among the nomadic warriors of Central Asia—a people "easy in the saddle [and] deadly with sword and bow"—it makes sense that the ancient Greek historian Herodotus identified Scythia (modern Iran) as the home of the legendary Amazons, who "go on horseback, hunting with their men . . . go to war too, and wear the same dress as the men do." (Modern archeology confirms Herodotus's sometimes truth-stretching reports: the excavated graves of a quarter to a third of nomadic, steppe-dwelling women contained the remains of active warriors, buried alongside their weapons.)

Closer to Pari's time, various European visitors to Iran during the fifteenth and sixteenth centuries remarked on the open and equal participation and presence of women in society, as well as their power. In 1404, Ruy Gonzalez de Clavijo—Castilian ambassador to the court of Iran's Turco-Mongol ruler Timur (Tamerlane)—attended a royal wedding at the invitation of the emperor's daughter-in-law, the Princess Khanzadeh. The ambassador was struck by how the princess "herself with many guests and other ladies who were in attendance on her," all sat together with male guests at the wedding feast. During his mission to Tahmasp's court in 1540, Venetian envoy Michele Membre declared that Safavid women, while agreeable in nature, were more hardnosed when it came to household budgets. "These ladies . . . keep all their husband's money. When the husband wants something he has to ask his wife for the money," he wrote. While in Qazvin, the Venetian diplomat also observed that "ladies ride through town like men and go with maids instead of grooms," albeit veiled "with a white handkerchief, so only their eyes are seen." Captivated by their appearance, Membre further reported that Safavid women were "very beautiful and wear beautiful, big, round pearls at their necks."

Venetian merchant Franceso Romano, who journeyed to Tabriz during the reign of Ismail I, was less enchanted with feminine Safavid sex appeal, which he found somewhat shocking. "The women are short in proportion to the men and as white as snow," he recorded. "Their dress is the same as always has been—the Persian costume—wearing it open at the breast, showing their bosoms and even their bodies, the whiteness of which resembles ivory. All the Persian women—and particularly in [Tabriz]—are wanton, and wear men's robes, and put them on over their heads, covering them altogether."

While subjective, Romano's observations offer yet more evidence of the highly visible and unrestricted presence of women in Safavid culture.

an influential role at court, they were entitled to equal amounts of booty and inheritances, and thus were, conceivably, eligible to rule. (Such equality *did* have had its downsides. Like their princely male counterparts, seventeenth-century Safavid princesses suspected of rebellion were blinded as a punishment.)

Pari was educated alongside her siblings—seven daughters and twelve sons from her father's multiple wives—in accordance with Safavid coeducational traditions. Curricula for both princes and princesses included study of the Qur'an, Islamic law, poetry, and painting, the latter intended to cultivate good taste. Additionally, both sexes received training in the military arts: archery, horseback riding, the use of arms, wrestling, and polo, introduced to Iran between 600 BCE and 100 CE by Central Asia nomads whose version of the game was part sport, part battlefield training. Young women of the court also received instruction in calligraphy and formal letter writing, a valuable skill when engaging in diplomacy.

According to contemporary court historian Iskandar Beg Munshi, Pari was notably "more intelligent than the other royal princesses." Intellectually, she leaned towards the sciences, Islamic law, and poetry, in which she took a keen interest. Under her patronage, the "number of poets who flourished at that time, either at court or in the provinces, was legion." Writing under the pen name of *Haqiqi* (Truth) she composed her own poems and corresponded (in verse) with leading poets of her day with whom she engaged in poetry contests.

Like her aristocratic Ottoman counterparts to the west (such as Roxelana), Pari and other, wealthy Safavid women also endowed public buildings, charitable institutions, and religious festivals, and funded the construction of caravansaries, underscoring the importance of trade to the welfare of the state and private enterprise.

But Pari's true gift was governing, a talent she seemed to inherit from the female side of her family. Tahmasp's mother, Shah Beg(i) Khanum, acted as one of her husband's most trusted counselors. Upon Ismail's death, she was regarded as the power behind her son's throne, ruling under the title Tajlu Khanum (Crowned Lady). Equally dynamic was Tahmasp's sister, Shahzada Sultanum, a "learned and wise woman," according to contemporary accounts. In keeping with the cultural traditions of her distant Turkic nomadic ancestors of the Central Asian steppes, she was routinely at her brother's side on hunting expeditions and in the council chamber.

"[A]ll the financial and administrative ... affairs of the state" in the words of Safavid-era chronicler Qazi Ahmad al Qummi—including the exchange of diplomatic letters with Roxelana—"were carried out according to her advice, and the shah would not do anything without consulting her and without her knowledge."

By the time Pari was in her early twenties, Tahmasp similarly came to rely on her counsel on all matters "trivial or major, domestic or foreign," wrote the sixteenth-century Safavid historian Muhammad Afushtah Natanzi. "[N]othing," Natanzi emphasized, "was done without her knowledge and consent." Such was her growing power and influence at court, Munshi remarked, that those "who had difficult problems asked her to intercede with the Shah, which she frequently did with success."

Even though Tahmasp betrothed Pari to his nephew, Badi al Zaman, governor of the southeastern Iranian city of Sistan, the doting shah refused to let her journey there (and thus consummate the marriage), preferring to keep her by his side in Qazvin, which he made his capital in 1555. The shah's obvious favoritism made her "the envy of her peers," especially her half brother, Prince Haydar, who came to resent her. As far as Pari was concerned, the feeling was mutual, as she "had no love in her heart" for him either, as Munshi reported. So when Tahmasp fell ill in October of 1574 without naming an heir to the throne, Pari did what she could behind the scenes to promote the candidacy of her older half brother, Ismail, as her father's successor.

Ethnic/family loyalty had something to do with Pari's objection to Haydar. His mother, Sultanzadeh Khanum, was Georgian while hers was Circassian. As rival members of the harem from different tribal backgrounds, the two mothers sought to empower their own relatives and countryman at court while bitterly competing for leverage over whose children would succeed. Some among the *Qizilbash* also took issue with Haydar's Georgian ancestry. Ethnically Turkic, they objected to the growing number of Georgians, Armenians and Circassians infiltrating the army, the harem, and court during Tahmasp's reign. While a handful of the *Qizilbash*, including those with Georgian connections, supported Haydar, most favored Ismail, whose Turco-Mongol, maternal ancestry (his mother, like Tahmasp's own, was a member of the powerful Turcoman Mawsillu tribe of Eastern Anatolia) assured them that the throne would remain a Turkic power base. Tahmasp's eldest son, Mohammad Khundabanda, was considered ineligible to succeed because he was nearly blind.

The trouble was, Ismail happened to be in jail at the time, locked up by Tahmasp for the past seventeen years in the remote, rockbound fortress of Qahqaheh Castle, a sort of Club Fed penitentiary for Safavid royals, about fifty miles northwest of Ardabil.

The reasons for Ismail's imprisonment seem to have been a combination of hubris and moral turpitude. Born in 1537, he began his political career as a model prince, "of robust frame and daring spirit, of great courage, and loving war . . . [who] proved his valour on many occasions against the Ottomans," in the words of Vincentio D'Alessandri, sixteenth-century Venetian ambassador to the Safavid court. Ismail's skirmishes with the Ottomans—which were both unauthorized by Tahmasp and carried out during peacetime—made him popular with the hawkish *Qizilbash* (another reason they favored him as Tahmasp's successor). But they raised concerns at court "that this young man had ambitious views." Though Ismail was "beloved by his father," the relationship began to sour when it dawned on Tahmasp "how ardently [his son was] desired as ruler by all the people." The shah also became increasingly concerned about Ismail's self-destructive weaknesses: he was an opium addict and a pedophile. Munshi's discreet reporting of the young prince's eventual downfall and imprisonment was that Ismail "displayed ingratitude toward the Shah's beneficence and committed certain acts displeasing to his father."

All through Tahmasp's convalescence, during which time he twice came close to death, Pari stayed at her father's side, nursing him back to health, an experience that brought them even closer. But while she had one eye on his recovery, she kept another sharply focused on the succession intrigues at court, in particular a plot hatched by Haydar to have his spies at Qahqaheh assassinate Ismail. When she reported this intelligence to Tahmasp, he dispatched a contingent of bodyguards to the prison to watch over his son.

Though Tahmasp recovered from his illness long enough to rule for about another year and a half, the shah finally passed away on the night of May 14, 1576. The usual chaos that ensued upon a monarch's death was exacerbated in this instance by the fact that he still had not named an heir. According to Sufi custom and tradition, as Munshi pointed out, if "the Shah should die before nominating any of his sons . . . the eldest son should be considered heir-apparent." But since the eldest, Muhammad, was blind, and the next in line, Ismail, still languished in prison, Haydar, "with the arrogance of youth, and natural ambition," promptly seized the throne for himself with the backing of his supporters at court and the slippery connivance of his mother. No sooner had he placed his father's crown upon his head and buckled the shah's personal sword to his belt than his mother produced a will that Haydar declared was "in the late Shah's own handwriting from beginning to end," naming him as heir. There were skeptical mutterings that the will was a skillful forgery (recall that the women of the harem received particular instruction in calligraphy and letter-writing). Defusing the situation, Haydar—your classic, glad-handing politician—"spoke warmly" to the assembled palace guards and other officers of the court, to whom he "distributed gifts . . . and uttered fair promises."

Pari, however, wasn't buying any of it.

She knew that she needed to act fast if she was going to preserve her status at court, and perhaps even her life. On the night of their father's death, Haydar gave orders that his half sister be confined to the palace and limited her access to companions and resources. How long would it be before she ended up at Qahqaheh like Ismail, or worse? Haydar had already tried to have him assassinated. Why not rid himself of Pari as well, who he always resented anyway and who opposed his ascension to the throne?

But Haydar wasn't quite aware of what he was up against. Decisive but dim, he made a series of fatal missteps during his first hours on the throne that Pari, like a chess player watching a novice fumble his way through his first game, utilized to her advantage. Per Safavid royal custom, different members from different tribes among the *Qizilbash* took turns standing watch over the palace each day. Blithely, not to mention foolishly, Haydar dismissed his own contingent of supporters from the palace, unaware that the guards on duty the day of his self-coronation just so happened to be made up of those loyal to Ismail. By doing so, as Munshi put it, he "made himself the prisoner of his opponents."

Keenly aware of the blunder, Pari knew that if she could free herself from her house arrest, she could find a way to help Ismail's supporters seize the palace and the throne. But first she had to convince her brother that she was no traitor—an appeal she made not to his better judgement but to his male vanity. Throwing herself at his feet, "with an air of helplessness and perturbation," she laid it on fairly thick, as Munshi reported.

"Women are foolish creatures," she coyly declared. "If, in my stupidity and short-sightedness, I have been guilty of any misdemeanor, I beg you to pardon me and spare my life. In that event, I will follow the path of obedience to you, and will not deviate by so much as a hair's breadth from the course of conduct which is pleasing to Your Royal Highness." She concluded the deceptive speech by bowing down to kiss the foot of the gullible monarch. Needing all the friends he could get at this point, Haydar told Pari, whether "out of desperation or trust," that he had always been fond of her. Swearing an oath on a Qur'an (at Pari's insistence), he promised that if she would rally her Circassian supporters to his cause, including her brother Suleiman Mizra and her powerful uncle (Tahmasp's brother-in-law), Shamkhal Sultan, he would hold her "even dearer" than he did during the late shah's lifetime—a bit of a stretch, considering that Haydar never liked her in the first place.

With that, he let her leave the palace. As promised, she went straight to her uncle and brother, not to convince them to support Haydar, however, but to hand them the keys to the harem garden gates. They returned with three hundred Circassian troops, all hostile to Haydar, who poured into the palace, searching for the hapless shah. They found him hiding in the harem dressed in women's clothes (not his finest machismo moment), a cowardly stratagem concocted by his mother. Once identified, possibly by Pari herself, Haydar was ignominiously dragged out into the open and hacked to death with "battle axes, swords, and daggers"—a ghastly, not to mention heretical execution, considering that, coward or not, he was still the son of a shah and an acknowledged descendent of Shias.

Chaos engulfed Qazvin for the next ten days, as rival factions of the *Qizilbash* clashed openly. Riots broke out, stirred up by "riffraff and unruly elements of various districts" while those seeking to settle old scores took advantage of the lawlessness to brazenly roam about the capital, murdering their enemies. As Munshi summarized, "[t]he city was in turmoil."

During this troubled period, Pari firmly took charge and restored order. Guards were posted throughout the city while those who threatened acts of violence were threatened themselves with the prospect of capital punishment. The streets were cleared, the "bazaar was reopened, and trade began again," reported Munshi—all reassuring signs of stability. Meanwhile, Pari dispatched an envoy to Qahqaheh castle to fetch Ismail. She then summoned the princes and high-ranking members of the *Qizilbash* to gather at the city's main mosque on May 23, 1576, to hear the *khutbah* read in Ismail's name, an act that affirmed him as the new shah, Ismail II.

During the twenty days it took her half brother to get to Qazvin, "it was Pari Khan Kanom who gave the orders" and oversaw all the affairs of state and the palace. Each morning, after prayer time, she held a private audience for a delegation of *Qizilbash* leaders who met with her at her residence to review the kingdom's most "pressing administrative and financial problems." While there may have been some debate among the amirs at these briefings, it was Pari who ultimately called the shots. "Not one of them," Munshi wrote, "dared to contravene her orders."

Though Ismail reached Qazin on June 13, 1576, a month after his father's death, he didn't enter the city right away and instead stayed for two weeks at the house of a trusted *Qizilbash* leader. The reason for the delay was written in the stars; his astrologers, in whom he (like most Safavid rulers at the time) placed great trust, advised him that the foretold hour of his coronation had not yet arrived. Meanwhile, regarding more earthly matters, he relied on reports from faithful *Qizilbash* leaders to keep him informed on the affairs of Pari's court, which the amirs still attended. As these daily reports trickled in, the new shah increasingly didn't like what he was hearing:

> Pari Khan Kanom's servants and stewards began to act with greater pomp and circumstance than during the reign of Shah Tahmasp, and her doorkeepers, chamberlains, and other retainers instituted ceremonies more appropriate to the court of a king. Pari Khan Kanom confidently expected that, since Shah [Ismail II] owed his throne to her, and since she had also been his supporter during the reign of Shah Tahmasp, she would have greater influence in matters of state than Tahmasp's sister [Shahzada Sultanum].

This was one of her few miscalculations. Ismail had no intention of sharing power with his half-sister, and said as much to the *Qizilbash* leaders.

"Have you not understood, my friends, that interference in matters of state by women is demeaning to the king's honor, and that for men to associate with the women of the Safavid royal house is an abominable crime?" he warned them, brushing aside the Turco-Mongol traditions of his ancestors when it came to respect for the status of women in society. It was abundantly clear that Ismail equally had little regard for family or loyalty as well. In Munshi's estimation, he "was a hard-hearted man, not possessed of normal feelings of affection toward his family [who] never displayed any kindness towards his brothers, male cousins, and nephews," all potential rivals to the throne.

Lying to their faces, he promised his nearest and supposedly dearest that "[i]f you treat me lovingly and justly, I shall, God willing, treat you in a way in which no other king has treated his brothers." Yet "in his heart he planned only to eliminate them, and in the end carried out what was hidden in his heart," i.e., a Mafia-style, in-house killing spree that followed soon after his coronation on August 22, 1576.

The sweeping and bloody purge began with the execution of prominent members of the Ustajlu tribe, one of the largest and most powerful clans in the *Qizilbash*. Whether any of them had actually supported Haydar—or him for that matter—was immaterial to Ismail. Long years of drug abuse and imprisonment left him acutely paranoid, "with the result that he saw enemies everywhere" he looked. In their colorful account of the carnage, written sometime after 1607, Carmelite friars—dispatched by Pope Clement VIII to the court of Abbas I to woo the shah into an alliance against the Ottomans, vis a vis the old "enemy of my enemy is my friend" geopolitical gambit—reported that Ismail:

> . . . also had put to death all the chief governors (sultans) who had been at his father's Court, saying that "the royal tents could not be held up by old ropes." He even reddened with blood his own hands, killing many of them with his own sword, saying that he wanted to see whether it would cut: wherefore, by the reckoning made, it was estimated that by his own hands or by his orders . . . there were killed about 12,000 persons, without counting those whom he deprived of eyesight and sent into exile.

The number of dead may be a gross exaggeration, but it certainly included members of his family, who he had disingenuously vowed to protect. Brothers, cousins, nephews—six relatives in one day on one occasion—were murdered, or blinded, in what contemporary historians characterized as "a reign of terror in which nobody felt safe."

Of all Ismail's male relatives, only his elder brother Mohammad—still considered harmless because of his blindness—and Mohammad's sons, too young to be a threat at that point, survived the purge (for the time being anyway). Pari also managed to stay off the paranoid ruler's hit list, though she was essentially banished from court. After Ismail advised his amirs that consulting with women on affairs of state was a dishonor, they stopped visiting her at her residence and cut her off from all the affairs of the palace. Still, while out of sight, she wasn't entirely out of her vengeful half brother's mind. In addition to seizing most of her assets and properties, he tried to slut-shame her by spreading rumors of her sexual indiscretions, a commonly employed smear. The indictment was especially egregious, given that Pari was still officially betrothed (if not already married) to her cousin, Badi al Zaman.

True to form, she pushed back and defended herself and her honor. In a letter to Ismail, composed around the time all this was happening, she condemned the "slander of our cuckoldry" (emphatically using the "royal we") as "unacceptable." Rumors circulating among the ulema that Pari plotted to overthrow him also reached Ismail's ears, an accusation she unequivocally denied:

> Another issue they [the Imams] have brought up is the question of women's involvement in state affairs . . . Women never wanted to rule, and if I had wanted to, then when I was in charge I would have chosen one of the princes whose mouths still smelled like milk [i.e., an infant], and I would have ruled without any problems . . . Or if I had wanted a husband like other princesses, I could have taken one of the two worthy princes remaining among Bahram Mizra's children* and then I would not have fought so much for [your] revival and survival.

Far from being a threat, she continued, she was a virtuous and valuable asset to the throne.

* Bahram Misra was brother to Ismail I.

> I have studied the books of jurisprudence all my life, and have memorized most of the [Qur'anic] exegeses, so why should I be labeled like this? Moreover, unlike other princesses I was never away from my father's court, I have never gone through the streets, I have never seen the city's bathhouses, and I have not gone hunting, but I am still being slandered like this. If the problem is that of protective jealousy . . . there are many others you should be more concerned about than me. If the problem is that you are afraid that I am the heir to the kingdom, then send a prince who is deserving of the kingship and is the best soldier among princes to come and wear the dagger and strike [me with] the sword in order to put your mind at ease. I am ready to die while others are ready to grab the kingship.

Taking a final jab at Ismail's scorched-earth approach to governing, she concluded, "Truly, it is not possible to rule through murder and destruction."

Predictably, her admonition fell on deaf ears.

Perpetuating his "reign of terror," Ismail ordered the massacre of five hundred Sufis, recently arrived in Qazvin from Anatolia, fearing they were brought to the city to overthrow him in a plot hatched by disloyal *Qizilbash* leaders. He also alienated his own Shia ulema by flirting with the teachings of a prominent Sunni scholar, Mizra Makhdum Sharifi, who he appointed to the office of *sadr* (minister of religious affairs).

When rumors reached his ears that some *Qizilbash* amirs wanted to replace him on the throne with Mohammad's eldest son, Prince Hasan, Ismail reversed his hands-off policy regarding his brother's children. With tragic irony, the murderous shah ordered members of the *qurchi* (the royal bodyguard) to garrote the young prince in Tehran. With Hasan dispatched, Ismail drafted orders in the fall of 1577 to execute the rest of the family.

Enough was enough. Before his orders could be carried out, the malevolent shah was found dead in his bed, on the morning of November 25, 1577. The cause of death appeared to be an opium overdose, but foul play was not ruled out. The evidence, in fact, pointed plainly in that direction.

The previous night, Ismail and one of his close companions, fellow drug addict Hasan Beg Halvachi, left the palace, fueled on opium. They spent the night wandering the streets of Qazvin, where they loaded up on sweets and pastries from street vendors before returning to Ismail's bedchamber for a specially prepared nightcap of opium and Indian hemp. Hasan, who usually blended the concoction, noted that the seal on the box containing the drug mixture was tampered with, but Ismail, fatally, ignored his companion's warnings. When palace physicians discovered traces of poison in the Shah's body the next day, some suspected that Pari had "conspired with the maidservants of the harem" to add the deadly ingredient to Ismail's recreational drug mix. By the time the Carmelites wrote their history of the Safavid dynasty, it was unquestionably the "shrewd and prudent" Pari who, aided by members the harem, "devised the poison," added it to "some pills of opium, which he (Isma'il) was wont to eat," and slipped them into "a wallet which was carried by the son of a captain trusted by him, who had always remained by him."

However Ismail died, a delegation of nobles wasted little time in approaching Pari to ask if she would consider succeeding her infamous half brother. She declined, on the premise that so long as Mohammad Khundabanda was alive, blind or no, he was the rightful heir. One dignitary suggested that she act as regent for Ismail's eight-month-old son, Shuja al Din, and that while he grew "she should be the real ruler of the state." Again, she declined, not because she had no desire to serve as interregnum once more, but because she could read a room. Most of the amirs looked more favorably on Mohammad's candidacy and chafed at the thought of putting a woman on the throne, at least publicly. Well aware of her capacity for governing, they came up with a compromise. Behind the closed doors of her private apartments, they proposed to her that she would reign until Mohammad arrived in Qazvin from Shiraz, where he had been under house arrest, after which "he would be the titular king, but the real power would reside in her hands."

And so, as Munshi related, Pari once more took "upon her own shoulders the responsibility for the conduct of state affairs." Governing an empire of more than a million square miles, with a population of some 20 million people, was no small task. It involved overseeing a vast bureaucracy of court officials, judges, governors, and financial officers tasked with collecting taxes, assigning salaries and pensions, and maintaining a paid army of around eighty thousand troops, also under command of the shah. The grand vizier, assisted by a cadre of civil servants, undertook many of the nitty-gritty details. But under the Safavids, as in most pre-parliamentarian Islamic states, the shah (or the sultan or the caliph) was the ultimate authority, and Pari was no exception. During her second reign as interregnum ruler, the "emirs obeyed her orders, and every day presented themselves at her house" to learn just what those orders were.

Still, there was always the unexpected to worry about. So, while keeping close tabs on the *Qizilbash* leaders, she gave orders that no one was to leave Qazvin without her permission (lest some might have second thoughts about her authority). To bolster support for her rule, she also freed all political prisoners who had been locked up under Ismail's reign.

Nonetheless, one court official managed to slip out of the capital: Mizra Salman Jaberi, Ismail's former vizier. Riding "hell for leather to Shiraz," Salman wanted to intercept Mohammad before he left the city. His motive, like that of most court officials, was the preservation of his own hide, as Munshi frankly related:

> Looking to his own interests, therefore, as all officers of the state and aspirants to high office have to do, he told the Shah and his wife the truth about events at Qazvin, and something about the powerful position of [Pari] Khan Kanom and the way in which the [*Qizilbash*] emirs obeyed her.

The key phrase there was "and his wife," i.e., Mohammad's spouse, Khayr al Nisa Begum, known formally as the Mahde Ulya (The Queen). Proud and imperious, she descended from a long line of prominent Shia imams and rulers of Mazandaran, a lush and mountainous province skirting the southern shores of the Caspian Sea. When her father was overthrown by a rival cousin, Madhe and her brothers fled to the safety of the Safavid court, where she soon married Mohammad.

"[W]ell cultivated and . . . acquainted with matters of state," she was not a woman accustomed to simply sitting idly on a throne. As she listened to Mizra Salman's report, it became increasingly evident to her and her husband that a Pari Khan Khanum shadow government was neither desirable nor sustainable.

> [Mizra Salman] made it clear to the Shah and Mahd-e Ulya that, as long as Pari Khan Kanom was mistress in the palace and controlled affairs of state, the Shah would possess nothing but the title of king, and his wife would not be admitted to the harem. The Shah and his wife, deciding that the 'Kanom had to be rendered powerless, deliberated as to how this might be achieved. All the reports that came from Qazvin confirmed them in this resolve. In short, Sultan Mohammad Shah and Mahd-e Ulya determined to remove Pari Khan Kanom from the scene . . .

Rumors of the royal couple's displeasure with Pari's presumptuous rule reached Qazvin during the month it took for Mohammad and Mahde to prepare for their journey to the capital. During this time, some *Qizilbash*, holding their fingers to the wind, abandoned Pari and, in defiance of her orders, left Qazvin to join the royal entourage. In advance of his arrival, Mohammad dispatched guards to the city to stand watch over the treasury. Meanwhile, those Qizilbash who remained loyal to the princess stood guard themselves at her residence to ensure her safety. Once more, the kingdom was dividing into factions.

The new shah and his followers finally arrived on the outskirts of Qazvin on February 1, 1578. Pari traveled from the city to greet them, ahead of her own entourage of some four- to five-hundred supporters. During her formal audience with Mohammad there was discussion of Ismail's tyranny, and condolences were exchanged over the death of their father, Tahmasp. Then, as Munshi related, Pari made an uncharacteristic faux pax: "I heard from some of the eunuchs who were present that [Mahde Ulya], as a point of courtesy, kissed the hand of Pari Khan Khanom, but that the latter, in her pride and folly, displayed no great regard for her in return."

How Mahde reacted to the obvious, public snub is unknown. How she felt about her sister-in-law was less of a mystery. In their account of the meeting, the Carmelites remarked on the "jealousy [Mahde] bore [Pari] for being so wideawake and sagacious a lady."

Whether her motivations were personal or political (and they were probably both), Mahde saw to it that Pari's fate was sealed. On February 3, Mohammad ascended the throne and took up residence in the palace. Before the coronation, the new shah gave orders to the princess's former bodyguard,

Khalil Khan Ashfar, to prevent her from returning to her residence after the ceremonies. As Pari was leaving the palace in her litter, she and her servants were surrounded by Khalil's men, who forced them to turn around. The two parties struggled, during which time Pari "was tossed to and fro" in the litter until Khalil shouted above the din that he was acting on the shah's orders. At that point, Pari understood what was happening and accepted her fate. She was taken to Khalil's house where her neck was broken via strangulation. That same day, just to tie up all loose ends, Mohammad and Mahde had Pari's loyal uncle, Shamkhal Sultan, and Ismail's infant son, Shuja al Din, also assassinated. For his bloody efforts, Khalil was rewarded with Pari's personal fortune and assets. At the time of her death, the princess was barely thirty years old.

Mahde promptly took on the role that Pari had envisioned for herself: running the kingdom on Mohammad's behalf. It was she who now made all political, administrative, and military decisions and who approved all royal decrees. Just as Pari had during her reign, Mahde issued daily orders to the *Qizilbash* amirs and civil dignitaries during a morning council held in her quarters. Like Pari, "no affair was conducted without her advice," Safavid historian Qummi observed, and her word on all matters pertaining to the governing of the kingdom was final.

Yet by the summer following her husband's coronation, Mahde's relationship with the Qizilbash began to sour. She blocked lucrative promotions among them, bestowing rich favors instead upon her own Mazandarani kinsmen. She also transferred revenues from Qizilbash-controlled provinces directly to the crown and was "known for her severe criticism of amirs," openly arguing with them, threatening them, and displaying her "disdain [for] their advice and opinion."

Frustrated, the amirs brought their case—and a blatant ultimatum—directly to the shah, in a petition tinged with misogyny:

> Your Majesty well knows that women are notoriously lacking in intelligence, weak in judgment, and extremely obstinate. Mahd-e 'Olya has always opposed us, the loyal servants of the crown, and has never agreed with us on matters of state policy; she has acted contrary, to the considered opinions of the qezelbdi elders, and has constantly attempted

> to humiliate and degrade us. We have not been safe from her actions, even though up to the present time we have not been guilty of improper conduct, nor have we done anything to cause her alarm. So how can we feel secure now, when our basic incompatibility has come out into the open, when she has lashed with her tongue the elders of the [Qizilbash] tribes, has called us mutinous, and has uttered dire threats against us? In short, we do not consider it proper that word should spread among neighboring rulers that no member of the royal family still remains in the care of the [Qizilbash] because a woman has taken charge of the affairs of state and is all-powerful. Mahd-e 'Olya's power and influence in the government of the realm is objectionable to all the qezelbdi tribes, and it is impossible for us to reach a modus vivendi with her. If she is not removed from power, in all probability revolts will occur that will be to the detriment of both religion and the state.

Mohammad, "a pious, ascetic, and gentle soul" and, as it seems, a people-pleaser, responded that if his wife's "intervention in state affairs to be not in the best interests of the state, then he would exclude her from them in the future." If that didn't satisfy the emirs, he promised to send her on a permanent vacation to visit their eldest son (and her favorite), Hamza Mizra in Qom, or perhaps even return her to her family in Mazandaran.

Mahde, however, "being of an aggressive temperament, strongly disapproved of the Shah's mild rejoinder to the emirs." She further "declared that she had no intention of changing her behavior nor would she swerve a hair's breadth, she said, from the line of conduct she had followed so far."

Fed up with her intransigence, the *Qizilbash* emirs resolved to dispatch her in the same way she had gotten rid of Pari: strangulation, which occurred in the harem on July 26, 1579. For good measure they killed her mother as well. To justify their murderous act, they spread false rumors of Mahde's infidelity with a Crimean prince residing at court and fears that she had transferred the royal treasury to Manzandaran. But what irked them the most was her refusal to surrender her power.

Despite the gruesome circumstances of both Mahde's and Pari's deaths, it is clear from contemporary sources that royal women, as we have seen, were respected and played a significant role in sixteenth-century Safavid society.

By the time Pari assumed control of the empire, the "idea of a woman openly active on the political scene and even governing the state in a period of crisis was fully accepted by Safavid elites."

Those same elites, however, were not comfortable with women remaining on the throne indefinitely. Women were openly accepted as close advisors or lieutenants of the shah. But as far as the *Qizilbash* was concerned, an available male relative—no matter how ruthless, ham-fisted, or corrupt—was the preferred choice for the office of shah itself, as both Pari and Mahde, under differing circumstances, learned at their peril.

While contemporary, or near-contemporary Safavid and European chroniclers described Pari as domineering (a double standard with which women in leadership roles still cope to this day), they also extolled her wisdom, judgement, and competence. Later historians recast her as something of a villain: a scheming, manipulative woman who plotted the murders of two of her brothers who blocked her pathway to power and the throne. Yet these assessments overlook the record. The need to preserve the kingdom at times of unrest, and not personal ambition, motivated her to assume responsibility for the empire. At the same time, she had too much respect for her father's memory and the Safavid dynasty itself to stand by and let it fall into the hands of her deeply flawed brothers. In retrospect, "[i]t seems clear that Pari Khān Khānom, a woman with a powerful, influential, and can-do personality, felt that she was far better able to handle the affairs of the Safavid government than the male princes."

As Safavid elites began to drift from their Turko-Mongol roots over the course of generations, upper class women in Iranian society became increasingly confined to the harem and excluded from public life.

But two continents away, in what is now the northwest region of Nigeria, another Islamic princess who lived around the same time as Pari not only ascended a throne, but expanded and enriched a kingdom.

CHAPTER 8

Amina (1533–1610)

Warrior Queen of Zazzua, Nigeria

Defenders of Nupeland—in what is today the Niger State's Bida Emirate, in north central Nigeria—braced themselves for attack. The Nupe were accustomed to conflicts: their founding father, Tsoede, became king by rising up against the Igala, his own father's tribe and Nupe's oppressors. Conquering a broad swath of towns and villages between the Niger and Kaduna river basins, he ultimately asserted his authority over the region, establishing Nupeland during the mid-sixteenth century.

Now a new adversary, from the neighboring kingdom of Zazzau (modern Zaria) to the north, threatened the Nupe: not a king, but a queen, Amina Sarauniya Zazzau (Amina, Queen of the Zazzau). Amina was a fierce warrior whose army consisted of a thousand cavalry and some twenty thousand armored foot soldiers, both male and female. Battle-hardened and trained to fight since childhood, she had been campaigning practically nonstop since her ascension to the throne in 1576. Her objective was straightforward enough: Zazzau hegemony over all the kingdoms of Hausaland, a collection of city-states spread out between the Niger River and Lake Chad, in what is now northern Nigeria.

Whether the Nupe fought or outright surrendered that day is unknown. But the Kano Chronicle—a compilation of traditional oral histories written down during the nineteenth century—does record that "Amina conquered all the towns" of Hausaland, from Kwararafa (Jukun) in the southeast to Nupeland in the southwest. In the end, all "paid tribute to her," the Chronicle reported. Upon his defeat, the Sarkin (King) of the Nupe* sent Amina forty eunuchs and ten thousand kola nuts. The eunuchs, or slaves, were a valuable commodity, while kola nuts were a luxury trade good, prized as an alternative to coffee and tea (beverages shunned by some devout Muslims as stimulants) long before they provided the key flavorant for one of world's most popular soft drinks.

With the fall of Kwararafa and Nupeland—two of Hausaland's seven "lesser" city-states—Amina achieved something no monarch had before: the unification of Hausaland's legendary seven major kingdoms (Daura, Kano, Katsina, Zazzau, Gobir, Rano, and Hadejia) into one vast state under control of the Zazzau throne. "[T]he most extensive among the kingdoms of Hausa," at approximately five hundred square miles in size, Zazzau stretched "to the sea in the south and the west," according to the nineteenth-century African historian and Sultan of Sokoto, Muhammad Bello, commissioner of the Kano Chronicle.

Amina's conquest of Hausaland was a resounding political, military, and economic victory. It was also, in many respects, her birthright.

Precedents for female rule in Hausaland date back long before Amina assumed the throne. Hausa legend speaks not of a founding father but a founding grandmother, the "*Magajiya*"—a Hausa word that translates as "overseer" or "woman leader"—who emerged sometime before the ninth century CE. (see "The Magajiyya Legend's Middle Eastern Roots," p. 140) In many African legends, the *Magajiya* is a politically active, aristocratic, and charismatic figure, a "Black Moses" who leads her followers to a fertile "promised land" and establishes there "the traditions of her people." According to Hausa legend, the *Magajiya*'s descendants—an uninterrupted dynasty of seventeen queens—gave rise to the Hausaland Empire in 1050 CE.

The research of modern historians and anthropologists supports the central premise of the *Magajiya* myth that "in olden times the Hausa states favored uterine descent." Studies have shown that in many pre-colonial West

* Possibly Tseode or one of his successors. Tsoede died in 1591, and the exact date of Amina's conquest of Nupeland is unknown.

African tribes and principalities, queen-mothers, queen-sisters, princesses, female chiefs, as well as female military commanders and monarchs, wielded significant, if not total, political power. If men proved to be ineffective or incompetent as leaders, it was not unknown nor unacceptable for women to usurp and replace them. Beyond the halls of the palace, local women also contributed significantly to the economic and infrastructural well-being of their towns and villages, weighing in on such critical matters as road construction and maintenance, drinking wells and streams, as well as conflict resolution. Via their roles as traders, merchants, members of trade and craft guilds, and agriculturalists, these industrious women were also "active in business, ruled the marketplace, set rates, and even imposed fines." Additionally they financially cared for widows and performed "the rituals necessary for the proper functioning of the market as a whole."

Zazzau's first queen, and its twenty-second monarch, was Amina's mother, Bakwa Turunku. Accounts of her ascension to the throne vary. In some histories, she was the daughter of the king, Sarkin Zazzau Nohir and succeeded her uncle, Nohir's younger brother, Kawanissa, upon his death in 1536. In other versions, she was not Nohir's daughter but his daughter-in-law. Her husband—Nohir's son, King Nikatau—was the father of Amina and her younger sister, Zaria. Bakwa's own father was not a royal but a high-ranking official from the nearby city of Kufena. However it came about, historians agree that she became Zazzaua's queen after seizing political power and the throne in 1536.

The translation of Bakwa's name—"the female stranger belonging to the Toronke people," i.e., inhabitants of the Zazzau city of Turunku—leans towards the latter version of how she came to rule the kingdom. Together with Kufena, Turunku was one of the major economic and administrative centers in the region. Around thc time of her ascension to the throne, Bakwa recognized that Turunku's limited water supply could not sustain its population and that people were migrating from there to Kufena, which lay within Zazzau's borders. Her solution to these migration shifts was to establish a new capital some twenty miles to the west, which she named Zaria, after her youngest daughter. Eventually, under British colonial rule, the entire kingdom of Zazzau came to be called Zaria, after its capital.

The city was (and still is) located about sixty miles south of Kano, on

The Magajiyya Legend's Middle Eastern Roots

The mythology of the Magajiyya and its connections to the founding of the seven Hausa states are intertwined with Middle Eastern, Palestinian, and North African history.

According to varying legends, the tenth-century prince Bayajidda either quarreled with his father, Abdullahi, King of Baghdad, and fled the city, or was exiled by an invading queen, Zidam. Journeying west across Africa with a contingent of three hundred troops, he eventually arrived in the West African kingdom of Bornu. Known to Arab geographers from the eighth century as Kanem, the medieval kingdom (700–1380 CE) stretched from southern Libya, across most of Chad and into northern Nigeria as well as parts of Niger and Cameroon. In still another account of Bayajidda's journey, he made war upon and conquered the Ziduwa, an African tribe whose territory abutted Bornu.

Fearing that Bayajidda might take over his kingdom, the king of Bornu proposed a marriage alliance, offering the invader a woman of the royal household, known as the Magira or Magaram. In most versions of the story, the bride is the king's daughter, though it could have been the king's sister or another female relative. Magira is not a name, but a title—similar to the Magajiyya—meaning a female royal and not necessarily a daughter.

Meanwhile, still fearful of Bayajidda's power, the king devised a plan to diminish the prince's military forces. Borrowing the invader's foreign troops to use on campaigns, the crafty king gradually left numbers of them behind to guard the conquered outposts. Eventually, Bayajidda was left with no one at his side but his wife and a single servant. When the Magira learned that the king planned to assassinate her husband, the couple fled, together with Bayajidda's servant, to Garun Gabas in what is now southern Nigeria. There, the Magira gave birth to a child, Biram. Thinking he was not yet safe from the king of Bornu's threatening reach, Bayajidda snuck out of the city in the middle of the night, leaving his wife and new baby behind. On his flight, he passed through Gaya near Kano (other sources say Gaya was in modern Niger), a city famed for its blacksmiths. There, he engaged the blacksmiths to craft a sword for him, similar to one he lost on his journey.

Continuing north, he arrived in Daura, in what is now Nigeria's Katsina State. Here, the story takes a Biblical turn. According to legend, the people of Daura were said to have originally migrated from Canaan (Palestine), led to sub-Saharan Africa via Egypt by Najib, grandson of Noah. From these original founders descended the seventeen Hausa queens, including the Magajiya Daurama (sometimes also called Daura), who sat on the city of Daura's throne by the time of Bayajidda's arrival.

Stopping at the first house he came to, Bayajidda asked its owner, an elderly woman named Ayana (in other versions, Waira) for some water for himself and his horse. She informed him that water could only be drawn on Fridays from the only well in the city, guarded by a snake called Sarki, which dwelt at the well's bottom. Because the snake was fearfully regarded as a kind of king (*sarki* meaning "king" or "chief" in Hausa), the weekly drawing of water was accompanied by songs and ceremonies to appease the tyrannical serpent.

Nonetheless determined to slake his thirst, Bayajidda persuaded Ayana to give him a bucket and went to the well. He lowered the bucket, striking Sarki, which angrily rose from the watery depths to the surface. Bayajidda promptly beheaded the serpent with his new sword, put the head in a bag, and returned to Ayana's house.

Hearing the news of Sarki's death, Queen Daurama went to the well and offered half her kingdom to the snake's killer. Several men in town falsely claimed credit, producing snake heads, none of which matched Sarki's body. Finally, Ayana told the queen that it was her guest, Bayajidda, who had killed the snake. As she promised, Daurama offered him half the kingdom. Bayajidda declined the offer, however, asking instead for the queen's hand in marriage. She accepted, on condition that they not sleep together, as it was the custom of Daura's queens to remain celibate. Instead, she offered him a concubine, Bagwariya, with whom Bayajidda had a son, Karbagari. Jealous of the child, Daurama abandoned her vow of celibacy and had a child of her own with Bayajidda, whom she named Bawo.

Bawo, in turn, sired six sons of his own who came to rule six of the seven great Hausa states: Daura, Gobir, Kano, Katsina, Rano, and Zazzau. The seventh state, Hadejia (aka Biram), was ruled by Biram, son of Bayajidda and his first wife, Magira. Meanwhile, Karbagari, the illegitimate son of Bayajidda and his concubine Bagwariya, had seven sons of his own who ruled over Hausaland's lesser states, collectively known in Hausa as the *Banza Bakwai* or the "seven illegitimate" kingdoms: Kebbi, Zamfara, Gwari, Jukun, Ilorin, Nupe, and Yauri.

Scholars have suggested that the legend of Bayajidda (Abuyazidu in Arabic) was inspired by the life of the tenth-century North African Berber Ibadi leader, Abu Yazid Makhlad ibn Kaydad. Ibadism—sometimes called a "third branch of Islam"—was an early Islamic sect that favored a more democratic election process for the role of imam than those practiced by both Sunnis and Shias.

In 937 CE, Abu Yazid led a rebellion against the Fatimids, who sought to suppress the Ibadis, regarding them as a dangerous and disaffected group. Gathering an armed following, Abu Yazid scored some victories such as the capture of Kairouan in 943 and the defeat of the Fatimid army at Al Akhawan. By the summer of 947, however, the Fatimid caliph al Mansur Billah (r. 946–953 CE) had the rebel forces cornered and on the defensive in the mountain fortress of Kiyana, in what is now northeastern Algeria. Abu Yazid was captured and died on August 19, 947, from injuries sustained trying to escape. What remained of his army "marched southwards into the desert and disappeared from the pages of North African history."

Though perhaps not entirely.

Superimposing the Magajiyya mythology over the historical facts, it "seems possible that it is the arrival of this force in Bornu" that gave rise to the Bayajidda legend. In this context, "Abu Yazid's defeated army could have been the rock on which [the Hausaland] empire was founded." Some have also seen Bayajidda's role in the founding of the Hausa states as a symbol of Bornu's economic and political dominance over Hausaland.

The slaying of the snake, a symbol of evil going back to Genesis, is a common motif found in many origin myths, from West Africa to the Middle East to Western Europe (e.g., St. George and the dragon). In terms of its function in the Bayajidda legend, it has been speculated that the defeat of Sarki may symbolize Islam's triumph over the Hausa states' animist religions. The marriage of Bayajidda and Daura may also represent the gradual merging of the Arab and Berber cultures of North and West Africa during migrations between 500 CE and 1400 CE.

the plain of Zazzau. This tropical, well-watered mixture of woodlands, open savannah, and rocky, mountainous outcroppings called inselbergs lies about 2,200 feet above sea level in the center of northern Nigeria. Describing the region during the early sixteenth century, Leo Africanus accurately observed that "[s]ome part of this kingdome is plaine, and the residue mountainous," adding that its "fields abounding in water are exceedingly fruitfull." But Zazzau's abundance, Leo also noted, came from other sources as well: "The inhabitants are rich and have great traffique unto [with] other nations."

Geography had a lot to do with Zaria's wealth and good fortune. The city stood at a major crossroad of the trans-Saharan trade route, a six hundred-mile network of camel caravan tracks and stopovers fanning out across the Sahel (sub-Saharan Africa) and the Sahara, linking the tropical forests of West Africa to the shores of the Mediterranean. From the late fifteenth century, Hausaland's walled city-states grew increasingly prosperous as centers of trade along the route, trafficking in gold, kola nuts, salt, horses, natron (a mineral used to make soap and prized as a desiccant by Egyptians for the mummification process), and slaves, in addition to locally manufactured leather goods and textiles. In exchange, Hausa merchants imported steel weapons and chain mail armor from Europe, glass beads from China, as well as silk and cowrie shells from the Indian Ocean.

Along with trade goods came new intellectual ideas, including Islam, which spread south across the Sahel as early as 750 CE. By 1400, the faith was well established in Hausaland, though it was more popular among the urban ruling classes than members of the rural agricultural population, who tended to cling to their traditional animist beliefs. The prestige associated with being part of the wider Islamic world, with its great empires, may have been a compelling reason for the conversion of Hausaland's ruling class. Nonetheless, the lower classes eventually blended Islamic principles and customs with lingering elements of their indigenous animist religion, "resulting for individuals in sets of beliefs and practices which were neither wholly Muslim nor non-Muslim." (Another distinctive manifestation of Hausaland's ultimate adoption of Arab/Muslim culture was the production, some centuries later, of a body of Hausa literature written in Arabic characters, a script known as ajami.)

Whatever the true depths of their devotion, the Zazzau royals embraced

Islam sometime around the second half of the fifteenth century. With that cultural shift and nod towards Cairo, Baghdad, and Mecca came significant rewards. By the time of Bakwa's ascension to the throne, the family had grown fabulously wealthy via trade with traveling Arab and North African Berber merchants who helped spread Islam throughout sub-Saharan Africa. That Bakwa chose Arab names for her children—Amina, (meaning "honest" or "faithful") born in 1533, and Zaria, (from the Arabic *zahr*, meaning "flower") born sometime later—reflects the influence of Arab/Muslim culture on the royal household.

Given her family's wealth and position, Amina might have lived the comfortable life of a coddled princess. But such was not her nature. Legends say that as soon as she could crawl, the infant Amina would make her way from the palace to her grandfather's council hall while Nohir was holding court. Brushing boldly past the legs of guards and courtiers, she planted herself on the dais, at the king's feet. Indulging her interest, and intrusion, the doting monarch would scoop her up and place her in his lap while he continued on with the business of the court. Her routine visits to the throne room continued as she grew. Thus, when other girls her age were beginning to learn domestic skills and how to be future wives and mothers, the young princess Amina's early childhood education was devoted to politics and the complex affairs of court: diplomatic receptions, the hashing out of trade agreements, the plotting of military campaigns.

These early lessons in statecraft, particularly the logistics of warfare, made a lasting impression on her. On one occasion, her grandmother, Marka—Nohir's favorite wife—saw young Amina clutching a dagger. Rather than being surprised or shocked, Marka remarked on how naturally and properly her granddaughter held the weapon, just as a warrior would. It's likely that Amina learned how to handle a knife, as well other military arts such as swordsmanship and horseback riding in the company of male youths in mixed-gender training sessions. Among her mentors were the many military commanders and prominent warriors who regularly attended her grandfather's court and personally tutored her in the arts of war.

When Amina turned sixteen, her mother designated her *Magajiya,* a title that had come to mean heir apparent and/or eldest daughter. With the honorific came a gift of forty *kuyanga*, or female attendants. Sixteen being the prime marrying age for young Hausa women, more gifts in addition to marriage proposals also began flooding in from prominent officers of the court. Zazzau's *Makaman* (chief advisor to the throne) pledged to send her ten slaves per day for every day she forestalled his offer of marriage. Another suitor, Kama Masu, the Emir of Kano, sent her fifty male and fifty female slaves along with fifty bags of costly, finely woven blue (probably indigo) and white cloth.

But Amina turned them all down. She was more committed to her role as *Magajiya* and the prospect of being queen one day, not just some foreign potentate's or bureaucrat's wife and companion. But what clearly interested her most was warfare. As she grew to adulthood, she spent increasing amounts of time in the company of the kingdom's most skilled military tacticians who educated her in the logistics of battle. She also continued to train with sword, spear, and bow and arrow, practicing how to cut down an opponent from the back of a charging horse.

In contrast, aside from a minor campaign or two, war had never been the purview of her mother, whose reign was known for its peace, prosperity, and culture. So while the kettle drums of battle appealed to some, Bakwa preferred the joyous beat of the hourglass-shaped *kalangu* ("talking drum") played to the lively rhythms of the *gada*, a women's dance celebrating marriages and the harvest. In what is today the Emir of Zaria's palace but is still sometimes referred to as *gidan Bakwa* (Bakwa's house), young women of the palace sang and performed the dance for the cultured queen on a daily basis. So peaceful was Bakwa's reign that stories were told of quivers slumped in corners, covered with clouds of spider webs, while swords and arrows grew rusty from neglect during her years on the throne.

All that changed upon the queen's death, around 1566. She was succeeded by her younger brother, Karama,* "a warrior who was never happier than when he was in the saddle." Now the weapons of war were dusted off, sharpened, and made ready for battle once more. Karama favored expansion, and during his reign he resumed the status quo by attacking the neighboring kingdoms of Hausaland which, from the fifteenth century on, sometimes engaged in peaceful trade but more often engaged in war with each other as

* Some sources claim that Karama was not Amina's uncle, but her younger brother.

they competed for access to resources and control of the trans-Saharan trade.

At his side during his campaigns was his niece, Amina, now a full-grown woman in her thirties and a famous warrior in her own right. As one of her uncle's ablest and most enthusiastic lieutenants, she "was always among the first to arrive at the palace with her horsemen when the war drums sounded." Her reputation as one of the leading warriors of the kingdom earned her the sobriquet *Amina, Yar Bakwa ta san Rana* ("Amina, daughter of Nikatau, a woman as capable as a man"). Already a rich woman, the spoils of war (slaves, estates, material goods) only added to her considerable wealth.

Amina's ascension to the throne when Karama died in 1576 was seamless and unchallenged. Jubilations, in fact, were held in her honor, celebrating her coronation, which, as far as the assembled nobles and court officials were concerned, "was a foregone conclusion." But once the parties were over, the new queen wasted no time in getting down to business, which essentially consisted of continuing Karama's program of territorial expansion as well as the political and economic domination of Hausaland. One effective strategy that helped her achieve these goals was the local production of chain mail and armor for her troops. Zazzau was already famed for its tanners, leatherworks, and textile production. Adding metalworks to these industries eliminated the expense of importing prefabricated armor from Europe.

To achieve this goal, Amina commanded her metalsmiths to copy the armor of the Kanem-Bornu Empire, to the north of Zazzau. These indigenous designs were as complex and as effective at deflecting sword thrusts, spears, and arrows as any of their European counterparts. They consisted of conical helmets, chain mail, and leather-lined cuirasses: iron-riveted metal breastplates and backplates that attached together and hung by straps over the shoulders. The chain mail was especially laborsome to craft, requiring a three-man team: two to make the rings and a master armorer to link them together. The job was also a quasi-spiritual one. Lingering Hausa animist beliefs associated the smelting and crafting of iron with the powers of life and death, powers that could be fatal if they fell into undisciplined or untrained hands. Thus blacksmiths were revered as a distinguished class in Hausa society, something like a medieval European guild, though more mystical, and as essential to the perpetuation of the kingdom as midwives.

Another one of her military strategies was to surround her encampments and the towns and cities she conquered with enormous earthen walls. She was the first to encircle Zaria with a city wall, and the many defensive structures she left in the wake of her conquests across Hausaland came to be known as *ganuwar Amina* (Amina's walls). Archaeologists who have studied the ruins of these fortifications have since established that they were built both before and after Amina's reign. Nevertheless, an enduring, complimentary saying in Hausa culture still credits their construction to Amina: *wane ya cika takma da tsufa kamar ganuwar Amina*, meaning "as proud and old as the walls of Amina."

Female troops were yet another asset of Amina's army, though not unique to Zazzau. Throughout history, the armies of many West African empires included women warriors. Medieval accounts of the Almoravid* siege of Christian Valencia in 1094 make mention of a company of three hundred "Moorish" warrior women from Ghana among the Muslim forces. Armed with Turkish bows, they possessed archery skills that one medieval chronicler described as "a wonder to behold." The Mino was a regiment of women warriors established in the seventeenth century in the Kingdom of Dahomy (in present-day Benin), renowned for their fierceness and bravery. By the mid-1800s, they numbered around four thousand troops, all under female command, and composed about a third Dahomy's standing army. Rulers in Central Africa also relied on women warriors. In his contemporary account of Vasco da Gama's expeditions along the coast of Africa during the first quarter of the sixteenth century, Portuguese official Duarte Barbosa reported that the King of Benematapa (modern Zimbabwe) "always takes with him into the field . . . a great band of warriors, and five or six thousand women, who also bear arms and fight." Between 1578 and 1589, Portuguese merchant Duarte Lopez traveled to Central Africa on behalf of Philip II of Spain in search of gold. In his report to the Crown, published in 1591, Lopez also noted that among Benematapa's troops, "those most renowned for their bravery, are the female legions, greatly valued by the Emperor, being the sinews of his military strength."

In the face of these and other descriptions of Africa's legendary women warriors, the record falls silent when it comes to Amina's appearance. Given her active lifestyle and rigorous physical training, however, she was probably a

* The Almoravids were a Berber Muslim dynasty based in Morocco during the eleventh and twelfth centuries.

fit woman, powerful and even muscular. Dresses made from the finely woven, colorful textiles for which Zazzau was renowned would have been preserved for state occasions or perhaps relaxation time in camp. Her jewelry case could have included ivory arm bands, carved from elephant tusk, necklaces strung with beads of carnelian (a brownish-red semi-precious stone from Egypt), as well as silver rings with glass inlays—all luxury items found in the burial sites of royal northern Nigerian women, dating from the thirteenth/fourteenth century to the fifteenth/sixteenth century CE. Less likely to don such finery in battle, she more commonly would have worn chain mail *sulke* (shirts) and armor, like her troops. Tunics, like those depicted in nineteenth-century engravings of female Mino soldiers, would also have been the practical choice for horseback riding. Her one nod to high fashion when it came to battle gear may have been strings of costly and imported cowrie shells—readily available via Zazzau's far-flung trading networks—sewn into her clothing, as seen in nineteenth- century photographs of Mino warriors. In keeping with Islamic traditions, she likely also wore some sort of turban-like hijab or cowrie shell cap to cover her hair.

Thus outfitted and riding at the head of her well-armed, well-trained army, Amina pressed further and further south and west, asserting Zazzau authority and influence. "She waged war in the Hausa lands and took them all," Muhammad Bello recounted, "so that the men of Katsina and the men of Kano brought her tribute. She made war in Bauchi and against the other towns of the south and of the west, so that her possessions stretched down to the shores of the sea."

Historians question whether the northern city-states of Kano and Katsina paid Zazzau much tribute, if any at all, though there is evidence that Kano and Zazzau did wage war with one another during the sixteenth century. What is more certain is the extent of Zazzau's influence and authority to the south and west under Amina's rule. A sixteenth-century hand-painted Portuguese map—the Planisphere of Domingos Teixeira—identifies a broad section of Western Africa, from present day Gambia to modern Chad, as "Castel O Damina" or "The Castle of Amina," meaning her domains. While Amina's kingdom never extended quite this far, her relentless campaigning did expand her empire from the Kaduna River to the border of the River Gurara in today's Niger State, some sixty miles northwest of the modern Nigerian capital of Abuja and some two hundred miles south of Zaria. Governmentally, many of the towns and cities in this vast region remained either under direct control of or maintained tributary relationships with the Zazzau state well into the eighteenth century.

Muhammad Bello's narrative also claims that Zazzau influence extended "to the kingdoms of Yirwu . . . and the kingdom of Baasa, and Kadawru," all of which "are under the sovereignty of the region of Zakzak [Zazzau]." These historic kingdoms, Bello noted, lie north of "the harbors of the ships of the Christians from two kingdoms who trade among the Sudanese" i.e., the Portuguese, the French, and the British,* who trafficked in slaves along the Bight of Benin in the Gulf of Guinea, aka the Slave Coast. If Bello can be believed, Zazzau's political control of these and other southern states, all of which "are on the shores of the sea and . . . came to be part of the land of Zozo [Zazzau]" put the kingdom in contact, however tangentially, with European slavers. This contact compounded Zazzau's already well established role in the slave trade as the primary source of slaves sold in Kano and Katsina to Arab and Berber merchants, who in turn transported them to the slave markets of North Africa.

While not solely responsible for Zazzau's territorial expansion, Amina's campaigns "marked the beginning of the process which culminated in it" and followed a distinctive pattern. Once conquering a region, she appointed local sarkins who ensured that tribute would be sent. The walls she built around the cities she conquered also played a vital role in establishing and maintaining her policies. Towering symbols of her power and of her ability to summon and command the labor necessary to build them, *ganuwar Amina* also offered protection against foreign attack. This security instilled a sense of well-being among the population while providing the necessary stability for increased industrialization and commerce, including the lucrative trade in kola nuts that Amina introduced into Hausaland's economy after the defeat of Nupeland.

In the thirty-four years Amina spent subjugating Hausaland, it was said that she never spent more than three months at a time in residence at her capital of Zaria. Her restlessness may have stemmed from her reputation

* Bello obviously conflates the two of them here.

as a hands-on administrator who "never relied solely on information about events and developments in the kingdom reaching her through messengers and courtiers," regarding such reports as hearsay. If there was news of trouble in a far-flung corner of her kingdom, she preferred to travel there and handle the situation herself. So absolute was her rule over these conquered territories that "the overriding authority of Zazzau provided something of an 'international' peace-keeping force among the numerous mutually hostile groups beyond the Kaduna River offering protection of life and property to people lacking the resources to achieve it themselves."

Such aggressive campaigning left her little time for marriage, and she continued to decline proposals from court officials and regional rulers throughout her reign. Rejecting one offer, from the Mai (King) of Bornu, she reportedly responded that "she would never be subject to any man." This is not to say, however, that she wasn't amorous. According to legend, she took a different lover in every town she conquered, only to have him beheaded the next morning so that her unfortunate paramour couldn't brag or share any details about his night of passion with the queen.

Amina died in 1610, fittingly in battle, "in a place called Ataagar" near the Igala Kingdom capital of Idah, nearly 350 miles south of Zaria. She was seventy-seven years old. To the end, she was looking after the economic welfare of her kingdom: her interest in subduing the distant trading center likely stemmed from its reputation as a source of brass rings and cowrie shells.

While the site of her grave is unknown, Amina is commemorated in Nigerian culture in manifold ways. In Lagos, a colossal bronze equestrian statue depicting the warrior queen, sword in hand and riding into battle, towers before the entrance to the National Arts Theater. Her life has also been celebrated in literature, festivals, films, plays, and even video games and television shows, serving as an inspiration for the character of Xena: Warrior Princess.

To historians of African Islamic feminist culture, Amina was "one of the last bastions of African Matriarchy and Feminism." Her military, political, administrative, economic, and entrepreneurial achievements as a Muslim Hausa leader were "unparalleled" and attest to the "historically strong, social rights and status" of Muslim women in Nigeria—rights so tragically abused and ignored in modern times by the likes of Boko Haram, an extremist group who one can only imagine Amina would have dealt with summarily and harshly.

But the Africa of her day was beginning to come under threat from European explorers and traders whose end game, unlike Muslim traders from the north, was exploitation and colonization. Fending off such powerful empires as Spain, Portugal, the Netherlands, and Britain required cunning, skill, and the sort of political willpower that matched their own. In northern India, around the same time as Amina's kingdom was expanding, another Muslim queen with these very credentials took charge of an empire built upon the conquered remains of the Sultanate of Delhi and named for its Turco-Mongol ancestors: the Mughals.

CHAPTER 9

Nur Jahan (1577–1645)

India's Fashion-Designing, Tiger-Hunting, Business-Savvy Empress

In the autumn of 1619, reports reached the Mughal capital of Agra in northern India that a Bengal tiger was attacking people in Mathura, a holy city and popular Hindu pilgrimage site in the Himalayan foothills, some forty miles to the northwest.

While tigers normally avoid humans, if wounded or somehow deprived of their regular food source (often due to habitat depletion) Bengals have been known to hunt people, with horrifyingly deadly results. With jaws capable of exerting around a thousand pounds of pressure per square inch—the most powerful bite of any cat, and greater than that of a great white shark—a Bengal tiger can crush a human skull to bits in an instant. Meanwhile, the razor-sharp claws of its powerful paws can decapitate a person with a single swipe.

Betwcen pilgrims traveling to Mathura's temples to pay homage to the Hindu god Lord Krishna and farmers laboring in the district's bountiful fields of barley, peas, sesame, and cotton, the region offered an abundance of prey for a famished tiger. Snatching their targets in the open, Bengals typically drag their victims into the seclusion of the jungle to feed on the carcasses, leaving shockingly little more than bits of bone and flesh for families to mourn let alone bury.

Something needed to be done.

Appealing to the emperor was the logical course of action. The hunting of tigers was a royal privilege, a tradition symbolizing the ruler's authority over both his subjects and nature, introduced during the Mughal dynasty (1526–1857). Stretching across much of current-day India, Pakistan, Afghanistan, and Bangladesh, the dynasty was founded by Turco-Mongol (hence "Mughal") descendants of the armies of Genghis Khan. During their reign, the Mughals governed a state famed for its bureaucracy, learning, religious and racial tolerance, plus its rich culture, culminating in the Taj Mahal, tomb of the Emperor Shah Jahan's beloved wife, Mumtaz Mahal (d. 1631).

At the time of the Mathura crisis, it was Shah Jahan's father, the Emperor Jahangir (r. 1605–1627), who sat on the throne. Responding to reports of the tiger attacks, he called for the organization of a *bargh shikar*, a royal tiger hunt. During these elaborate, monthlong expeditions, practically the whole court—including thousands of noblemen, courtiers, soldiers, cooks, and servants—traveled by horse and elephant to the hunting grounds. Once there, the royal entourage set up camp in shimmering, embroidered tents of red silk velvet and gold brocade. Mounted on elephants and horseback, wielding spears, bows, and—by Jahangir's day—matchlock muskets, the emperor and his royal huntsmen pursued their prey, forced into the open by beaters who would corner the animals using dogs and specially trained cheetahs.

The Mathura expedition was hardly Jahangir's first wild animal hunt. From the age of twelve until he turned fifty (in lunar years) in 1619, he reckoned that he had personally bagged more than seventeen thousand wild game, including eighty-six tigers, sixty-four wolves, ninety boar, nine bears, and ten crocodiles. Yet on his fiftieth birthday, he vowed "to give up hunting with guns and not harm any animal" by his own hand. The gesture was a sacrificial one: by sparing the lives of animals, he hoped Allah would cure his four-year-old grandson, who suffered from epilepsy.*

And so he turned to the last, and most beloved, of his estimated nineteen wives, Nur Jahan—Persian for "Light of the World"– and asked her to shoot the rampaging tiger. Trained from an early age in archery and firearms, it was not unusual for royal women of the Mughal court to accompany the emperor on hunts. In his personal memoir and record of his reign, the *Jahangirnama*,

* Politics may have been a secondary reason for the vow. Jahangir may have been trying to appease his nonviolent Jain subjects, whom he had treated harshly earlier in his reign.

begun in 1605, Jahangir remarked on several occasions how he "set out with the ladies of the harem" to hunt tigers.

But of all the women of the court, and in fact all the hunters in the emperor's service, in Jahangir's opinion, it was Nur Jahan, then forty-two years old, who was the finest shot, famed for her ability to handle herself, and a weapon, from the teetering perch of an elephant litter. On one particular hunt, two years earlier, she shot four tigers with six bullets, hitting "two of them with one shot each and the other two with two shots," before any of the ferocious cats had an opportunity to spring or escape. Until that day, "such marksmanship"—firing from atop an elephant and inside a litter without missing a single shot—"had not been seen," Jahangir remarked with awe and admiration.

Now, as the hunting party approached the dense jungle surrounding Mathura with Nur Jahan in the lead, her elephant, sensing the tiger's presence, began to nervously grunt and shift back and forth. "An elephant is not at ease when it smells a tiger and is continually in movement, and to hit with a gun from a litter (*imari*) is a very difficult matter," Jahangir reported from first-hand experience. Sure enough, the elephant's frantic motion sent Nur Jahan's litter pitching to and fro, just as the enraged tiger emerged from the jungle thickets. Steadying her nerves—and her trigger finger—the skilled hunter took aim and fired. The charging tiger crumpled to the ground, hit "so well on the first shot that it died of the wound," as Jahangir recalled in his eye-witness account. The episode reaffirmed his wife's reputation as a sharpshooter, praised in verse by one contemporary poet:

> Though Nur Jahan be in the form of a woman,/
> In the ranks of men she's a tiger-slayer.

Yet she was so much more than that. A loving, caring wife, she was also a tactile politician, an astute businesswoman, a fashion designer and trendsetter, a fragrance inventor, an urban developer and garden planner, a philanthropist devoted to women's issues and helping the poor, a battlefield commander, and, during the first quarter of the seventeenth century, the virtual ruler of the Mughal Empire, one of the most powerful and celebrated states in Islamic history.

Legends swirl around the story of how this remarkable woman became the de facto ruler of an empire that at its height far surpassed its contemporary European counterparts in terms of population, wealth, and military might. Some of this folklore intersected with actual recorded events, such as the appearance of a fiery red comet—later dubbed the Great Comet—that streaked across the skies above Asia and Europe in 1577, the year of Nur Jahan's birth. While the comet didn't foretell her nativity (she was born in the winter of that year, months before the comet appeared in October), its significance did impact her future. Observing the blazing object's progress in the heavens, astrologers at the Mughal court predicted that its "effects would not be felt in Hindustan,* but probably in Khurasan and Irak," strongholds of the (Persian) Safavid Empire. Sure enough, "great troubles arose in Persia" during the calamitous and bloody reign of Shah Ismail II, Pari Khan Khanum's mentally unstable half brother, following the death of their father, Shah Tahmasp in 1576 (see Chapter 7).

That same year, Nur Jahan's father, Mizra Ghiyas Beg—an erudite aristocrat from a cultured family of high-ranking Safavid officials—fell into disfavor and left Persia seeking opportunity in the Mughal Empire. The reason for Ghiyas's fall from grace are unknown;** yet his situation was precarious enough for him to leave the comforts of his home in Herat with his family in tow: two sons, a daughter, and his wife, Asmat Begam, pregnant at the time with Nur Jahan.

The journey from Persia to northern India was difficult—months of trekking through rugged mountain passes, river valleys, and across burning desert—though not unfamiliar. By the time Ghiyas and his family left Herat, Persian traders, adventurers, mercenaries, artisans, intellectuals, and clerics had been routinely emigrating to the wealthier, more tolerant Mughal Empire for more than two hundred years. Though Ghiyas and his family were

* Today's north-central India, as well as modern Pakistan, Bangladesh, and sections of Afghanistan.

** Ghiyas's offense might have been nothing more than his family's association with Tahmasp's court—enough of a transgression in Ismail's paranoid mind to warrant exile, imprisonment, or execution during his bloody purge of royals and courtiers alike. Plus, Ghiyas was also known to be a liberal free-thinker, which might have run afoul of Ismail's hard-line makeover of Safavid society. His decision to leave Persia under these circumstances and during Ismail's purge makes sense.

Shias, he knew he would be welcomed, and most likely find employment, in the Sunni court of Jahangir's father, Akbar (the Great), the third Mughal emperor, who ruled from 1556 to 1605. "Followers of various religions had a place in the broad scope of his peerless empire," Jahangir recalled. "Utter peaceableness was his established way. He conversed with the good of every group, every religion, and every sect and gave attentions to each in accordance with their station and ability to understand."

The roots of this religiously and intellectually pluralistic society reached back to Akbar's great grandfather, Babur (r. 1526–1530), founder of the Mughal Empire and himself a descendant of Timur (known in the west as Tamarlane), the Turkic conqueror who in the late fourteenth century wrested control of the Delhi Sultanate from Razia's dynastic heirs (see Chapter 3). A pragmatic man, Babur sought peace with local Hindu and Muslim rulers who accepted his sovereignty, while cracking down on those who didn't. Akbar continued his ancestor's policy of tolerance and diplomacy as more productive alternatives to war, though he was known to respond brutally to rebellion. On one shocking occasion, he ordered a minaret to be constructed from the severed heads of insurrectionists as a warning against future treason. Nonetheless, during his long reign, he tripled the size of the empire to include most of the Indian subcontinent. In doing so, he enriched the state and engaged in trade with both the Gulf region and Europe. Culturally, he supported the arts and sciences, and his courts at Delhi, Agra, and nearby Fatehpur Sikri became flourishing centers of poetry, scientific inquiry, and artistic creativity, enhanced by generations of migrants from the Safavid Empire. Thus, thanks to this diaspora, Persian culture, language, sensibilities, and bureaucratic efficiency permeated Mughal society, which meant a soft and familiar landing for transplants like Ghiyas and his family.

In fact, the most challenging part of relocating to the Mughal Empire for Safavid refugees was getting there. The journey was not only long, but dangerous. Lone travelers or small groups like Ghiyas and his family were easy targets for bandits, who lurked in remote mountain passes and isolated byways. Seeking safety in numbers, travelers often joined lumbering horse and camel caravans led by merchants who regularly made the journey between the two empires. But even this was no guarantee. Near Kandahar, in modern Afghanistan, robbers attacked Ghiyas's party, leaving the family with nothing but a pair of mules to carry what goods they had left, along with a hugely pregnant Asmat, who was about to give birth any moment.

That moment came just outside the city in the winter of 1577 when Asmat delivered a baby girl who the family named Mihr un Nissa (the Sun of Women). This much is reliable history. Beginning about a century later, chroniclers, both Indian and European, felt the need to embellish Nur Jahan's birth narrative, starting with Venetian adventurer Niccolao Manucci, who arrived in India in 1653, passing himself off as a doctor, though he had no medical training whatsoever. In his 1705 *Storia Do Mogor* ("History of the Mughals"), the Catholic Manucci compared the misfortunes of Ghiyas and his kin to the Holy Family's flight into Egypt as related in the Gospel of Matthew (2:13–23), a story with which Indians, thanks to Jesuit missionaries, were familiar: "He [Ghiyas] brought with him his wife who was [pregnant]. On the way, near the fortress of Candar (Qandahār), she was delivered of a child, and one of the merchants lent him an ass on which to convey the woman in that state of distress."

A quarter century or so later, Khafi Khan, an Indo-Persian historian of the Mughal Empire, injected a bit of drama into his version of the story. In his account—the earliest to include what has come to be known as "the abandonment of Nur Jahan" motif—Mihr's parents, penniless, desperate, and unable to feed one more mouth, left the infant to her fate by the side of the road. Fortunately, Malik Masud—the caravan director who provided Ghiyas and his family protection on their journey from Herat—happened upon the abandoned baby. Taken with the child's beauty and demeanor, he determined to rescue her. Seeking out a wet nurse, he unwittingly returned Mihr to her own mother, Asmat. Consulting Khafi and later Persian texts, Alexander Dow, an eighteenth-century Scottish writer and military officer in the East India Company, added even more drama to Nur Jahan's birth narrative. In a pathetic passage in Volume 3 of his *History of Hindostan*, Dow related how Mihr's disconsolate parents left her nestled in a pile of leaves beneath a tree.

> When they had advanced about a mile from the place, and the eyes of the mother could no longer distinguish the solitary tree under which she

> had left her daughter, she gave way to grief; and throwing herself from the horse on the ground, exclaimed "My child, my child!"

Moved to pity, Ghiyas turned back to fetch his daughter. When he got to the tree, he was horrified to find a black snake coiled about the infant, its fatal jaws poised to devour the child. Fortunately, at Ghiyas's approach, the startled snake slithered away and Mihr was saved.

None of these fables were found in contemporary accounts of Nur Jahan's life. As with many historical figures (think George Washington throwing a silver dollar across the Potomac), it was Nur Jahan's "later fame and renown [that] led the imaginative mind of the common folk to fabricate such stories."

When the family finally arrived in the Mughal capital of Fatehpur Sikri, the well-connected Malik Masud, who was "said to have been known to Akbar," formally introduced Ghiyas to the emperor. Asmat's uncle, already in Akbar's service, may also have pulled some strings. Skilled "both in writing and in transacting business," Ghiyas steadily rose through the ranks of government, from *diwan* (treasurer) of Kabul province to the office of *diwan i buyutat*, in charge of roads and government buildings (similar to a US cabinet post). The prestigious appointment not only paid well (in the top tier of civil service paychecks) but placed him at the lavish court in Fatehpur Sikri, a city famed for its distinctive red sandstone gateways, pavilions, and domes and cupolas notching the skyline. Wealthy merchants and court officials like Ghiyas lived in the heart of the city in palatial townhouses and mansions called *havelis* (from the Arabic, *hawali*, meaning "private space") lining the main avenue that ran through the central marketplace. Sprawling and elegant, with gardens and central fountains splashing in hushed courtyards, *havelis* offered residents sanctuary from the heat of day and the dusty clamor of the busy souk beyond their walls.

It was in such a setting that young Mihr was educated "with the utmost care and attention," sequestered from the men of the household, in the women's quarters. In addition to learning how to read and write both Persian and Arabic, her studies included music, dancing, painting, as well as the poetry and literature of her Persian heritage and the memorization of Qur'anic verses. Her history lessons would also have included stories of her Safavid past, including accounts of the troubled reign of Pari Khan Khanum.

As Dow related, she was a superlative student, if not a bit of a handful: "Her disposition was volatile, her wit lively and satirical, her spirit lofty and uncontrolled."

When Mihr was around eight years old, Ghiyas moved his family to Agra, a major administrative center and "a very large city . . . situated in the very heart of the Empire," in the words of seventeenth-century Flemish geographer Johannes de Laet, one of the directors of the Dutch East India Company. According to de Laet's intelligence, gathered by agents in the field, Akbar relocated his capital from Fatehpur Sikri to Agra because of the latter's inadequate water supply. A "mere village" beforehand, Akbar transformed Agra into "a spacious and very populous city." The emperor lived in an alabaster fortress featuring windows of gold, from which he would watch elephant fights on the grounds below, while his nobles inhabited rows of "[m]any beautiful palaces" overlooking the Yamuna river, the Ganges' second-largest tributary. In just such a palatial setting, Mihr resumed her daily routine: lessons, playing with other girls (including the children of house servants), and engaging in the social life of the city, such as the public celebration of holy days and various festivals like Nowruz, the springtime Persian New Year, sacred to Shias. As she approached adolescence, she was said to be "a remarkable beauty" whose attractiveness surpassed "all the ladies of the East," as Dow put it (with obvious hyperbole). Physical descriptions by later chroniclers described her as "a tall, attractive woman of proportionate limbs." These accounts may be unreliable since contemporary images depict her as a person of somewhat below-average height, perhaps even petite, with dark hair, a high forehead, a delicate smile, and large, almond-shaped eyes. Tall or short, her good looks, intelligence, wit, and charm made her an exceptionally desirable candidate for marriage when the time came for Ghiyas and Asmat to begin considering a match for their daughter.

In Mughal society, that time generally came around the age of puberty for most upper- class girls, i.e., around fourteen years of age. So at seventeen, Mihr was a bit on the mature side when she was given in marriage in 1594 to Ali Quli Khan Istajlu, a fellow Safavid transplant. Ali Quli served Ismail II before fleeing Persia amid the chaos that ensued following the troubled shah's death in 1577. Once in Mughal territory, he joined the army, distinguished himself in battle, and was "promoted to a rank befitting his station."

The year of his betrothal, he served as a retainer to Akbar's son, Prince Salim (the future Jahangir), on a campaign to Mewar in northwest India against rebellious Rajputs—the same Hindu warrior class that plagued Razia during her reign. The prince was so impressed with Ali Quli's courage in battle that he conferred upon him the title *Sher Afghan* (Tiger Slayer). Marrying into Ghiyas's family was another big step up for the heroic army officer, who couldn't have found a better match than the clever, lovely daughter of one of the empire's highest-ranking and most highly respected government officials.

After the nuptials, the couple moved to Burdwan, a military outpost on the eastern Mughal frontier, in Bengal, where Ali Quli was stationed. His "job," as it were, kept him away from home a lot: campaigning on behalf of the emperor, protecting trade routes from thieves, supervising the collection of taxes. He did manage to spend enough nights at home for the couple to have Mihr's one and only child, a daughter, affectionately named Ladli (the Loved One), born in 1600 or 1601.

Meanwhile, back in Agra, family life among the royals was less sanguine. Troubles were brewing among Akbar's sons, especially Salim, and rival heirs. In the five hundred years that had transpired since Arwa sat on the throne in Yemen, primogeniture was still not a universally accepted custom in Islamic dynasties, and the Mughals were no exception. While eldest sons were often preferred, the emperor was free to choose any male member of the family he saw fit to succeed him, and often did. Akbar's own grandfather, Babur, designated his eldest son, Humayun (Akbar's father), as his successor, only to change his mind towards the end of his life in favor of his youngest son. On his deathbed, the fickle ruler reversed his decision, placing Humayun back on deck, though after much internal strife and pressure from rival factions.

Though Salim was not the firstborn, he was the eldest surviving son after his twin older brothers died in infancy. Regarding himself the presumptive heir to the throne, he began acting as such, building a power base of supporters at court. This didn't escape the attention of Akbar, who feared it might lead to rebellion.

Then there were Salim's personal problems.

At the age of eighteen, he had his first taste of wine, which quickly escalated into a full-blown alcohol addiction, as he recorded in his memoirs:

> I started drinking wine, increasing it day by day until I no longer got a kick out of grape wine and started drinking liquor. Little by little, over nine years, it increased to twenty phials of double-distilled spirits, fourteen during the day and the rest at night . . . In this state no one had the power to stop me. Things got so bad that in my hangovers my hands shook and trembled so badly I couldn't drink myself but had to have others to help me.

Mistrusting his eldest son's ambitions and with an eye on the prince's alcoholism, in 1594 Akbar began heaping honors on Salim's son, Khusraw, then seven years old. The emperor's open declaration that he "loved grandchildren more than sons" clearly indicated his views on the succession. Salim understandably grew bitter and resentful. With his mind clouded "from drunkenness and bad companionship," as Akbar's prime minister, Abul Fazl Allami, observed, the disgruntled prince began heeding the advice of "evil-minded persons" at court who—just as Akbar feared—egged him on to rebellion in 1599.

At first, Ali Quli supported Salim, his princely benefactor, who set up his own court in Allahabad, a strategically located, fortified city at the confluence of the Ganges and Yamuna rivers, half way between Agra and Bengal. Ghiyas, meanwhile, closer to the center of imperial power in Agra, remained loyal to Akbar. Ultimately, Ali Quli abandoned Salim after it seemed to him that the winds were blowing in Khusraw's favor.

From her husband's fortress in Burdwan, Mihr kept a watchful eye on these political intrigues via dispatches from her father in Agra and conversations with her husband whenever he was home. She studiously learned the ins and outs of provincial politics and governing while gaining an appreciation for how shifting loyalties on an imperial level impacted the lives of those in the provinces, especially women, children, and the poor—demographics that became of particular concern to her as she gained power herself.

Before he died in 1605, Akbar forgave Salim, who that same year ascended the throne. Bestowing upon himself the royal title Nur ad Din Jahangir (Light of Faith, Conqueror of the World), among his first official acts was to pardon criminals and extend clemency towards those who opposed his rebellion against his father. These included Ghiyas, who Jahangir honored with the title "Itimad ud Daula" ("Pillar of the State"). Ali Quli was likewise exonerated. "After my accession I was manly enough to overlook his faults and gave him a *jagir* [a feudal land grant] in the [province] of Bengal," the emperor wrote, with self-congratulatory noblesse oblige.

Yet the succession crisis wasn't quite over.

Despite Jahangir's blanket pardon, at least one former opponent remained in custody—his son, Khusraw, confined to the fortress at Agra under house arrest. Tired of being bottled up and seething with resentment, the young prince—by now a teenager—escaped from the fortress and launched a revolt on April 6, 1606, just five months after his father's ascension to the throne. While Jahangir fumed, Khusraw remarked that the emperor had a short memory. Hadn't he himself rebelled against Akbar? "If I offend, it will only be by following the example of my own father," the rebellious prince remarked, acerbically.

The revolt was messy, short, and unsuccessful.* Yet in its wake, rebel factions who supported Khusraw continued to nurse grudges against the emperor and conspired to assassinate him in 1607. A rash of executions and prison sentences followed Jahangir's discovery of the plot in which Mihr's family was implicated. Her elder brother, Mohammad, was executed on suspicion of joining the conspiracy, while Ghiyas, also a suspect, was temporarily demoted and imprisoned, ultimately paying a fine for his release. Last but not least, Mihr's own husband, Ali Quli, was listed among the conspirators—a personal blow to Jahangir, who regarded the Tiger Slayer as one of his most trustworthy subjects.

Upon advisement, the emperor determined that "it was not proper to station the likes of such troublemakers" in a position of provincial authority. He ordered his close friend and foster brother, Qutbuddin Khan, the new governor of Bengal, to summon Ali Quli for questioning. The Tiger Slayer refused, prompting Qutbuddin to journey to Burdwan with a detachment of soldiers to deal with the matter firsthand.

Learning of the governor's arrival on the outskirts of town, Ali Quli rode out to greet him accompanied by two attendants. When he saw the large

* Jahangir had his son blinded and imprisoned, but not before the rebellious prince was led in chains by an elephant and forced to look upon the impaled bodies of his supporters lining the road to Agra. He died in 1622, by order of his younger brother, Khurram (the future Shah Jahan), who ultimately succeeded Jahangir.

company of soldiers at Qutbuddin's side, the Tiger Slayer quickly realized that this was no cordial state visit and went into defense mode. Surrounded, he drew his sword and, true to character, attempted to fight his way out of the situation, mortally wounding the governor in the melee. Outnumbered, Ali Quli was quickly overpowered by the governor's soldiers who "chopped him to pieces, and dispatched him to hell."

Suddenly widowed, Mihr may have had concerns about her future, though not her welfare. It was Mughal tradition for the widow and children of imperial retainers to be cared for. In the case of defeated enemies or traitors, like Ali Quli, it was also customary to seize their property and assets for the royal treasury and make room in the imperial harem for the women of their households such as wives, daughters, sisters, and sometimes mothers. Nonetheless, according to protocol, surviving women were to remain unmolested. So when Haidar Malik Chadurah, an administrator and a high-ranking soldier in Qutbuddin's army, learned that some of the rougher elements of the governor's foot soldiery were plundering Mihr's quarters, he rushed to her defense and promptly put a stop to it. He provided shelter for her and her family in his own home for forty days, the religiously mandated period of mourning, during which time, as he wrote, he "did not spare any moment in honoring and serving her."

Haidar and his brother personally accompanied Mihr and her daughter and attendants to the Bengal capital of Rajmahal, where an imperial escort guided the party the rest of the way to Agra. Near Hajipur, according to legends recorded by contemporary Dutch cloth merchant Pieter van den Broeke, it was said that Mihr stopped to consult "a certain dervish" whose prophesies "always came to pass." His prediction was "that the king would be exceedingly gracious to her, and that her future would be brilliantly successful."

The future Nur Jahan's path to the ultimate fulfilment of the dervish's prophecy began in the imperial harem, her home for the next four years. There, she became a close companion of Ruqayya Sultan Begam, one of Jahangir's stepmothers, who "conceived a great affection for [Mihr]," as van den Broeke reported. Like most imperial harems dating back to the days of Khayzuran, the Mughal harem was a self-sufficient entity, with "an immense staff" consisting of everything from servants to scribes, astrologers to bookbinders, perfumers to masons, in addition to cooks, nannies, and housemaids, all dedicated to catering to the needs of its royal residents, many of whom were the elderly widows (like Ruqayya) of Jahangir's late father.

With her daughter, Ladli, by her side, Mihr, now a mature woman of thirty, settled into a comfortable enough life, passing the time, like most harem residents of her social status, writing poetry (at which she was fairly good), discussing politics, or gazing at the stars in lamplit, open courtyards while lazily puffing on hookah pipes.

She also spent time in public sections of the palace, beyond the confines of the harem, visiting with her parents. It was on one such occasion, van den Broeke reported, that Jahangir noticed her and boldly drew back her *chaddar* (*hijab*) so he could see her face, the beauty of which captivated him.

This was just one of many prenuptial encounters between the couple reported by both Indian and European sources, each one more dramatic than the other. According to Khafi Khan, the relationship dated back to Mihr's youth, when Janhagir, then young Prince Salim, first noticed her on visits to the royal palace with her mother. Managing to get Mihr alone, Salim attempted to make love to her, but the frightened girl fought him off. She reported the incident to Salim's mother, who subsequently informed Akbar of his son's behavior. The emperor advised Ghiyas that he should quickly find a husband for his daughter, which, according to this narrative, is how she ended up in the arms of Ali Quli.

In Dow's account of the couple's early encounters, the Scottish chronicler stereotypically casts Mihr as the temptress who drives a libidinous young Salim to distraction with her charms. When she sang, "he was in raptures"; when she danced, "he could hardly be restrained, by the rules of decency, to his place."

> Her stature, her shape, her gait, had raised his ideas of her beauty to the highest pitch. When his eyes seemed to devour her, she, as by accident, dropped her veil; and shone upon him, at once, with all her charms. The confusion, which she could well feign, on the occasion, heightened the beauty of her face. Her timid eye by stealth fell upon the prince, and kindled all his soul into love.

A common plotline in these and other highly romanticized versions of the couple's backstory connects the dots between Jahangir's obsessive passion for Mihr and the death of Ali Quli. According to Manucci, Jahangir long coveted the Tiger Slayer's talented and attractive wife. On one occasion, the emperor was at his palace in Lahore, looking out over the Ravi River, when he noticed Mihr drifting by in a boat. In that moment, he "fell so violently in love with her that he had no sleep nor rest." Still married to Ali Quli at the time, Mihr rebuffed Jahangir's emissaries, "nor would she hear a word from any other man so long as her husband remained alive." So the king dispatched Ali Quli to Bengal with a letter for Qutbuddin, the governor, dictating "that as soon as Sher Afghan should arrive there with [the] letter he must be slain."

These and other such David-and-Bathsheba tales of Jahangir's illicit and manipulative desire for Mihr are not only "unsupported by contemporary testimony" according to modern historians, they also fail to stand up to scrutiny. It is unlikely that Jahangir would have heaped honors upon the man whose wife he coveted, or waited twelve long years—the time between Mihr's marriage to Ali Quli and his death—to finally act on his passion and have his rival killed.

Contemporary sources do agree, however, that Jahangir was indeed lovestruck the first (documented) time he set eyes on Mihr, during the New Year's Festival in late March of 1611: "[H]er appearance caught the King's far-seeing eye, and so captivated him that he included her amongst the intimates of his select harem," recorded Mutamad Khan, official diarist of Jahangir's memoirs. They were married less than two months later, on May 25. She was just shy of 35, while he was 41. One of several hundred residents of the harem, Mihr quickly became the emperor's favorite and chief consort. Royal honors and titles soon followed. "Day by day her influence and dignity increased," Mutamad Khan observed. "[S]he received the title of *Núr Mahal*, 'Light of the Harem,' but was afterwards distinguished by that of *Núr Jahán Begam*, 'Light of the World.'"

That "Light" soon shone on "all her connexions," as Mutamad Khan subtly noted. Not long after the wedding, Ghiyas was made prime minister, Asmat became chief matron of the harem, Asaf Khan, Nur Jahan's brother, was appointed master of the household, while her niece, Arjumand (Asaf's daughter) was married to Prince Khurram (the future Shah Jahan). Granted, "[t]here was nothing new in this," since governing in medieval India "was primarily a family affair." Nonetheless, the "Nur Jahan junta," as historians have labeled it, was highlighted in reports by European spice traders and textile merchants residing in India. Such accounts spelled out, in no uncertain terms, who was now clearly in charge.

"[Jahangir] is King in name only, while [Nur Jahan] and her brother Asaf Khan hold the kingdom firmly in their hands," recorded Francisco Pelsaert in his report to the Dutch East India company, written within a decade and a half of Nur Jahan's marriage. "If anyone with a request to make at Court obtains an audience or is allowed to speak, the King hears him indeed, but will give no definite answer of Yes or No, referring him promptly to Asaf Khan, who in the same way will dispose of no important matter without communicating with his sister, the Queen."

Muhamad Hadi, another of Jahangir's diarists, also left a detailed description of life at the Mughal court under the new regime: "[Nur Jahan] sat at the *jharoká* [a lattice window overlooking the royal reception area, to preserve the Queen's modesty,] and the nobles came to make their salutations and receive her commands. Coins were struck in her name [the only Mughal woman so honored], and the royal seal on *farmáns* [official edicts] bore her signature." Prior to this, the signatures of Mughal royal women on official documents always included the prefatory qualifier "mother of," "sister of," "daughter of," or "wife of" the ruler. Abandoning this custom, Nur Jahan signed decrees with her name, and her name alone. In an even more definitive display of her authority, her movements through the hallways and ceremonial spaces at court were preceded by drums and banners, "a profound and public affirmation of her high political ranking."

"In short, by degrees she became, except in name, undisputed Sovereign of the Empire," Hadi summarized, while "nothing was wanting to make her an absolute monarch but the reading of the *khutbah* in her name."

Predictably, just as they had with Roxelana, Nur Jahan's power and authority inspired jealous rumors at court that seduction or witchcraft ("Sorceries practis'd by her upon [Jahangir]," as Italian traveler Pietro Della Valle noted in 1623) were the only possible explanations for her ascendency. Yet, such "prejudice against Nur Juhan and the charge of meddling in imperial affairs reflected the deep seated anti-feminist bias of many contemporary historians which has often been repeated uncritically by a number of modern historians," as one twentieth-century scholar of medieval India has observed.

A closer look at the record shows that it was mostly European chroniclers of the day who tended to think this way. Contemporaneous Mughal dynastic histories "were relatively free of misogynist prejudice" while their "authors readily acknowledged that women were capable of governing."

Still, there were Europeans at court who recognized ugly rumors about Nur Jahan for what they were: "vulgar report[s] and common received opinion" of street-corner gossipers, as seventeenth-century British merchant Peter Mundy surmised. Similarly, Manucci ignored the slanders and regarded Nur Jahan as "a woman of great judgement . . . worthy to be a queen." There is also evidence that the currents of Nur Jahan's relationship with Jahangir ran much deeper than those of a wife seeking to "wholly gouerneth" her husband (as English ambassador to the Mughal court, Thomas Roe, put it). The emperor was ill. A self-confessed alcoholic who had since added opium to his daily regimen of substance abuse, Jahangir "used to say that Núr Jahán Begam has been selected and is wise enough to conduct the matters of State" while all he desired was "a bottle of wine and piece of meat to keep himself merry," as Hadi reported.

As Jahangir's health declined, he increasingly relied, to the exclusion of all others, on Nur Jahan to get him through the day. In a touching passage in his memoir, the emperor praised his most beloved wife's "skill and experience" as "greater than those of the physicians," crediting her "affection and sympathy" for diminishing "the number of my cups [and keeping] me from things that did not suit me."

In this context, Nur Juhan comes across as less of a Lady Macbeth and more like a devoted, exceptionally capable wife, married to a chronically ill husband—with all the draining, emotional anguish that involves—who juggled the job of keeping Jahangir alive with the demanding duties of running his empire.

"It is impossible to describe the beauty and wisdom of the Queen. In any matter that was presented to her, if a difficulty arose, she immediately solved it," Mutamad Khan reported.

The sheer range of her accomplishments are proof. To begin with, she was a shrewd and thrifty businesswoman. She turned land grants given to her by Jahangir into profit-making operations, collecting duties on imported goods ("grain, butter, and other provisions" as Pelsaert noted). She owned her own ships that sailed the Indian Ocean and the Red Sea to Arabia, Persia, and North Africa, trading spices, ginger, and dyes for perfumes, ceramics, ivory, amber, and pearls. She also played the English off the Dutch and the Portuguese off them both, granting trade concessions (primarily for indigo and embroidered cloth) for sizeable fees, greased by the age-old business custom of bribes.

"In Asia, the great are never approached empty-handed," observed Francois Bernier, a French physician at the Mughal court. Like many of his fellow European merchants, Pelsaert warned investors back home not "to be surprised at this, for it is the custom of the country."

Nur Jahan selflessly used her great wealth to support painters, poets, musicians, and architects in whose work she took a particular interest and even dabbled herself, leaving a distinct impact on Mughal architecture (see "Nur Jahan and Mughal Architecture," p. 170). Her fondness for the domestic art of embroidery, for example, is reflected in the finely crafted ornamental reliefs seen in the tomb of her father at Agra, which "bears in every part of it the imprint of the refined feminism of this remarkable queen." Her exquisite taste was also evident in the "very expensive buildings" she erected "in all directions—*sarais*, or halting-places for travellers and merchants, and pleasure-gardens and palaces such as no one has ever made before . . . " as Pelsaert remarked. She designed, among others, the famed Achabal Gardens in Kashmir state, with its lavish array of fruit trees, fountains, and a man-made waterfall, illuminated from behind by "innumerable lamps" at night, wrote a gobsmacked Bernier.

Yet Nur Jahan could also be as thrifty as a village housewife and knew how to stretch a rupee. On one occasion, recounted Khafi Khan, Jahangir questioned the expense of the finely embroidered caparisons for the royal elephants. He was pleased to learn that Nur Jahan spent "practically nothing on them" and had them "made by palace tailors" from used mail bags.

When it came to her own couture, she was just as innovative, and pioneered what would be regarded today as a designer line of clothing. She designed silver-threaded brocades (*badla*) and lace (*kinari*), lightweight, floral-patterned cotton and muslin textiles (*panchtoliya* and *dudami*) for veils and gowns, and her own signature scent, *atr i Jahangiri* (rose perfume), all of which set fashion trends at court. For the cost-conscious bride (and groom), she is also credited with creating the (now traditional) *nurmahali*, an

Nur Jahan and Mughal Architecture

Like their Safavid counterparts, with whom they shared many tastes, the Mughals were lovers of elegance and sophistication in the arts and culture. Among the dynasty's most enduring cultural legacies is its distinctive and tastefully elaborate architecture, characterized by graceful domes, archways, and detailed inlays, the Taj Mahal being perhaps the most famous example. While this iconic structure was the project of Shah Jahan, Nur Jahan's influence on the building may be traced to the tombs that she had built in her lifetime, namely those for her mother and father and herself.

Her plans for her parents' tomb in Agra originally called for a building of pure silver, though the builders ultimately convinced her that pure white marble would be more durable and resistant to India's sultry climate. The building sits in the center of a memorial garden of orchards and pools—considered the most sophisticated in Mughal history—evenly divided into four square sections. This symmetry is reflected in the buildings design, which features four octagonal towers capped by domed kiosks, offset by a square pavilion in the center of the roof, also domed with four finials responding to the towers. The most spectacular element of the building is its decorative marble surface, inlaid with semiprecious stones and mosaic tiles in floral patterns, creating a bejeweled effect. The technique, known as *pietra dura*, may have come to India from Florence or derived from the brilliantly colored tile work of Safavid Persia. Architectural historians believe that the tomb of Nur Jahan's parents was the first in India to feature the technique.

Her own tomb in Lahore mimicked many of the same symmetrical features, as did that of Jahangir's, though she may have had less input in its design. Still, all three tombs are, architecturally, "of one mind." When the time came for Shah Jahan to construct a fitting mausoleum—the Taj Mahal—for his own wife, some years later, he chose a spot directly across the Yamuna river from the tomb of Nur Jahan's parents. Though this most famous of all Mughal buildings is larger than that that of Ghiyas and Asmat, its lines, its setting, and many of its decorative features, "down to the details of the red lilies and rose petals in the paintings and inlays," nonetheless reflect Nur Jahan's enduringly tasteful vision.

inexpensive set of wedding clothes. More than a gesture, her concern for the poor—especially poverty-stricken young women—was genuine.

"She was an asylum for all sufferers, and helpless girls were married at the expense of her private purse," Hadi recorded. "She must have apportioned about 500 girls in her lifetime, and thousands were grateful for her generosity."

Yet this cultured queen was just as ready to swap flowery gowns for battle gear when the need arose. Ambushed by rebel forces on her way to Kabul with Jahangir in 1626, Nur Jahan directed the Imperial Army's defensive maneuvers from atop a war elephant. When a female servant, riding the elephant with her, took an arrow in the arm, the queen "herself pulled it out, staining her garments with blood," Hadi reported.

The rebellion of 1626 was an outcome of earlier unrest stirred up by Prince Khurram, who was jealous of Nur Jahan's influence over his father. When Jahangir died in 1627, yet another war of succession followed, during which Nur Jahan attempted to enthrone her son-in-law (Ladli's husband) Shahryer, youngest of Jahangir's sons. The coup failed, Shahryer was slain, and Prince Khurram ascended the throne as Shah Jahan.

The "Light of the World" accepted her downgraded status and lived out the remainder of her days in quiet retirement in Lahore with her daughter. Putting aside her elegant finery, she is said to have worn plain clothing and abstained from parties and social functions, though she continued to "spend lavishly on the needy and the poor" with money from her personal wealth. She died on December 17 or 18, 1645, at the age of sixty-eight and is buried in Lahore, in a mausoleum of her own design, where this epitaph to her grace and modesty is etched on her tomb:

> "On the grave of this poor stranger, let there be neither lamp nor rose.
> Let neither butterfly's wing burn nor nightingale sing."

CHAPTER 10

Tajul Alam Safiatuddin Syah (1612–1675)

Sumatra's Beloved Queen of Diamonds

On September 20, 1644, after months of negotiations, Arnold de Vlamingh van Oudtshoorn, special envoy of the Dutch East India Company (the *Veerinigde Ooostindische Compagnie*, or VOC for short), finally reached an agreement over a debt owed to the company by Iskandar Thani, sultan of Aceh, an Islamic state on the island of Sumatra, in what is today Indonesia.

A fiscally freewheeling sultan, Thani was especially fond of jewels, universal symbols of royal power and prestige, which Dutch diamond cutters and jewelers were world-renowned for producing. His insatiable lust for diamonds, emeralds, and the like extended well beyond his dazzling, jewel-encrusted clothing and royal regalia, including a golden throne weighing nearly a ton. Many of the extravagant sultan's personal items such as his waterpipe, saddle, and even bathing scoop were likewise richly adorned with precious stones.

In 1640, Thani placed a hefty order with the VOC that included some 15,000 taels* worth of custom cut diamonds and jewels from the Netherlands. A year later, he was dead. Yet his jewelry bill, which Vlamingh was dispatched to collect, remained unpaid.

* 1 gold tael = 4 silver Dutch *rijksdaalders*.

The debt now fell to the sultan's widow and successor, thirty-one-year-old Tajul Alam Safiatuddin Syah, to resolve. The first woman to ascend the throne of Aceh, though not the first—or last—female to rule in the Indonesia Archipelago (see "A Long Tradition of Female Rule," p. 179), Safiatuddin had been on the throne for three years by the time of Vlamingh's arrival. During this period, she grew skilled at dealing firmly yet diplomatically with foreign traders such as the Dutch and the Portuguese, who she mistrusted and despised, much as her earlier counterparts, Morocco's Sayidda al Hurra and India's Nur Jahan, had.

Unlike her profligate late husband, Safiatuddin was more interested in the promotion of *ilm* (Islamic knowledge), good governance, and boosting the economy than in gaudy displays of diamonds. She was also a hard bargainer, as Vlamingh soon learned. After her ministers initially dismissed some of the VOC jewels as being worth "no more than pebbles," the Sultana offered the Dutch 3,000 taels for the lot, with the proviso that she would go no higher than 4,000. Negotiations dragged on over the course of the summer, during which the original Dutch counteroffer of ten thousand taels was finally whittled down to an agreed-upon six thousand from the sultana: one thousand to be paid in cash, with the balance in tin—one of Aceh's principle trade goods—along with discounts on tolls for Dutch ships.

To finalize the deal, Safiatuddin had one last request of Vlamingh and his delegation. She asked that he and his companions honor their bargain by dancing for her and the women of the court. "Doubtless mortified," Vlamingh and his fellow VOC officials had no other choice but to hop and bounce about ridiculously for the assembled ladies who couldn't contain their laughter at the spectacle.

Whether or not Safiatuddin intended to humiliate the Dutch is unknown. What was clear is that because of Aceh's role as a major trading center for gold, tin, silks, sandalwood, and spices—especially pepper—the Dutch, and their rival European powers, needed her more than she needed them. Two centuries later, the tide would turn, and Aceh and all of the "East Indies" (as the Dutch called what would become Indonesia) fell under European colonial control.

But during the late seventeenth century, the riches and political might of the Sultanate of Aceh—a major Southeast Asian regional power—rested in the hands of a woman at whose command European envoys danced and local Islamic states bowed.

Safiatuddin was born Putri Sri Alam in 1612 in the Aceh capital of Banda Aceh. She was the daughter of Sultan Iskandar Muda, whose reign (1607–1636) is regarded as Aceh's golden age. Known as Aceh Darussalam (Abode of Peace), the sultanate emerged at the end of the fifteenth century with the unification of two smaller Muslim principalities in northern Sumatra. As the "western gate of the Indonesian Archipelago," Aceh's strategic location at the northern end of the island attracted an international cross section of traders over the centuries, from China to India. It was traveling merchants from Gujarat (the northwestern Indian state where medieval Muslim missionaries settled under the patronage of Yemen's Queen Arwa) who introduced Islam to northern Sumatra in the eleventh century. The close Indian connection inspired later geographers to refer to the region as Further India, or the "East Indies."

By the sixteenth century, Banda Aceh's reputation as a "commercial emporium" not only attracted Indian and Chinese merchants but "Arabs, Persians, Ottomans, [and] Abyssinians" as well. Meanwhile, Europeans, who long chafed at Muslim control of the flow of luxury goods from the East, actively sought their own exclusive sea routes to Indonesia. Their objective was to gain direct access to spices such as cloves, cinnamon, nutmeg, mace, and pepper. The medicinal as well as culinary demand for these exotic spices—the world's "first truly global commodity"—yielded enormous profits back in Europe, with markups of as much as 1,000 percent.

Europe's effort to establish direct oceangoing channels to Indian and Southeast Asian spice merchants was spearheaded by Portugal, following the pioneering late-fifteenth-century voyages of Dias and de Gama around Africa's Cape of Good Hope. After settling in west Indian ports like Goa, the Portuguese began eyeing "the still greater potential richness of Sumatra's natural resources." These included "great quantities of gold, camphor, benzoin, cinnamon, ginger 'better than that of Malabar,' sandalwood, silk 'like that of Persia' and sulphur," according to reports by Jorge de Lamos, sixteenth century secretary to the Portuguese viceroy of Goa.

Along with gold and tin, black pepper—native to India and introduced to Sumatra in the early fifteenth century—was one of East's most sought-after commodities. In Roman times, it was as prized as frankincense, one of the three precious gifts brought by the wise men to the baby Jesus. When spice merchants formed a guild in London in 1180, it was called the Guild of Pepperers, while debts such as "rents, taxes and dowries were often paid" with sacks of the pungent spice.

An oversupply of pepper following De Gama's voyage glutted the market. Still, Sumatran pepper was enough of "an essential element in [Portugal's] interoceanic trade" for the Portuguese to seize Malacca from the Muslims in 1511. One of the most "prosperous and powerful" entrepôts in the region, the Indonesian sultanate lay south of Aceh, across the Strait of Malacca on the southern Malay peninsula. During the Ming dynasty (1368–1644) it was the "entrepot of choice by traders from the east, particularly the Chinese." By the second half of the fifteenth century, Malacca's influence extended across most of the Malay Peninsula as well as Sumatra's east coast and surrounding islands. Its capture by the Portuguese signaled a direct threat to the numerous Muslim states in the archipelago.

In response, Aceh's sultans, beginning with the state's founder, Ali Mughayat Syah (r. circa 1514–1530), began to push back militarily against the European invaders. The resistance continued under successive Aceh sultans, reaching its peak under Muda, dubbed *sayf al muluk*, the "sword of kings." The warrior sultan ultimately conquered most of Sumatra, including regions under Portuguese influence on the Malacca Peninsula. His one failed campaign was attempting to seize the strategic port of Malacca itself in 1629. During the disastrous mission, hundreds of Aceh warships were lost, along with thousands of Muslim troops.

As many of the other major trading ports on the Malay Peninsula and along Sumatra's west coast fell under Aceh's authority, the domineering sultan was able to monopolize commerce in the region. For example, in order to capitalize on the pepper trade, he expanded the plant's production in and around various western Sumatran trading ports under his control as well as the agricultural regions south of the capital.

Tightening his grip on the markets, Muda concentrated all foreign trade in the capital, with strict rules forbidding overseas traders from dealing directly with regional ports. If foreign merchants, such as the Dutch—who first arrived in Aceh in 1599—wanted access to tin, or silks, or pepper (which Muda marked up considerably), they had no choice but to come to Banda Aceh. There they were required to obtain a trading permit from the sultan, who kept close tabs on the production and transportation of pepper from the plantations to the capital. These strict regulations on foreign trade and pepper production, in addition to hefty harbor fees in the capital plus tribute from the regions Muda conquered, all contributed significantly to Aceh's booming economy. At the time of the sultan's death in 1636, the sultanate was the wealthiest and most powerful Muslim state in the western Indonesian Archipelago.

The "sword of kings" was succeeded by his son-in-law, Iskander Thani, a prince from Pahang, one of the sultanates on the east coast of the Malay Peninsula, subjugated in 1618. Brought to Aceh as a captive at the age of seven, Thani was married to Putri Sri Alam two years later. He tried to emulate his father-in-law's reign, but it was a hard act to follow. Though he lacked his predecessor's military prowess, he did share the late sultan's taste for iron-fisted autocracy. By "nullifying or reversing many of the religious, economic, and social policies that his late father in-law had enacted," the young, inexperienced new sultan quickly began to make enemies among Aceh's powerful and influential nobles, merchants, shipowners, and dockmasters, collectively known as the *orang kaya*.*

Immensely wealthy, the *orang kaya* lived in "large stately Houses, with canon at their Gates, and great Numbers of Slaves to serve and guard them," observed the French general Augustine de Beaulieu, who led an expedition to the East Indies in 1619. The "Grandeur and Authority" of their "magnificent Garments" and showy, "pompous retinues" not only impressed the common people: such public displays served to remind the sultan that the *orang kaya* could be "fatal to his Person" should he cross them.

Tempting just such a fate, Thani's convulsive shift in policies, coupled with his extravagant, treasury-draining taste in jewelry, led to an assassination attempt by poisoning in August of 1637, just eight months into his reign. Surviving the attempt, the vengeful sultan's retribution was swift and horrifyingly bloody. British merchant Peter Mundy, who arrived at Aceh three to four months after the failed coup, reported that some four hundred conspirators were publicly executed,

* An Indonesian term meaning a rich person or "man of wealth" in the same way that the word for the ape "orang-utan" (orangutan) means "man of the forest." Today, orang kaya is gender neutral and can describe a rich woman as well as a man.

> . . . with sundry sorts off exquisite torments, *viz.*, divers cutt in peeces, others sawne in 2 . . . some hung on Iron hookes by the heeles, stretched wide abroad, and Molten lead powred into the Fundamentts of the Men and privities of the women to cause them [to] Conffesse where their Masters or husbands treasure lay.

The tyrannical sultan's sudden death four years later was suspicious though not surprising, given that "his short reign had many opponents" not the least of whom were the *orang kaya.* It was now left to them to determine who should succeed, since Thani left no heir. One thing was certain: they would have no more foreign-born rulers on the throne. But with no male heir, who among them would rule? Contentious disputes broke out among the nobles, "for each one . . . wanted to be king" according to Dutch physician Nicolaus de Graaff, who was in Aceh at the time of Thani's death. The arguments led to bloodshed and chaos, during which time no trading could take place in the city, forcing the VOC to shut its office doors. Realizing that the succession crisis was bad for business, the members of the *orang kaya* put aside personal ambition and reached a consensus: the throne would go to Thani's widow, Putri Sri Alam.

While she was Aceh's first female ruler, the elevation of women to positions of power in the sultanate "was not unusual for that place and time." During the reign of Sultan Ala al Din Riayat Shah al Mukammil (r. 1589–1604), the admiral of the navy was a woman, Laksamana Keumalahayati, while the sultan's "Chiefest Counsellers" were all female, including the head of his personal guard, "for hee will trust no men," as John Davis, navigator for England's East India Company (EIC), observed during the company's maiden voyage abroad in 1601. With Al Mukammil's blessing, Laksamana Keumalahayati raised an army of two thousand widows whose husbands, like her own, had died in battle. Their military barracks/training center cum widows' home, on a hilltop overlooking Aceh's Krueng Raya Bay, became known as *Kuta Inong Bale*, the "Widows' Fort."

Women continued to serve in the military under Muda. His personal guard was composed of three thousand women who accompanied "him on Foote with bowes and arrowes in their hands" whenever he was in residence in the palace. Added to these precedents of empowered women in Acehnese

A Long Tradition of Female Rule

Long before Safiatuddin ascended the throne, many high-born women in Austronesian societies—from Polynesia to Madagascar, Indonesia to the Philippines—occupied positions of supreme political power from the late medieval period onward. In Pasai, a northern Sumatran sultanate just east of the territory that would become the kingdom of Aceh, two successive queens ruled from 1405 to 1434. Since the fourteenth century, six of the thirty-two rulers of the Sulawesi Sultanate of Bone, in the former Celebes, were women. It was a queen, Shinsawbu (1453–72), who occupied the throne of Myanmar (Burma) and oversaw the rise of the city of Pegu as a major shipping port in the Bay of Bengal. Japara, on Java's north coast, rose to prominence during the third quarter of the sixteenth century as an important maritime power under the command of its famous queen, Kali-nyamat. Women also presided over the economies of "the diamond-exporting center of Sukadana in Southwest Borneo (c. 1608–22), pepper-rich Jambi in East Sumatra (1630–C. 1655), and the sandalwood base of Solor, to the East of Flores (c. 1650–70)" during the years these Indonesian principalities were thriving regional commercial centers. And like Aceh, the Sultanate of Patani, on the Malay Peninsula, was ruled by a succession of four queens who reigned from 1584 to 1688. Like Safiatuddin and her successors, Patani's queens "conducted trade and diplomatic ties with the Portuguese, Dutch, [and the] English" as well as Japan and the rest of Southeast Asia, bringing "peace and prosperity to their kingdom."

Female rulership in these and other Indonesian societies throughout history were not merely the results of "accidents of succession." Women earned the respect, support, and loyalty of their subjects, especially the wealthy merchant classes, because of the stability their tenures on the throne provided. In contrast to male rulers such as Thani, who could be reckless when it came to the kingdom's finances, women could be relied upon to "understand market forces, to drive hard bargains, and to conserve [the kingdom's] capital" resources.

society was the fact that Putri Sri Alam's pedigree "as the widow of Thani and a daughter of Muda by a royal wife" was "impeccable."

If there was a potential roadblock to her enthronement, it was a religious one. Was there justification in Islam for a woman to rule? Searching for an answer to this question, the *orang kaya* turned to religious scholarship of the day. A passage in the *Taj al Salatin* ("The Crown of Kings")—"an ethical guide for rulers with advice on how [to] correctly to govern . . . in tandem with Islamic tradition" composed in 1603—allowed for female rule "during turbulent times; that is when the ruler of the country has passed away without leaving a male heir." Certainly, Thani's sonless marriage and the state of affairs following his death checked both of these boxes.

The judgments of Aceh's ulema provided further justification for Putri Sri Alam's elevation to the throne. Gujarati-born Nuruddin al Raniri, whose writings are considered to be the oldest Islamic scholarship in Southeast Asia, resided in Aceh from 1637 until 1644. So respected were his opinions that Thani appointed him *Sheikh al Islam* (chief religious judge). In his seven-volume *Bustan as Salatin* ("The Garden of Kings"), the conservative scholar defended Putri Sri Alam's worthiness for the throne based on her devotion to Islam and support for shariah as the de facto law of the land. His public praise for her as "*khalīfat Allāh*" (God's deputy) unequivocally legitimized her right to rule and carry out "our Lord's orders in the blessed (*mubārak*) country of Aceh Dār al-Salām."

Abdul Rauf al Singkel, a contemporary of Raniri, was born in West Sumatra but traveled and studied widely throughout the Middle East, including stints in the Persian Gulf, Yemen, Mecca, and Medina. His views on the permissibility and fitness for women to rule a Muslim state were based on his interpretation of Islam's support for "equality between men and women as a component of our humanity, opportunity and rights." These included the right to govern and for women to occupy the position of *hakim* (judge) in Muslim society.*

Skeptics may point to the fact that both these scholars benefitted from Putri Sri Alam's favor once she became queen. She had a close relationship with Raniri, who tutored her in Islam, while she appointed Singkel *Sheikh al*

* His opinions on the equality of the sexes were not absolute. He still regarded men as heads of the family.

Islam, once Raniri left Aceh. Still, the support of such prominent members of Aceh's ulema, coupled with that of the *orang kaya*—who regarded female rule as an effective safeguard against despotic kings and one of the best ways to "make the state safe for international commerce"—ensured her ascendency to the throne within days of her husband's untimely death on February 15, 1641. Once crowned, she took the royal title *Tajul Alam* (Crown of the World) Safiatuddin (Purely Faithful), two of her father's affectionate names for her.

Among the first orders of business on the new queen's agenda was maintaining the independence of the throne in the face of growing, external threats from European traders, who sought to gain a more dominant foothold in the region. Internally, she also needed to manage the expectations of the *orang kaya* who could, as they made clear, depose her at any time should she not balance their economic interests with those of the state.

Power shifts in the region soon put her new rule to the test. The year of her coronation, the Dutch captured Malacca from the Portuguese, one of the final nails in the coffin of Portuguese colonial supremacy in the East Indies. To Safiatuddin, the news came as a mixed blessing. Much like Morocco's Hurra, the Acehnese queen hated the Portuguese, regarding them as "religious enemies and foreign intruders." Yet once the Portuguese were out of the way, the Dutch and the English aggressively began to fill the void left by their ousted colonialist competitor.

Keeping a watchful eye on the situation, Safiatuddin recognized that international diplomacy required a subtler hand than that employed by her father and certainly her late husband. One of her strategies was to expand VOC trading concessions along Sumatra's west coast. By doing so, she was in fact using the Dutch to help oust their mutual enemy, the Portuguese. Meanwhile, she wrote to England's King Charles II, extending an invitation to the EIC to establish a warehouse in Banda Aceh together with the privilege of sending three ships annually to trade in the port. A greater English presence in Aceh, she calculated, would effectively keep her ersatz allies, the Dutch, in check. To this end, she stirred the pot by informing King Charles that, despite her efforts to offer the English protection, the "accursed" Dutch were known to board EIC ships and seize their costly cargoes of pepper.

Being able to read between the lines of a diplomatic correspondence himself, King Charles ultimately decided against being "drawn into a brawl between the Acehnese and the Dutch." Nonetheless, Safiatuddin's strategies proved that she was just as skilled as Dutch capitalists and English monarchs at playing the chess game of international relations.

With the rise of Dutch colonial power in the region, some historians have suggested that the queen's trade agreements with the VOC, particularly along Sumatra's west coast, ultimately led to Aceh's downfall. While it is true that she was forced to surrender some of the territories conquered by her father, such as Pahang, Safiatuddin was able to retain control over the vital, tin-producing center Perak on the Malay peninsula's west coast. As for the exclusive deals with the VOC, some had been struck not by her but by her late husband. If anything, Safiatuddin expanded trade concessions to include English and Gujarati merchants who offered Aceh better deals on manufactured goods like cloth.

The affair with the VOC jewels also demonstrated that, when the need arose, she was not afraid to play hardball. In 1649, when the VOC-appointed commissar to Aceh, Johan Truijtman, requested the cancellation of all export tariffs on pepper for Dutch ships doing business along the entire west coast of Sumatra—a sum amounting to thousands of taels annually—the outraged queen refused.

"How could I accept a condition never before applied that could take the bread out of the mouths of my people?" she responded angrily.

And her people appreciated it. Many of her vassals in the states conquered by her father resented his policy that restricted them from trading directly with the VOC. She was willing to loosen those restrictions, while standing firm on the question of toll exemptions for pepper, thus enriching her subjects while protecting Aceh's interests.

Her relations with the *orang kaya* were equally strategic. Aware of how much "the very name of a Kinge [had] longe since become nautious unto them" after "the Tyrannicall Goverment of theire last Kinge" (her late husband), she governed less like an autocrat and more like the chair of a board, which the *orang kaya* closely resembled. In placing her upon the throne, the nobles and wealthy merchant class agreed that they "[s]hold cause noe act or law (now Established) to be Violated, or any Other to be made without the Queene [granting] her Consent and good likeinge thereunto."

Rather than being an issue of concern, her gender set her apart from the "male-dominated political factions" of the *orang kaya* elite, "and thus was not bound to any." Consequently, "the orangkaya found they could govern collectively with the queen as sovereign and referee, and there was something of the quality of Elizabethan England in the way they vied for her favour but accepted her eventual judgement."

Those who didn't learned the hard way what it meant to test her limits. In 1641, when one of the *orang kaya* appropriated the choicest lands of the Pidie region, south of the capital, for himself, leaving nothing for the crown, Safiatuddin made him stand meekly before her with his hands on his head, a sign of submission, while she chastised him in front of the court.

Yet so long as her nobles behaved themselves, everyone benefitted from what was clearly "a more decentralized system of government" than her father or late husband would have recognized, let alone endorsed—a system that nonetheless worked.

Under her rule, the sultanate "was extremely prosperous . . . foodstuffs were very cheap, and everybody lived in peace," according to Raniri. The sheikh further noted that "she was fair in all matters of the law, and . . . was very serious in everything she did."

Some of Aceh's good fortune under Safiatuddin's reign was sheer luck. Raniri reported that during her rule, "gold mines were discovered in several mountains and the proceeds were so abundant that it made the Kingdom of Aceh a rich and prosperous country." The location of the mines was a closely guarded secret and the queen retained the right, without asking permission of the *orang kaya*, to mint coins from the bountiful deposits of gold. The new coins contained exceptionally high percentages of the precious metal, further boosting the Sultanate's already robust economy.

Nowhere was Aceh's wealth and power was on greater display than during royal audiences for ambassadors and VOC/EIC envoys, as William Marsden, an agent for the EIC described:

> [T]he royal elephants are sent down to carry him and his letters to the monarch's presence; these being first delivered to the hands of a eunuch, who places them in a silver dish, covered with rich silk, on the back of the largest elephant, which is provided with a [litter] for that purpose.

> Within about an hundred yards of an open hall where the king sits, the cavalcade stops, and the ambassador dismounts, and makes his obeisance by bending his body and lifting his joined hands to his head. When he enters the palace, if an European, he is obliged to take off his shoes, and having made a second obeisance, is seated upon a carpet on the floor, where *betel** is brought to him.

When Safiatuddin ascended the throne, these protocols were adjusted somewhat, in accordance with mandates spelled out in the *Taj al Salatin*, which specified that "a female ruler was neither to be seen in public, nor could she meet with a man face to face." So an audience with Safiatuddin, as Marsden reported, was conducted before "a curtain of gauze . . . which did not obstruct the audience, but prevented any perfect view" of the queen, who sat in an elaborate lodge upon a throne "of ivory and tortoise shell."

Even as trade remained central to the Acehnese economy, Safiatuddin wisely recognized that diversification was essential to the Sultanate's survival in the face of rising competition from the Minangkabau peoples of Sumatra's west central highlands, together with tougher VOC trade policies. Like her father, she expanded the production of pepper in the interior, as well as rice, a staple crop that could not only feed many hungry mouths but held "immense cultural significance in Indonesia," historically regarded "by many Indonesians as a miraculous gifts of the gods."**

Feeding her nation spiritually was another of Safiatuddin's priorities. Sharing her views on moral behavior with the Dutch governor of Batavia*** in 1659, she wrote, "God says since antiquity there are no better things as these two things; namely, think always about God above all and always do good to other people." Living this dictum, "she feared Allah and read Allah's Book and had instructed her people to do good deeds and forbade them to commit felonies," Raniri reported in the *Bustan*. To outsiders, the impact

* Betel nuts were another of Aceh's valuable trading commodities. When chewed together with slaked lime and betel leaves, they act as a stimulant.

** Respect for Sumatran rice extended to at least one of America's founding fathers. Famed English botanist and naturalist Sir Joseph Banks supplied Thomas Jefferson with three varieties of the crop, which Jefferson planted in the garden of his Parisian townhouse, the Hotel de Langeac.

*** Capital of the Dutch East Indies; modern-day Jakarta.

of her pious leadership was evident. On a visit to Aceh during Safiatuddin's reign, the Muslim traveler al Mutawakkil remarked that "a very gracious, perfect Muslim woman, generous with money, rules them. She can read and knows science, beneficence and agreement on the Qur'an."

She also encouraged and supported religious scholarship. During her reign, Aceh "became the most productive center of literary activity in *alam Malayu* [the Malay world]," especially the composition of Islamic literature. It was in Aceh that the Qur'an was first translated into Malay, by Singkel, along with other religious texts. In addition, original works flowed from the pens of major scholars such as Raniri, who wrote no less than twenty-nine volumes on such topics as Islamic law and jurisprudence in both Malay and Arabic. Added to this rich corpus were translations of imported Persian and Arabic poetry, whose syntax and poetic genres exerted a strong influence on Malay literature. With its reputation as the "porch of Mecca," Aceh played a critical role as "the major center of transmission of religious knowledge in the region."

Safiatuddin died peacefully of natural causes on October 23, 1675, "after reigning, with a degree of tranquility little known in these countries, upwards of thirty-four years." She was sixty-three years old, and childless, though, unlike the demises of many of the rulers we have seen, "her death was not accompanied by crisis or chaos at court." Instead, the *orang kaya*—knowing a good thing when they saw it—elevated another woman to the throne, Sultana Nurul Alam Naqiatuddin Syah (r. 1675–1678), whose blood relationship to Safiatuddin remains unclear. She herself would be succeeded by two more sultanas.

"The people being now accustomed and reconciled to female rule, which they found more lenient than that of their kings, acquiesced in general in the established mode of government," Marsden wrote.

Safiatuddin's reign established this acceptance of women on Aceh's throne and her manner of governing, in fact, "became somewhat of a template for her female successors." Naqiatuddin's successor, Ratu Inayat Zakiatuddin Syah (r. 1678–1688), dealt with the European powers in much the same way as Safiatuddin. When English traders, based in Madras, arrived in Aceh in 1684 seeking permission to open a fortified trade office, Zakiatuddin wisely denied their request for a fortress but agreed to let them conduct business in the

Sultanate. Trade and tariffs were one (good) thing. Foreign forts, on the other hand, were potential threats to Acehnese sovereignty and the sultana knew it.

This balanced approach to governing was Safiatuddin's legacy. Through deftly negotiated treaties and alliances that served the needs of the Dutch and the English, but also those of her people, she was able to maintain Aceh's "political and commercial autonomy." She may have surrendered some territories and trade privileges, but she always "ensured that customs duties and tolls for her vassals were protected." Most critically, like those of her royal predecessor, Yemen's Arwa, her policies sought to avoid "wasteful and dangerous wars."

But Acehnese society was changing. The growing presence and influence of conservative-minded, Meccan-based Arab traders in the capital led to a shift in attitude towards women on the throne. These sentiments gained traction in 1693 after the death of Singkel—a leading religious authority and a longtime supporter of female rule—together with the arrival in the capital of a letter from Mecca declaring women unfit to rule under Islamic law.

Falling back on the familiar, albeit repeatedly disproven, philosophy that the realm of politics and the governing of an Islamic state was "male by default," in 1699 the members of the *orang kaya* turned their backs on their fourth consecutive woman ruler, Sultana Zainatuddin Kamalat Syah, and installed a sultan in her place. With the sultana's death a year later, the age of Aceh's queens came to an end.

Epilogue

But it was hardly the end of female political leadership in the Islamic world. Not by a long shot.

In the centuries since the last sultana sat on the throne of Aceh, there have been dozens upon dozens of Muslim women who ruled outright, acted as regents, served as advisors to their husbands, or led shadow governments, primarily in India and Central and Southeast Asia (with its long history of female rule) as well as other corners of the Muslim world.

India's Mamola Bai stepped in as de facto ruler of the Rajput state of Bhopal, India, from 1730 to 1745, after the death of her husband, overseeing all government affairs and making military decisions in the name of her stepson, who was more inclined to a life of religious contemplation than governing. Lalla Aicha, widow of the Sultan of Tuggurt, a historic Algerian state in the Sahara, assumed power after her husband's brother, Ali, murdered him in a failed coup in 1831. Ordering Ali's poisoning, she served as regent in her son's name from 1833–1846, ably governing the state. A colorful figure, she was known for her equestrian skills, wore pistols on her belt, and was fond of smoking hemp. Ghaliyya Al Bogammiah (d. 1818) was a Saudi military leader who earned the title "Amira" (the feminine form of Emir, a high-ranking military or political officer) after successfully defending Mecca from Ottoman attack at the head of Arab forces during the Wahhabi War (1811–1818). The conflict was Saudi Arabia's first step towards independence, paving the way, ironically, for the ultra-conservative Wahhabist movement in the kingdom that for decades severely restricted women's rights.

More recently, there have been female heads of state—presidents or prime ministers—in numerous Muslim-majority countries, such as Pakistan,

Indonesia, Turkey, Tunisia, Kosovo, Kyrgyzstan, and others. In addition, women have served as cabinet ministers in a wide cross section of Muslim nations, such as Egypt, Bahrain, Morocco, and Jordan, which incidentally still has a queen, Rania, a passionate advocate for the empowerment of women.

Certainly many extremist Muslims and Muslim governments continue to misappropriate and loosely interpret Islamic texts "to justify discrimination against women and to impose social and legal restrictions on women's rights and freedoms," as Tamara Kharroub, Deputy Executive Director and Senior Fellow of the Arab Center Washington DC, has written. Oppressors of women in these Muslim-majority countries and societies display a willfully appalling ignorance of the Islamic faith, not to mention Islamic history—a history in which women have played a crucial role from the very beginning, starting with the Prophet's wife, Khadija, Islam's first convert and follower.

Given the current record of human rights violations against women in countries such as Afghanistan, where women's education is forbidden and in 2024 extremists issued a ban on women baring their faces or speaking out loud in public, or Iran, with its abysmal post-revolutionary record of abusing "the rights of women and girls, including the rights to freedom of expression, often with the use of excessive force," it is easy enough for Western critics to condemn Islam as inherently misogynistic.

Yet has Western society not been guilty of patriarchy and the oppression of women, even into the modern era? Up until 1882 and the passage of the Married Women's Property Act, women in England were forced to surrender their property to their husbands upon marriage. Muslim women, on the other hand, "enjoyed property rights centuries before women in the West" under Islamic law which "prescribes equality in women's ability to own, manage, and dispose of property."

At a time when proto-feminists in England and the United States were struggling to win the right to vote, a succession of four powerful female Muslim Nawabs (Governors) of Bhopal ruled from 1819 to 1926, embodying "feminism much before it gained prominence." The last of the line, Sarkar Amman, like her predecessors, instituted numerous social reforms, including free and compulsory public education for boys *and* girls, the funding of institutes of higher learning, the expansion of public works, and access to public health, including statewide programs to vaccinate and inoculate the public against infectious diseases.

In an era when women in America could not open bank accounts, let alone secure mortgages, without a male's permission, Egypt's Rawya Ateya (1926–1997) became the first parliamentarian in the Arab world, remembered as a pioneering figure in the history of Egyptian and Arab feminism.

Since its introduction in 1923, the Equal Rights Amendment—guaranteeing equal rights for all American citizens regardless of gender—has yet to be officially acknowledged as a part of the U.S. Constitution. Meanwhile, jurists at Dar al Ifta, an Islamic legal institution in Egypt, have since stipulated in a fatwa (legal ruling) that because "women have continued to occupy lofty positions throughout the centuries" as "rulers, judges, warriors, teachers, muftis, etc.," they have "every right to occupy" the position of head of state, as "[a]ny honest student of Islamic history can testify."

In contrast, the United States has yet to elect its first female president, while "a majority of all Muslims in the world are living in countries that have, at some time, elected women as their leaders."

And while misogynist mullahs and the Boko Harams of the Muslim world are clearly responsible for the abuse of women's rights, Western colonialism and its legacy have also played a role. When nineteenth-century Christian European missionaries to Africa encountered indigenous women engaged in the public sphere as chiefs, local leaders, and policy makers, they were shocked. To the Western mind, women served two—and only two—functions in society: as homemakers and child bearers.

Thus, in addition to the saving of souls, "[c]onversion was aimed at transforming the division of labour in African homes in order to fulfil these Victorian ideals of devout domesticity." As Western colonialism spread across the wider Muslim world, the imposition of "appropriate gender roles remained central to imperial stability." Politically savvy, politically powerful, not to mention armed and educated women who insisted on a seat at the table threatened the "patrimonial colonial domination" upon which the whole system was erected.

As noted above, some indomitable Muslim women rulers resisted this paradigm. Today, Muslim women in leadership roles in both Muslim-majority and Muslim-minority countries (especially the US) are becoming increasingly accepted as their numbers continue to grow, in spite of the hurdles they still face. "It is clear that women's engagement in politics and the economy," economists and sociologists have concluded, "is crucial for achieving the government's objectives in the rapidly evolving global economy."

The *orang kaya* weren't so far off.

The paths today's Muslim women have traveled to public office were blazed by the women profiled in this book. Their courage and determination, their dignity and achievements, serve as examples and inspirations for women everywhere, no matter what their faith, while their stories emphatically answer the question, "Were there really any Muslim women rulers?" Yes, there were. There were indeed.

Acknowledgements

Writing, as they say, is a lonely occupation. Still, no writer ever works entirely alone.

My thanks to Aramco Americas and *AramcoWorld* magazine for permission to utilize some of the copyrighted material from the original series I wrote for the publication in 2016, upon which this book is based—a series that would never have seen the light of day without the encouragement and support of former executive editor, Richard Doughty. The same goes for Interlink publisher Michel Moushabeck who believed in this project from the moment I proposed it to him.

Appreciation also goes to scholars Richard Bulliet, Metin M. Coşgel, Hasna Lebaddy, Alan Mikhail, Letizia Osti, Sevket Pamuk, Yves Porter, Yasser Tabbaa, and Vanessa Van Renterghe for their guidance and advice along the way. Any errors in the text are my own and not attributable to those who offered me their kind assistance. Thanks as well to Sofia Ali-Khan, Jean Bauer, Brian McGlynn, Lori Taylor, Matthew Teller, Priscilla Warner, and Alia Yunis for their frank feedback and encouragement.

Tracking down and securing research material for this book would have been a much steeper climb without the dedicated and dogged assistance of the staff of the Stonington Free Library in Stonington, Connecticut, in particular interlibrary loan librarians Ivy Burns and Molly Linder, whose help was closer to that of research assistants than circulation desk staff persons.

Lastly, heartfelt gratitude goes to my best editor, my wife Kate, whose honesty is a gift and whose love is a blessing.

Endnotes

Preface

an academic journal: Tom Verde, "Cairo: Histories of a City. By Nezar Al Sayyad," review, The Historian, vol. 74, 2012, issue 3, p. 553–554.

"the first and only woman": Nezar Al Sayyad, *Cairo: Histories of a City* (Cambridge: Belknap Press, 2011), p. 77.

various Islamic extremist groups: Heraldo Munoz; Marzuki Darusman; Peter FitzGerald, "Report of the United Nations Commission of Inquiry into the facts and circumstances of the assassination of former Pakistani Prime Minister Mohtarma Benazir Bhutto," UN Secretary General, April 15, 2010, www.refworld.org/reference/factfinding/unsecgen/2010/en/76590.

"the first woman to lead a Muslim country": Owen Bennett Jones, "Benazir Bhutto assassination: How Pakistan covered up killing," BBC, December 26, 2017, www.refworld.org/reference/factfinding/unsecgen/2010/en/76590. Last accessed October, 10, 2024.

CHAPTER 1

"Commander of the Faithful" and "God's Power on Earth": André Clot, *Harun al-Rashid and the World of the One Thousand and One Nights*, John Howe, tr. (London: Saqi Books, 2005), p. 38.

Forgoing royal finery: Al Tabari, *The History of al-Tabari*, C.E. Bosworth, tr., The Abbasid Caliphate in Equilibrium, Volume XXX of XXXVIII volumes, (Albany: State University of New York, 1989), p. 107; see also Nabia Abbott, *Two Queens of Baghdad: Mother and Wife of Harun al Rashid* (University of Chicago Press, 1946), pp. 125–126.

Protocol of the day: Fatima Mernissi, *The Forgotten Queens of Islam*, Mary Jo Lakeland, tr. (Minneapolis: University of Minnesota Press, 1993), pp 51–52.

The district was home: Jacob Lassner, *The Topography of Baghdad in the Early Middle Ages: Text and Studies* (Detroit: Wayne State University Press, 1979), p. 116; see also Guy Le Strange, *Baghdad During the Abbasid Caliphate from Contemporary Arabic and Persian Sources* (Elibron Classics, reprint of 1900 edition by Clarendon Press, Oxford), pp. 192–193. Lassner's translation is of Khatib al Baghdadi's eleventh century *History of Baghdad.*

the Khayzuran Cemetary: Lassner, p. 116.

donned a pair of boots: Al Tabari, p. 107; see also Abbott, p. 126.

He summoned [one of his close aides]: Al Tabari, p. 107.

most medieval chroniclers: Mernissi, p. 52.

She may have been born in Mecca: Abbott, p. 26.

no more than fifty: Abbott, p. 125.

while he was performing the hajj: F.E. Peters, *Mecca: A Literary History of the Muslim Holy Land* (Princeton University Press, 1994), p.117.

"for childbearing": Abbott, p. 26.

She was bought up there: Abbott, p. 22.

Other accounts say: Kathryn A. Hain, "Avenues to Social Mobility Available to Courtesans and Concubines," in *Concubines and Courtesans: Women and Slavery in Islamic History*, Matthew S. Gordon and Kathryn A. Hain, eds. (Oxford University Press, 2017), p. 324.

Some slaves were captured in battle: Hain, p. 325.

"Demand for slave women": Ibid.

"Indians," Butlan wrote, possessed "great beauty": Quoted in Taef El Azhari, *Queens, Eunuchs and Concubines in Islamic History, 661–1257* (Edinburgh University Press, 2019), pp. 88–89.

blended the most desirable qualities: Butlan, quoted in El Azhari, p. 88.

"concubines whose readiness": Abbott, p. 8.

she learned the Traditions: Al Tabari, p. 56.

She also gained a reputation: Abbott, pp. 40–41.

stopped short of buying her himself: Abbott, p. 26.

"Born at Mecca": Ibid.

had his tongue fed to a cat: Benson Bobrick, *The Caliph's Splendor: Islam and the West in the Golden Age of Baghdad* (New York: Simon and Schuster, 2012), p. 12.

the City of Peace: The name "Baghdad" is actually Persian in origin, from "Bagh" (God) and "Dadh," meaning "founded," so a city "Founded by God."

"Have you seen in any corner of the world": Reuvin Snir, tr. & ed., *Baghdad: The City in Verse* (Harvard University Press, 2013), p. 93.

"covered with parks": William Stearns Davis, *Readings in Ancient History: Illustrative Extracts from the Sources, Volume II: Rome and the West"* (Boston: Allyn and Bacon, 1913), p. 365.

"adorned with exquisite taste": Ibid.

"overlook[ed] courtyards with open doors": Snir, p. 94.

"tastefully furnished": Davis, p. 365.

"This is the Tigris": Quoted in George Hourani, *Arab Seafaring in the Indian Ocean in Ancient and Early Medieval Times*, 3rd edition, rev. and expanded by John Carswell (Princeton University Press, 1995), p. 64.

"It was the place": Quoted in Sabah Mohammad, "Baghdad and the Silk Road: A study on the commercial function of Baghdad in the middle ages," online publication, last accessed September 3, 2024, p. 2, en.unesco.org/silkroad/sites/default/files/knowledge-bank-article/baghdad_and_silk_route.pdf.

"the pinnacle of Islamic strength and splendor": Justin Marozzi, *Baghdad: City of Peace, City of Blood–A History in Thirteen Centuries* (Boston: De Capo Press, 2014), p. 37.

"larger than Constantinople": Snir, pp. 5–6.

"The least province in my empire": Al Muqaddasi, *The Best Divisions For Knowledge of the Region*, Basil Collins, tr., (Calcutta: Asiatic Society of Bengal, 1897) p.105, archive.org/details/al-muqaddasi-the-best-divisions-for-knowlegde-of-the-region/page/n1/mode/2up. Last accessed Oct. 10, 2024.

Under the early Abassids: Hugh Kennedy, *When Baghdad Ruled the Muslim World: The Rise and Fall of Islam's Greatest Dynasty* (Boston: De Capo, 2005), p. 160.

"seamlessly between the private world": Adam Ali, "Slave, Queen, and Mother of Caliphs: The Story of Khayzuran," Medievalists.net. www.medievalists.net/2019/04/slave-queen-and-mother-of-caliphs-the-story-of-khayzuran/. Last accessed October 10, 2024.

trained as musicians: Hain, p. 325.

Taught how to read and write: Ali.

"Pretty girls": Mernissi, p. 58.

spent most of their days: Hain, p. 324.

functioned in different ways: Ali.

"The harem," it's been said: Marozzi, p. 46.

most highly educated: Ali.

not to mention Europe: Though completely different on many obvious levels, the only contemporary Western European, self-sustaining, all-female institutions where women pursued and achieved levels of education similar to residents of the Muslim harem were convents. See Shirley Kersey, "Medieval Education of Girls and Women." *Educational Horizons* 58, no. 4 (1980): 188–92, www.jstor.org/stable/42924397. Last accessed October 25, 2024.

rolicking high life: Abbott, pp. 4, 43; Bobrick, p.19; Clot, p.22.

mocking Mansur's sour-faced temperament: Kennedy, p. 181.

known to be demanding: El Azhari, pp. 92–93.

On one occasion: the episode is recounted in both Abbott, pp. 45–46 and El Azhari pp. 92–93.

inherent "crookedness": Abbott, p. 46.

"deal justly": Qur'an 4:3.

Mahdi reportedly paid: Mernissi, p. 54.

"I never had such fear . . .": Ibid.

bloodless transition: Marozzi, pp. 25–26.

"In this year": Al Tabari, *The History of al-Tabari*, Hugh Kennedy, tr., Al Mansur and Al Mahdi, Volume XXIX, (Albany: State University of New York, 1990), p. 107.

The manumission of slaves: Hain, p. 328.

"a bold break with convention": Kennedy, *Baghdad*, p. 182.

"accommodated his wife's ambitions": El Azhari, p. 92.

"become a strong presence . . .": Ibid.

At her own palace: Ali; El Azhari, p. 94; Mernissi, p. 61.

"in many ways the public face": Kennedy, *Baghdad*, p. 43.

"man with no patience": Ibid.

laboring "into nightfall": Ibid.

"Al-Khayzuran was the one": Al Tabari (Bosworth), p. 98.

her mother: Abbott, p. 29.

when Mahdi's emissaries: Ibid.

"this affair with Asma": Abbott, p. 38.

"Your wife": Ibid.

Jafar, known as "the Younger": Al Tabari (Kennedy), p. 149.
"on account of her plumpness": Ibn Khallikan, *Ibn Khallikan's Biographical Dictionary*, Baron MacGuckin de Slane, tr., 4 vols, v. 1 (Paris: Printed for the Oriental Translation Fund of Great Britain and Ireland, 1843), p. 533.
"weave a power base at court": El Azhari, p. 91.
***Khayzuran's biggest* coup d'tat:** Mernissi, p. 55.
Of the thirty-nine Abbasid caliphs: Ali.
"tacit recognition": Abbott, p. 25.
"in the Lady's service": Abbott, p. 58.
eighteen thousand finely embroidered silken gowns: Al Tabari (Bosworth), p. 42.
numerous properties in and around Baghdad: Abbott, p. 120.
"an honour . . . not given to any other": El Azhari, p. 98.
as far away as Egypt and Mesopotamia: Clot, p. 183.
Her immense wealth: Abbott, p. 124.
By the time of her death: Al Masudi, *Meadows of Gold and Mines of Gems*, Tarif Khalidi, tr. Vol. 1, p. 192. Online edition, www.khalidilibrary.org//public/files/server/1615293155.pdf. Last accessed October 10, 2024.
These projects: Abbott, pp. 118–120.
ordered a shelter: Clot, p. 37.
Several of them were in her palace: Al Masudi, p. 164.
"had been brought up": Kennedy, *Baghdad*, p. 182.
"handsome and good looking": Al Masudi, p. 164.
eloquent diction: Ibid.
"even those tattered garments": Ibid.
"[Y]ou spoke harshly to me": Ibid.
"be shown kindness": Ibid.
"your sisters in my palace.: Ibid.
"You shall have the same privileges": Ibid.
"women folk [of the harem]": Ibid.
she favored Harun: Abbott, p. 60; Kennedy, *Baghdad*, p. 57.
Both princes were said to be tall and handsome: Abbott, p. 61; Bobrick, p. 37.
he had a fondness for literature: Al Masudi, p. 179.
enjoyed debating the finer points: Abbott, pp. 62–63.
assigned a special servant: Mernissi, p. 65.
ill-tempered, moody, and prone to violent outbursts: Al Masudi, p. 179; Kennedy, *Baghdad*, p. 57.
"staunchly supported": Bobrick, p. 27.
Yahya, characteristically, shouldered: Kennedy, *Baghdad*, p. 57.
"the first time that we see": El Azhari, p. 94
"exercise her authority": Al Tabari, p. 42.
"very obedient to his mother": Al Masudi, p. 182.

"met all her requests": Ibid.

"her door was never free": Ibid.

appointed governor of Yemen: Al Tabari, pp. 73–74.

"Do not step beyond the boundaries": Al Tabari, p. 42.

"You must grant my wish": Al Masudi, pp. 182–183.

Gathering them together: Al Tabari, pp. 44–45.

Musa sent her a rice dish: Al Tabari, p. 44.

"You can't have eaten it": Ibid.

There are stories: Al Masudi, pp. 188–189.

far jucier rumors: Al Tabari, p. 44.

"If Musā's dead": Quoted in Richard Kimber, "The Succession to the Caliph Mūsā al-Hādī," *Journal of the American Oriental Society*, Vol. 121, No. 3 (Jul.–Sept. 2001), p. 437.

Historians have rightly regarded: E.g. Kimber.

political payback might explain: Kimber, p. 433, n. 3.

"These measures by Khayzuran": El Azhari, p. 96.

"charity was ample, her conduct virtuous": Ibn Kallikan, pp. 532–533.

"one-tenth of it daily": Ibn Kallikan, p. 533.

ran to fifty million dinars: Al Zubayr, *Book of Gifts and Rarities,* Ghada al-Hijjawi al-Qaddumi, tr., (Harvard University Press, 1996), p. 121.

"whose value could not be assessed": Ibid. Such sumptuousness and stark wealth inequality are hardly things of past in Near Eastern cuture. In July of 2024 in Mumbai, members of the wedding party of Anant Ambani, son of billionaire businessman Mukesh Ambani—said to be the richest man in Asia—wore "outfits embroidered in gold along with . . . golf-ball sized rubies, diamonds and emeralds." "What a $600 million wedding says about India's attitude to wealth," *The Economist*, vol. 452, no. 9406, July 20, 2024, p. 51.

"the first to introduce the fashion for slippers": Al Masudi, p. 268.

"could scarcely walk": Wiebke Walther, *Women in Islam*, (Princeton: Markus Wiener Publishing, 1993), p. 199; Clot, p. 49.

"she replied that she was decided": Ibn Kallikan, p. 533.

"people of Mecca and the pilgrims": Quoted in Abbott, p. 251.

"a forceful and glamorous character": Abbott, p. 257.

CHAPTER 2

some 90 percent of the world's Muslim population: worldpopulationreview.com/country-rankings/sunni-countries. Last accessed October 10, 2024.

its two main branches: Andrew J. Newman, *Twelver Shiism: Unity and Diversity in the Life of Islam, 632 to 1722*, (University of Edinburgh Press, 2013), p. 2.

Considered unorthodox by Sunni standards: Azim Nanji, "Ismaili Philosophy," in *The Internet Encyclopedia of Philosophy*, online resource, https://iep.utm.edu/ismaili/ Last accessed on September 4, 2024.

"gazira in Arabic": Samer Traboulsi, "The Queen Was Actually a Man: Arwa Bint Aḥmad and the Politics of Religion," *Arabica* 50, no. 1 (2003), p. 99, n. 6. www.jstor.org/stable/4057749. Last accessed October 10, 2024.

"who wore power and pearls": Mernissi, p. 139.

"The lower classes admired": Robert W. Stookey, *Yemen: The Politics of the Yemen Arab Republic*, (Boulder, Colorado: Westview Press, 1978), p. 61.

"To maintain order": El Azhari, p. 222.

"poisoned by a slave girl": Ibn Kallikan, vol. 2, p. 345.

"one of the most famous": Mernissi, p. 145.

"with her face uncovered": Umarah ibn Ali al Hakami, *Yaman: Its Early Medieval History*, Henry Cassels Kay, tr. (London: Edward Arnold, 1892), p. 35.

"indisputable criteria of sovereignty": Mernissi, p. 71.

"had few equals in beauty": Umarah, p. 21.

"of a generous and noble disposition": Umarah, p. 22.

"fair beauty who is generous as a raincloud": H. F. Al Hamdani, "The life and times of Queen Saiyidah Arwa the Sulaihid of the Yemen," *Journal of The Royal Central Asian Society*, *18*(4), 1931, p. 508. doi.org/10.1080/03068373108725173. Last accessed October 10, 2024.

"a sovereign woman": Mernissi, p. 115.

"a liberated woman": Leila Al Imad, "Women and Religion in the Fatimid Caliphate: The Case of al-Sayyidah al-Hurrah, Queen of Yemem," in Micel M. Mazzaoui and Vera B. Moreen, eds., *Intellectual Studies in Islam: Essays Written in Honor of Martin B. Dickson*, (Salt Lake City: University of Utah Press, 1990), p. 140.

"Asma's bath obscured": Al Hamdani, p. 508.

Among Yemenis: Mernissi, pp. 140–141.

clearly pro-Sulayhid chronicler: Della Cortese and Simonetta Calderini, *Women and the Fatimids in the World of Islam*, (Edinburgh University Press, 2006), p. 128.

a dashing warrior and eloquent orator: Stookey, p. 67.

"great with child" Umarah, p. 31.

"to vindicate the honor of their tribe": Umarah, p. 32.

nearly seven to one: Umarah, p. 34.

slaughtered in great numbers: Ibid.

the piled-up bodies: Umarah, pp. 34–35.

boats he had standing by: Mernissi, p. 147.

"May God safeguard and perpetuate": Umarah, p. 35.

"Welcome our Lord al-Mukarram": Ibid.

"the wind" followed by a shudder: Ibid.

"conducted the affairs of [the] kingdom: Umarah, p. 148.

directly corresponded with Sulayhid governors: Ayman Fuad Sayyid, Paul E. Walker, Maurice A. Pomerantz, eds., *The Fatimids and their Successors in Yaman: The History of an Islamic Community* (London: I.B. Tauris, 2003), p.64; Cortese and Simonetta, p. 129. Sayyid et.al. is an Arabic edition and English summary of volume 7 of Idris Imad al Din's *Uyun al akhbar*, a fifteenth-century history of the Ismaili community from its origins up to al Din's own time.

"al Hurra, the noble": Quoted in El Azhari, p. 226.

"her loyalty": El Azhari, p. 227.

Yemeni chroniclers: Mernissi, p. 117.

whose positive impact: al Imad, p. 142.

oversaw her education: Umarah, p. 38.

"the wives [of the caliph] and the noble women": Quoted in Heinz Halm, *The Fatimids and Their Traditions of Learning* (London: I.B. Tauris, 1997), p. 45.

"the simple people and strangers in the city": Ibid.

"the culture and education of girls": Halm, p. 27.

"of fair complexion": Umarah, p. 39.

"well-read and a skillful writer": Ibid.

"shalt sweep away the dynasty": Ibid

"respect . . . for, by Allah": Ibid.

"the pleasures of music and wine": Umarah, p. 40.

"for the marriage bed": Ibid.

"May Allah prolong the days of al-Hurrah": Mernissi, pp. 115–116.

she had coins minted in her name: Mernissi, p. 73.

"Nought . . . but the lightening flashes": Umarah, pp. 40–41.

at the head of a large army: Umarah, p. 40.

"energetically took up the responsibilities": Al Hamdani, p. 511.

"a period of some brilliance": G.R. Smith, "Sulyahids," *The Encyclopedia of Islam*, New Edition, C.E. Bosworth et.al. eds., Vol. 9 (Leiden: Brill, 1997), p. 816.

The broad pavement of well-shaped stones: H. Ingrams, *The Yemen* (London: John Murray, 1963), pp. 29–30.

"scholars and teachers were well paid": Mernissi, p. 148.

A story related by Umarah: Umarah, pp. 26–27.

"was now the most powerful king": Umarah, p. 41.

"the two armies": Umarah, p. 42.

"Oh that thou hadst eyes": Ibid.

"a place where maritime and market risks": Roxani Eleni Margariti, *Aden and the Indian Ocean Trade: 150 Years in the Life of a Medieval Arabian Port* (Chapel Hill: University of North Caolina Press, 2007), p. 2.

"there were no less than twenty thousand shops": Quoted in Sadru K. Hassam, "The Socio-Economic Aspects of the Fatimid Caliphate," Simerg—Insights From Around the World. simerg.com/literary-readings/the-socio-economic-aspects-of-the-fatimid%C2%A0caliphate/. Last accessed October 10, 2024.

"the entrance hall of China": Quoted in Tim Mackintosh Smith, *Yemen: Travels in Dictionary Land* (Woodstock, NY: The Overlook Press, 1999), p. 160.

"the guardians of believers": Quoted in El Azhari, p. 230.

"far corner of the southern Arabian peninsula": El Azhari, p. 222.

politically, economically, and religiously: Shahla Haeri, *The Unforgettable Queens of Islam: Succession, Authority, Gender* (Cambridge University Press, 2020), p. 95.

"the fates of [their] two states": Haeri, p. 101.

"In his external appearance": Umarah, p. 43.

If news reached the tribes: Haeri, p. 89; Traboulsi, p. 98.

"to act in her son's interest": Quoted in Haeri, p. 89.
"the noble lady": El Azhari, p. 231.
"the religious figure": Traboulsi, p. 99.
No other woman in the Islamic world: Haeri, p. 90.
"the Sulayhid and Zuwahid sultans": Quoted in Traboulsi, p. 100.
"to abide by his wishes": Quoted in Traboulsi, p. 101.
"who followed her and her young son": Ibid.
"al-Hurra, *the Queen*": Ibid.
***"Of all Mustansir's surviving* sigils":** Ibid.
"the queen did not really need a husband": Cortese and Simonetta, p. 131.
The formality of a wedding: Ibid.
"perhaps the most sought after woman of her time": Haeri, p. 93.
"ministers . . . secretaries and officials of the state": Umarah, p. 46.
"Queen Sayyidah . . . Sovereign Lady": Umarah, p. 47.
"Our Lord the Prince of the Faithful": Ibid.
"Verily a gracious letter hath been conveyed unto me": Qur'an 27:29.
"true Religion": Qur'an 27:31.
"And behold it saith": Umarah, p. 47. The nested quotations are from the Qur'an 27: 29, 30.
"endued with strength": Qur'an 27:33.
Kings, when/They enter: Qur'an 27:34.
"their Mistress": Umarah, p. 48.
"savant in the sciences": Quoted in El Azhari, p. 233.
"Prince of the Faithful": Umarah, p. 47.
"Pillar of the Khalifate": Ibid.
"sat without ever raising his eyes": Umarah, p. 48.
"Tell our Lady": Ibid.
"some say manipulative": Haeri, p. 97.
"rare epistle between two queens": El Azhari, p. 233.
"In all things reliance was placed": Umarah, p. 51.
"The citadel is yours": Quoted in El Azhari, p. 235.
"The rebel Sunni jurist": Umarah, p. 54.
"had become weakened": Umarah, p. 60.
the dissemination of fake news: Haeri, p. 99.
"Percievest thou": Umarah, p. 61.
Some accounts: S. M. Stern, "The Succession to the Fatimid Imam Al-Amir, the Claims of the Later Fatimids to the Imamate, and the Rise of Ṭayyibi Ismailism." *Oriens* 4, no. 2 (1951), pp. 198–202. doi.org/10.2307/1579511. Last accessed October 26, 2024.
Others offered theological explanations: Stern, p. 200; Haeri, p. 100.

"That the minoritarian Musta'li-Tayyibi community of the Ismai'lis exists at all today": Farhad Daftary, "Sayidda Hurra: The Isma'ili Sulayhid Queen of Yemen," in Gavin R. G. Hambly, ed., *Women in the Medieval Islamic World* (New York: St. Martin's Press, 1999), p. 127.

"may be attributed largely to Sayyida's foresight": Daftary, p. 128.

"[T]he human body": Quoted in Al Imad, p. 141.

"brought light to a place of darkness": Quoted in Cortese and Simonetta, p. 134.

"the radiant and the pure": Cortese and Simonetta, p. 135.

CHAPTER 3

"a youth of great worth and promise": Minhaj al Din Siraj Juzjani, *Tabaqat-I Nasiri*, Maj. H. G. Raverty, tr., vol 1 (London: Gilbert & Rivington, 1881), p. 633.

"My brother killed his brother": Ibn Battuta, *The Travels of Ibn Battuta, A.D. 1325–1354*, H.A.R. Gibb, tr., vol. III (Cambridge University Press, 1971), p. 631. Hereafter, IB.

"there and then": IB, p. 630.

"held a public audience or rode out": Ibid.

"[S]tirred up to excitement": IB, p. 631.

"by hundreds of thousands": Juzjani, p. 512.

"with bow and arrow": Juzjani, p. 513.

"readily available": K.A. Nizami, "The Early Turkish Sultans of Delhi," in Mohammad Habib and Khaliq Ahmad Nazami, eds., *A Comprehensive History of India*, 12 vols., vol. 5 (Delhi: People's Publishing House, 1970), p. 206.

"endowed with comeliness": Juzjani, p. 599.

"who took note of the handsome youth's bearing": Haeri, p. 108.

"treated him like a son": Jamila Brijbhushan, *Sultan Raziya Her Life and Times: A Reappraisal* (New Delhi: Manohar, 2016), p. 8.

"displayed great valour": Juzjani, pp. 604–605.

"An oath of loyalty": Ibn Battuta, pp. 629–630.

"[H]is inclinations were wholly towards buffoonery": Juzjani, pp. 636–637.

a contemporary history: Most historians—medieval or modern—of the Sultanate of Delhi and Razia's reign rely on Juzjani as a primary source. He knew Razia and her family personally and witnessed, or was at least alive during, many of the events that took place in the Sultanate during the early 13th century and is generally regarded as reliable, taking into account the usual hagiography of medieval chroniclers. For more on Juzjani's credibility see Rafiq Zakaria, *Razia: Queen of India* (Oxford University Press, 1999), p. 132; A.B.M. Habibullah, "Sultanah Raziah," *The Indian Historical Quarterly*, vol. 16 (1940), p. 755; C.E. Bosworth, "Tabaqat-e Naseri," *Encyclopædia Iranica*, online edition, 2010, available at iranicaonline.org/articles/tabaqat-naseri. Last accessed October 10, 2024.

"entirely enslaved by dissipation and debauchery": Juzjani, p. 636.

"impersonators, effeminate men and eunuchs": Haeri, p. 135.

"indications of sovereignty and high spirit": Juzjani, p. 638.

"[I]n her father's lifetime": Mohamed Kasim Ferishta, *History of the Rise of the Mahomedan Power in India Till the Year A.D. 1612*, John Briggs, tr., in 4 vols., vol. 1 (Calcutta: R. Cambray & Co., 1908), p. 218.

"Inasmuch as he has grown-up sons": Juzjani, pp. 638–639.

"his sons [give] themselves up to wine and every other excess": Ferishta, p. 218.

"was better than twenty such sons": Ibid.

"Nomadic tribes lived in harsh environments": Ali, "Sultana Raziya of Delhi: Pillar of Women and Queen of the Eras," Medievalists.net. www.medievalists.net/2018/11/sultana-raziya-delhi/ Last accessed on September 4, 2024.

"[f]rom the 10th century onwards": Habibullah, p. 751.

During the 12th century: Habibulllah, p. 752.

"a daughter succeeding her father": Habibullah, p. 753.

"departure from current political ideas": Habibullah, p. 754.

he had his Secretary of State draw up a decree: Juzjani, p. 638.

He also issued a commemorative coin: Habibullah, p. 754; see also L. P. Sharma, *History of Medieval India (1000–1740 A.D.)*, 3rd ed., (Delhi: Konark Publishers, 1997), p. 44.

Some historians: E.g. Brijbhushan, p. 13; Sharma, p. 44.

"the people had their eyes upon": Juzjani, p. 631.

"apocryphal" addition: Peter Jackson, "Sultan Radiyya Bint Iltutmish," in Hambly, pp. 183–184.

"the people may have had their eyes on [Firuz]": Juzjani, p. 631, n. 9.

Juzjani composed his text more than twenty years after the events: Habibullah, p. 755.

bribing them with rich gifts: Juzjani, p. 631.

On the very night Iltutmish died: Abdul Malik Isami, *Futuh-us-Salatin*, Agha Mahdi Husain, ed., in 3 vols., vol 2, (London: Asia Publishing House, 1977), pp. 246–247.

but to the harem: Isami, p. 247.

"monster of cruelty": Ferishta, p. 247.

"Every morning, he threw open the [state] treasury": Isami, p. 248.

"dancing women, comedians, and musicians": Ferishta, pp. 213–214.

"stripling of unripe judgement": Isami, pp. 248–249.

Here I am, daughter of His Majesty: Isami, pp. 250–251.

"as he does a few paragraphs later": Isami, p. 252.

no Muslim jurist in the court: Sudha Sharma, *The Status of Muslim Women in Medieval India* (Los Angeles: Sage Publications, 2016), p. 178.

A daughter is better than an ill-bred son: Isami, p. 251.

seated Razia on a golden throne: Isami, p. 252.

"all things returned to their usual rules and customs": Henry Miers Elliott & John Dowson, eds., *The History of India, as Told by Its Own Historians*, in 3 vols., vol. 2 (London: Trubner & Co., 1869), p. 333. Elliott and Dowson (hereafter E&D) is another translation of Juzjani's *Tabaqat*.

"Sultan [Razia] was a great monarch": Ibid.

"together with the word* nusrat*" sarmaya.in/objects/numismatics/delhi-sultanate-silver-tanka/. Last accessed October 26, 2024

a reputation for reciting the Qur'an: Haeri, p. 109.

"the duty of every Muslim to seek knowledge": Abu Amina Elias, "Hadith on Learning: Seeking knowledge an obligation on every Muslim," August 30, 2012, Daily Hadith Online, www.abuaminaelias.com/dailyhadithonline/2012/08/30/talab-ilm-wajib-faridah/. Last accessed October 10, 2024.

The schools that she and her father established: Haeri, p. 109; Brijbhushan, p. 65.

"[i]ntellectuals and creative people from many regions of the Muslim world": Abraham Eraly, *The Age of Wrath: A History of the Delhi Sultanate* (New York: Penguin/Viking, 2014), p. 381.

some 300,000 people: Tim Dyson, *A Population History of India From the First Modern People to the Present Day* (Oxford University Press, 2018), pp. 49–50.

whose lavish homes outshone those of their Muslim competitors: Habibullah, *The Foundation of Muslim Rule in India*, 3rd rev. ed. (Allahabad: Central Book Depot, 1976), p. 248.

by Juzjani's day: Haeri, p. 109.

"a vast and magnificent city": IB, p. 618.

"extensive in length and breadth": Quoted in Brijbhushan, p. 62.

composed of stone foundations: IB, p. 621.

"out of which most are for the Hanafites": Quoted in Brijbhushan, p. 62, 69.

a large, terraced reservoir: IB, p. 624.

three gardens, each twelve miles long: Brijbhushan, p. 63.

Stone pavillions with benches: IB, p. 624.

Domed pavillions: IB, p. 622.

twenty-one different varieties of rice: M. S. Asimov and Bosworth, eds., *History of Civilizations of Central Asia, Vol IV, Part One; The historical, social and economic setting* (Paris: UNESCO Publishing, 1998), p. 284.

dozens of varieties of sweets: Ibid.

Shir-i-murgh, the "milk of birds": Quoted in Brijbhushan, p. 70.

[W]ell-known reprobates: Quoted in Brijbhushan, p. 66.

"[h]ere was a co-mingling of nationalities": Brijbhushan, p. 72.

"from the territory of Lakhanawati": Juzjani, p. 641.

"all the Maliks and Amirs": Ibid.

"[m]any of the faithful were slain": E&D, p. 336.

"Everywhere people are my supporters": Isami, quoted in Haeri, p. 122.

"What the multiple narratives": Haeri, p. 111.

"laid aside [her] female dress": Juzjani, p. 643.

sitting with them in the souks: Mernissi, p. 96.

"in the manner of a king": Habibullah, "Sultanah Raziah," p. 765.

"became jovial": Ismai, p. 253.

"a purely Turkish throne": Brijbhushan, p. 12.

"plenty of disorders": Brijbhushan, p. 77.

"A very great degree of familiarity": Ferishta, p. 220.

"was suspected of relations": IB, p. 631.

the record shows: Habibullah, "Sultanah Raziah," p. 766.

"[c]onfidence should not be placed in women": Isami, p. 254.

To wear the crown: Isami, pp. 254–255.

evidence of Razia's innocence: Habibullah, "Sultanah Raziah," p. 772.

"take possession of the kingdom": Juzjani, p. 647.

"Realizing from this": IB, p. 632.

"reign was full of murder, treachery and intrigue": Ishwari Prasad, *A Short History of Muslim Rule in India*, rev. ed., (Allahabad: The Indian Press, 1965), p. 89.

an ideal which is only just being realized: Report, "Religion in India: Tolerance and Segregation," June 29, 2021, Pew Research Center. www.pewresearch.org/religion/2021/06/29/religion-in-india-tolerance-and-segregation/. Last accessed October 10, 2024.

Some have speculated: E.g. Haeri, see p. 130.

CHAPTER 4

"unmatched in beauty among women": Gotz Schregle, *Die Sultanin von Ägypten:Šağarat ad-Durr in der arabischen Geschichtsschreibung und Literatur* (Wiesbaden:Otto Harrassowitz, 1961), p. 44.

the queen's fondness for pearls: Winifred Holmes, *She Was Queen of Egypt* (London: G. Bell & Sons Ltd., 1959), p. 147. Holmes bases her description on contemporaneous images of medieval female singers and courtiers painted on ceramics.

"the Blonde Ones": Karl Heinrich Menges, "The Oriental Elements in the Vocabulary of the Oldest Russian Epos, The Igor' Tale," *Word: The Journal of the Linguistic Circle of New York*, Vol. 7, December 1951, pp 3–4.

"renowned for her beauty": *The Chronography of Bar Hebraeus*, Book X, "Concerning the enthronement of Ghoyuk [Guyuk] Khan in the place of the Khan his brother" Earnest A. Wallis Budge, tr. vol. 1 (London: Oxford Univerity Press, 1932).

"I have witnessed in this country": IB, Vol. 2, (Cambridge, 1962), pp. 480–1.

"All of this is done in full view": Ibn Battuta, quoted in Ross E. Dunn, *The Adventures of Ibn Battuta: A Muslim Traveler of the Fourteenth Century* (University of California Press, 2012), p. 168.

"The sultan . . . loved her so desperately": Al Maqrizi, "Extracts From An Arabian Manuscript," Appendix to de Joinville, *Chronicles of the Crusades: Contemporary Narratives of the Crusade Of Richard Cœur De Lion by Richard Of Devizes and Geoffrey De Vinsauf and of the Crusade of Saint Louis by Lord John De Joinville,* (London: George Bell and Sons, 1888), p. 553.

"the Mamluks became such a dominating and powerful force": Al Sayyad, p. 79.

Their outpost on the river: Al Sayyad, p. 296, n. 3. See also Kenneth M. Setton, ed., *A History of the Crusades*, Vol. 2, (Madison: University of Wisconsin Press, 1969), p. 738.

"the most cunning woman of her age": Schregle, p. 44.

"shameful" retreat: Ibn Wasil, "Saint Louis' Crusade," in Franceso Gabrieli, *Arab Historians of the Crusades*, tr. E. J. Costello (University of California Press, 1984), p. 285.

"at his pillow day and night": Ibn Wasil, p. 287.

"in order that the Franks should not get information:" Schregle, p. 50, citing Ibn Wasil, *Mufarrij al-kurūb*, MS. Bn. 1703 (Paris, Bibliotuèque Nationale), f.75v.

"All three resolved to keep the sultan's death a secret": Al Maqrizi, p. 546.

fought to his death in nothing but a towel: Ibn Wasil, p. 290; al-Maqrizi, p. 548.

"He had no confidence but in a certain number of favourites": Al Maqrizi, p. 552.

"jars full of wine": Syedah Fatima Sadeque, *Baybers I of Egypt* (Oxford University Press, 1956), p. 80. Sadeque's work is a translation of al-Zahir's *Sirat al-Zahir Baibars* (Life of al-Zahir Baibars), an Egyptian folk epic on the life of Baybars, fourth Sultan of Egypt in the Mamluk Bahri dynasty (r.1260–1277).

"So shall I deal with the Bahris!": Robert Irwin, *The Middle East in the Middle Ages*, (Carbondale and Edwardsville: Southern Illinois University Press, 1986), p. 21. Irwin is citing C. Cahen, "Les Mémories de Sa'd al-Din Hamawiya Djuwayni," in *Les Peuples Musulmans dans l'historie médiévale*, (Damascus, 1977), pp. 476–7; also in *Bulletin de la Faculté des Lettres de Strasbourg*, vol. 7 (1950).

"The sultana, in alarm, implored the protection of the Mamlukes": Al Maqrizi, pp. 552–3.

"Thus iron, fire, and water": Ibid.

"The Sultan's decrees were to be issued at her command": Ibn Wasil, pp. 297–8.

"understanding the affairs of the kingdom": Mernissi, p. 98. Mernissi is citing writer Khayr al-Din al-Ziriklī in *al-A'lam*, his monumental biographical dictionary of famous Middle Eastern figures, published in Cairo between 1954 and 1959. Mernissi provides no page citation.

"If you are left with no man fit to rule but this woman": Quoted in Amalia Levanoni, "Shajar al-Durr: A Case of Female Sultanate in Medieval Islam," in *Egypt And Syria in The Fatimid, Ayyubid And Mamluk Eras*, Proceedings of the 6th, 7th and 8th International Colloquium organized at the Katholieke Universiteit Leuven in May 1997, 1998 and 1999 U. Vermeulen and J. Van Steenbergen, eds, (Uitgeverij Peeters Leuven 2001), p. 215.

"She dominated him, and he had nothing to say": Schregle 79. See also R. Stephen Humphreys, *From Saladin to the Mongols: The Ayyubids of Damascus, 1193–1260* (Albany: State University of New York Press, 1997), p. 303.

"the real power": Quoted in Sadeque, p. 35.

"Hall of the Columns": Doris Behrens-Abouseif, *Islamic Architecture in Cairo* (Leiden: E. J. Brill, 1992), p. 81.

"she was the first to introduce the tradition": Behrens-Abouseif, p. 92.

performing acrobatic feats by torchlight: Behrens-Abouseif, pp. 81–2.

pilgrims often painted mahmals on their doorways: Desmond Stewart, *Cairo: 5500 Years* (New York: Thomas Y. Crowell Company, 1968), p. 109; Holmes, p. 173.

"not the queen, but the woman": Stewart, p. 106.

"The co-wife is bitter": Hilma Natalia Granqvist, *Marriage Conditions in a Palestinian Village* (New York: AMS Press, 1975), p. 186.

"he will kill both you and us": Michael Haag, *Guide to Egypt* (London: Travelaid, 1981), p. 117.

A steamier version of the story: Dramatically retold in Amin Maalouf, *The Crusades Through Arab Eyes*, tr. Jon Rothschild (New York: Schoken Books, 1984), pp. 244–5.

"However highly romanticized": Ibid..

it was talked about in Europe: Peter Thorau, *The Lion of Egypt: Sultan Baybars I and the Near East in the Thirteenth Century*, P.M. Holt, tr. (London: Longman, 1992), p. 52.

Aybak's murderers ended up being crucified: Humphreys, p. 330.

The "sweetness" of Umm 'Ali's revenge: Max Rodenbeck, *Cairo: The City Victorious* (New York: Knopf, 1999), p. 59.

"dragged by the feet": Quoted by Rodenbeck, ibid.

the first Egyptian journal to focus on woman's rights: Beth Baron, *The Women's Awakening in Egypt: Culture, Society, and the Press* (Yale University Press, 1994), pp. 22–3.

"the central point between two epochs": Schregle, p. 143.

"how completely women were involved in affairs of state": Susan Jane Staffa, "Dimensions of Women's Power in Historic Cairo," in Robert Olson, ed., *Islamic and Middle Eastern Societies* (Brattleboro, VT: Amana Books, 1987), p. 68.

CHAPTER 5

from the interior: "Medina of Tétouan (formerly known as Titawin)" Unesco World Heritage Convention. http://whc.unesco.org/pg.cfm?cid=31&id_site=837 Last accessed on September 5, 2024.

outside the capital: Nada Mourtada-Sabbah, and Adrian Gully, "'I Am, by God, Fit for High Positions': On the Political Role of Women in al-Andalus," *British Journal of Middle Eastern Studies* 30, no. 2 (2003), p. 199. www.jstor.org/stable/3593222. Last accessed October 10, 2024.

Some sources say her name was Fatima: Hasna Lebbady and اللبادي حسناء, "Women in Northern Morocco: Between the Documentary and the Imaginary / النساء في شمال المغرب: بين التسجيلي والتخييلي." *Alif: Journal of Comparative Poetics*, no. 32 (2012), p. 131. www.jstor.org/stable/41850741. Last accessed October 10, 2024.

how she was identified on her marriage certificate: Ibid.

"eloquent, strong and witty Andalusian-Moroccan": Interview with Hasna Labbady, October 10, 2016.

not entirely unfounded: Khamakar News Agency, "A Morisco Appeal to the Ottoman Sultan," September 7, 2015. altahrir.wordpress.com/2015/09/07/a-morisco-appeal-to-the-ottoman-sultan/; see also Matthew Carr, *Blood and Faith: The Purging of Muslim Spain* (New York: The New Press, 2009), p. 123.

"the saddest sight in the world": Quoted in Carr, p. 160.

"pestilential horde": Quoted in Carr, p. 188

"[T]he Almighty not being pleased to grant victory to their cause": Ahmed Ibn Mohammed Al Makkari, *The History of the Mohammedan Dynasties in Spain*, Pascual de Gayangos, tr., 2 vols., vol. 2 (Delhi: Idarah-I Adabiyat-I, reprint, 1984), p. 392.

by a Rashid cousin, Abdul-Hasan ibn Muhammad: Jamil M. Abun Nasr, *A History of the Maghrib in the Islamic Period* (Cambridge University Press, 1993), p. 208.

"This girl will rise high in rank": Quoted in Chantal de La Verrone, "Sidda El-Horra, La Noble Dame," in *Hesperis*, Annee 1956, Tome XLIII, p. 223.

"For 80 years it remained abandoned": Leo Notes, Expeditions in Morocco, www.leoafricanus.com/expeditions/expedition2_2-2001/Tetouan_Leo.html. Last accessed September 5, 2024; cf. Al Hasan Muhammad al Wazzan, *The History and Description of Africa*, John Pory, tr., Robert Brown, ed., 3 vols., vol. 2 (London: Printed for the Hakluyt Society, 1896), p. 511.

"He was given the authority to restore the city": Ibid.

"is still in many ways an Andalusi city": Lebbady, *Feminist Traditions in Andalusi-Moroccan Oral Narratives* (New York: Palgrave Macmillan, 2009), p. 17.

"She was trusted by her male relatives": Lebaddy interview.

***contemporary Spanish records as* Sida el-Horra:** See for instance, *Les Sources Inedites de Les Histoire du Maroc*, H. De Castries, ed., vol. 1 (Paris: Ernest Leroux, 1921), p. 106.

"reached an unheard of level of prosperity": German Vasquez Chamorro, *Mujeres Piratas* (Madrid: Algaba Ediciones, 2004), p. 132. Chamorro translations by Rachel Sprouse.

women's dresses being particularly sought after: Ibid.

Like the women in al-Andalus: Labaddy, *Feminist Traditions*, p. 21.

"like a lion to the last": Stanley Lane-Poole, *The Barbary Corsairs*, 4th ed. (London: T. Fisher Unwin, 1890), p. 52.

"much booty and the taking a number of prisioners": De Castries, "Lettre D'Abou Hassoun a Francisco Verdigo," n. 1, p. 89. Castries translations by Rachel Sprouse.

"prayed for God to allow them to see her hanged": Chamorro, p. 134.

"a very aggressive and bad-tempered woman": Castries, "A copy from the aforementioned Contreras," p. 107, n. 4.

"Piracy was rampant in the sixteenth century": Lebaddy interview.

"diplomatic game": Mernissi, p. 18.

News of her wedding: Lebaddy, "Women in Northern Morocco," pp. 132–133.

nearing fifty: Hossain Kamaly, *A History of Islam in 21 Women* (London: One World, 2019), p. 90.

"emphasize their competence": David G. Smith, Judith E. Rosenstein, and Margaret C. Nikolov, "The Different Words We Use to Describe Male and Female Leaders," May 25, 2018, Harvard Business Review. hbr.org/2018/05/the-different-words-we-use-to-describe-male-and-female-leaders; see also Anna Presnall, "Political Women: A Double Standard," January 21, 2021, UAB Institute for Human Rights Blog. sites.uab.edu/humanrights/2021/01/21/political-women-a-double-standard/. Last accessed October 10, 2024.

CHAPTER 6

"a most extraordinary event": Richard Davey, *The Sultan and His Subjects*, 2 vols., vol. 1 (London: Chapman and Hall, 1897), p. 25.

"a slave woman from Russia": Ibid.

"cost thousands of pounds": Davey, p. 26.

The ceremony took place: Davey, pp. 25–26.

"[f]rom the very edge of Europe": Leslie Pierce, *Empress of the East: How a European Slave Girl Became Queen of the Ottoman Empire* (New York: Basic Books, 2017), p. 29.

stories circulating at the Ottoman court: Galina Yermolenko, "Roxolana: 'The Greatest Empresse of the East,'" *The Muslim World* 95 (April 2005), p. 234.

The region was also known at times as Red Rus: Ibid.

Writing in his memoirs: Quoted in Mahlia Lone, "Suleyman The Magnificent & Hurrem Sultan," Good Times, August 16, 2017, www.goodtimes.com.pk/2017/08/16/suleyman-the-magnificent-hurrem-sultan-2/. Last accessed October 10, 2024.

estimates run as high as 40,000: Pierce, p. 21.

"amazed at the great numbers of these slaves": Quoted in Lone.

"There a mother is severed from her son and daughter": Quoted in Pierce, p. 23.

A Polish proverb of the day: Ibid.

Modern Lviv and the residents of its surrounding countryside: Laura King, "Lviv was once a safe haven for Ukrainians fleeing the war. Now it's suffering too," Los Angeles Times, November 26, 2022, www.latimes.com/world-nation/story/2022-11-26/ukraine-lviv-refugees-face-hardships-russian-attacks; see also Cassandra Vinograd and Victoria Kim, "Russia Targets Kyiv and Lviv With Attack Drones," The New York Times, June 20, 2023, www.nytimes.com/2023/06/20/world/europe/russia-drones-kyiv-lviv-ukraine-war.html. Last accessed October 10, 2024.

"[t]he current wife of the Turkish sultan": Quoted in Lone.

"young but not beautiful": Quoted in Pierce, *The Imperial Harem: Women and Sovereignty in the Ottoman Empire* (New York: Oxford University Press, 1993), p. 59.

"black hair . . . bow-like eyebrows": Philip Mansel, *Constantinople: City of World's Desire 1453–1924* (New York: St. Martin's Press, 2006), p. 86.

fair-skinned, with light-colored hair: Yermolenko, ed., *Roxolana in European Literature, History and Culture* (Farnham: Ashgate 2010), p. 4.

"stopped to talk with her": Harold Lamb, *Suleiman the Magnificent: Sultan of the East* (Garden City, NY: Doubleday, 1951) p. 80.

"the Magnificent, the Lord of his age": Robert Gossip, *Turkey and Russia: Their Races, History, and Wars*, vol 1 (Edinburgh: Thomas C. Jack, Grange Publishing Works, 1878), p. 91..

"She laughed merrily": Lamb, p. 80.

When the Sultan decides to go to the Serai: Quoted in Antony Bridge, *Suleiman the Magnificent: Scourge of Heaven* (New York: Franklin Watts, 1983), p. 111.

"invested with almost imperial power": Lucy M. J. Garnett, "Famous Sultanas," *The Scottish Review* 34 (July and October 1899), p. 112.

Padishah [Sultan] requires: Ibid.

"no longer paid attention": Pierce, *Harem*, p. 59.

reported a few decades later: Ibid.

"the surest pledge of a legal marriage": Ogier Ghiselin de Busbecq, *The Turkish Letter of Ogier Ghiselin de Busbecq*, Edward Seymour Forster, tr. (Baton Rouge: Louisiana State University, 1927), p. 28

"Having . . . become her own mistress": Busbecq, p. 118.

"she felt secure enough": Pierce, *Harem*, p. 60.

"There has never been in the history of the Ottoman house": Quoted in Mansel, p. 83.

the average daily stipend: For Roxelana's income and that of harem residents see Pierce, *Harem*, pp. 127–130; *Empress*, p. 242; Yermolenko, "Greatest Empresse," p. 241; Godfrey Goodwin, *The Private World of Ottoman Women* (London: Saqi Essentials, 2006), pp.125–126.

"I am begging Allah with the loudest cry": "Historical Letter from Hurrem Sultan to Kanuni Sultan Suleyman," Muhtesem Yuzyil English Translations, muhtesemyuzyilenglish.blogspot.com/2014/06/historical-letter-from-hurrem-sultan.html. Last accessed September 6, 2024.

Throne of my lonely niche: Quoted in Evren Kutlay, "The Sultan Image in Selected Ballets of the Eighteenth and Early Nineteenth Century (1772–1836)," in Michael Hüttler & Hans Ernst Weidinger, eds., *Ottoman Empire and European Theatre vol 5: Gluck and the Turkish Subject in Ballet and Dance* (Vienna: Hollitzer, 2019), p. 236, n. 25,

Suleiman would also send Roxelana presents: Christopher de Bellaigue, *The Lion House: The Coming of a King* (New York: Farrar, Straus and Giroux, 2022) p. 114.

"His Majesty the Sultan loves her [Roxelana] so much": Quoted in Lone.

The Greek youth was charming: Yermolenko, *Roxolana in European Literature*, p. 9.

"You asked why I am angry": Quoted in Pierce, *Harem*, p. 64.

"was much hated": Quoted in Pierce, *Harem*, p. 74.

"a matter of conjecture": Yermolenko, *Roxolana in European Literature*, pp. 9–10.

"prayer halls, baths, gardens and other comforts": Quoted in Gulru Necipoglu, *Architecture, Ceremonial, and Power:The Topkapi Palace in the Fifteenth and Sixteenth Centuries* (Cambridge, MA: MIT Press, 1991), p. 163.

"a small walled garden": Quoted in Barnette Miller, *Beyond the Sublime Porte: The Grand Seraglio of Stanbul* (Yale University Press, 1931), p. 94.

"[S]end news quickly": Quoted in Pierce, *Harem*, p. 64.

"Thus with the pasha's key": Yermolenko, "Empresse," p. 241.

"envy of all the princes": Quoted in Pierce, *Harem*, p. 81.

"The young Sultan is born to the saddle": Lamb, p. 244.

"[T]he entire court hate[s] her": Quoted in Miller, p. 87.

"great potency in love affairs": Busbecq, p. 49.

"gossip fed to Europeans": Goodwin, p. 123.

"tend to overlook the fact": Yermolenko, "Empresse," p. 236.

By the end of the sixteenth century: Pierce, *Harem*, p. 119.

"new role as a principal division": Ibid.

"from a state geared to expansion": Pierce, *Harem*, p. *x*.

Her stipend of three thousand aspers per day: Pierce, *Harem*, p. 126.

"Knowing the lofty place Your Highness holds": Quoted in Pierce, *Harem*, p. 227.

"her majesty's [Elizabeth's] picture": Quoted in Jerry Brotton, *This Orient Isle: Elizabethan England and the Islamic World* (London: Allen Lane, 2016), p. 189.

"a suit of princely attire": Quoted in Brotton, pp. 189–190.

"a robe, a sash, two large gold-embroidered bath towels": Quoted in Pierce, *Harem*, p. 228.

"I [Safiye] will take action": Ibid.

The intimate correspondence: Ibid.

"communication among female royalty": Pierce, *Empress*, p. 297.

"a new type of a Ukrainian woman": Yermolenko, "Empresse," p. 241.

In 2019, at the request of the Ukrainian embassy: "Reference to Roxelana's Russian origin removed from label near her tomb in Istanbul at Ukraine's request," *Interfax-Ukraine*, January 26, 2019, en.interfax.com.ua/news/general/561610.html. Last accessed October 10, 2024.

CHAPTER 7

"Pari," a cognate for the English word "fairy": Kamaly, pp. 94–95.

believed to depict Pari in her mid-twenties: Abolala Soudavar, "The Age of Muhammadi," *Muqarnas* 17 (2000), p. 60 doi.org/10.2307/1523290. Last accessed October 10, 2024.

exceptionally skilled miniaturists: Zainah Mahmood, "Mongol Illustrated Manuscripts: The Jami al 'Tawarikh and the Shahnama," Asia Society, asiasociety.org/mongol-illustrated-manuscripts. Last accessed on September 7, 2024.

"the active role of females": Kathryn Babayan, "The 'Aqaid al Nisa': A Glimpse at Safavid Women in Local Isfahani Culture," in Hambly, p. 351.

females served in the military: Joshua J. Mark, "Women in Ancient Persia," World History Encyclopedia, January 30, 2020, www.worldhistory.org/article/1492/women-in-ancient-persia/. Last accessed October 10, 2024.

Such councils were recognized as influential seats of power: Maria Szuppe, "Status, Knowledge, and Politics: Women in Sixteenth-Century Safavid Iran," in Guity Nashat and Lois Beck, eds., *Women in Iran from the Rise of Islam* (Urbana: University of Illinois Press, 2003), p. 153.

"synthesis between Turko-Mongol nomadic steppe-traditions": Babayan, p. 351.

rode in hunting parties and military expeditions alongside men: Szuppe, p. 161.

"a trait that both men and women could possess": Marc David Baer, *The Ottomans: Khans, Caesars and Caliphs* (London: Basic Books, 2021), p. 124.

Lady Chichek: See Geoffrey Lewis, tr., *The Book of Dede Korkut* (London: Peguin Books, 1974), pp. 10–11; 64–66.

"forty slender-waisted": Lewis, p. 43.

scattering the enemy: Lewis, p. 106.

"from one end to the other": Lewis, p. 129.

"do not sit passively in their tents": Lewis, "Heroines and Others in the Heroic Age of the Turks," in Hambly, p. 149.

"Father, a girl": Lewis, *Book Of Dede Korkut*, p. 65.

"easy in the saddle": Anthony Sattin, *Nomads: The Wanderers Who Shaped Our World* (New York: W. W. Norton, 2022), p. 72.

"go on horseback, hunting with their men": Herodotus, *The History of Herodotus*, David Grene, tr. (University of Chicago Press, 1987), p. 322.

the excavated graves: Adrienne Mayor, *The Amazons: Lives and Legends of Warrior Women across the Ancient World* (Princeton University Press, 2014), p. 11; see also Jeannine Davis-Kimball and Mona Behan, *Warrior Women: An Archaeologist's Search for History's Hidden Heroines* (New York: Grand Central Publishing, 2003), p. 54.

"herself with many guests and other ladies": Gonzalez de Clavijo, *Embassy to Tamerlane, 1403–1406*, Guy Le Strange, tr. (London: George Routledge & Sons, 1928), p. 245.

"These ladies . . . keep all their husband's money": Michele Membre, *Mission to the Lord Sophy of Persia (1539–1542)*, A.H. Morton, tr. (London: SOAS, 1993), p. 31.

"ladies ride through town like men": Ibid.

"very beautiful": Ibid.

"The women are short in proportion to the men": Quoted in Szuppe, p. 143.

equal amounts of booty and inheritances: Szuppe, p. 141.

Curriculae for both princes and princesses: Szuppe, p. 149.

introduced to Iran between 600 BCE and 100 CE: "History of Polo," Museum of Polo and Hall of Fame, www.polomuseum.org/sport-polo/history-polo. Last accessed October 10, 2024.

"more intelligent than the other royal princesses": Eskander Beg Monshi [Munshi], *History of Shah Abbas the Great*, in 2 vols., vol. 1, Roger M. Savoy, tr. (Boulder, CO: Westview Press, 1978), p. 198.

"number of poets who flourished": Monshi, p. 274.

"under the pen name of Haqiqi (Truth)": Nazak Birjandifar, "Royal Women and Politics in Safavid Iran," Master's Thesis, Institute of Islamic Studies McGill University, December 2005, p. 35. escholarship.mcgill.ca/concern/theses/6682x4295. Last accessed October 10, 2024.

she composed her own poems and corresponded: Birjandifar, pp. 35; 52.

endowed public buildings: Kishwar Rizvi, "Gendered Patronage: Women and Benevolence During the Early Safavid Empire," in *Women, Patronage, and Self-Representation in Islamic Societies*, D. Fairchild Ruggles, ed. (Albany: State University of New York Press, 2000), p. 129.

acted as one of her husband's most trusted counselors: Szuppe, p. 145.

"learned and wise woman" Birjandifar, p. 45.

at her brother's side on hunting expeditions: Begam Gulbadam, *The History of Humayun*, Annette S. Beveridge, tr. (London: Royal Asiatic Society, 1902), pp. 169–170.

"[A]ll the financial and administrative . . . affairs of the state": Quoted in Birjandifar, p. 45.

letters with Roxelana: Birjandifar, p. 43; see also Szuppe, p. 154.

"trivial or major": Quoted in Shohreh Gholsorkhi, "Pari Khan Khanum: A Masterful Safavid Princess," *Iranian Studies* 28, no. 3/4 (1995), p. 147, www.jstor.org/stable/4310940. Last accessed October 10, 2024.

"without her knowledge and consent": Quoted in Birjandifar, p. 51.

"who had difficult problems": Monshi, p. 218.

refused to let her journey there: Some sources say she did join her husband in Sistan but returned to Qazvin shortly thereafter to assist her father. See Nozhat Ahmadi, "The Status of Women in Safavid Iran," in Rudi Matthee, ed., *The Safavid World* (London: Routledge, 2022), p, 315.

"the envy of her peers": Monshi, p. 198.

"had no love in her heart": Ibid.

for Safavid royals: Gholsorkhi, "Ismail II and Mirza Makhdum Sharifi: An Interlude in Safavid History," *International Journal of Middle East Studies* 26, no. 3 (1994), p. 478, www.jstor.org/stable/163700. Last accessed October 10, 2024.

"of robust frame and daring spirit": Vincentio D'Alessandri, "Narrative of the Most Notable Vincentio D'Alessandri," in Charles Grey, tr. and ed., *A Narrative of Italian Travels in Persia, in the Fifteenth and Sixteenth Centuries* (London, Printed for the Hakluyt Society, 1873), p. 214, archive.org/search?query=external-identifier%3A%22urn%3Aoclc%3Arecord%3A263034296%22. Last accessed October 25, 2024.

"that this young man had ambitious views": Ibid.

"beloved by his father": D'Alessandri, p. 215.

opium: Monshi, p. 326.

a pedophile: Kioumars Ghereghlou, "ESMAIL II," *Encyclopædia Iranica*, online edition, 2016 www.iranicaonline.org/articles/esmail-02. Last accessed on September 7, 2024.

"displayed ingratitude": Monshi, p. 214.

in particular a plot: Monshi, p. 199.

"the Shah should die": Monshi, p. 198.

"with the arrogance of youth": Monshi, p. 215.

the slippery connivance of his mother: Kamaly, p. 98.

"in the late Shah's own handwriting": Monshi, p. 284.

"spoke warmly": Ibid.

"made himself the prisoner of his opponents": Monshi, p. 283.

"with an air of helplessness and perturbation": Ibid.

"Women are foolish creatures": Ibid.

"out of desperation or trust": Gholsorkhi, "Pari Khan Khanum," p. 150.

"even dearer": Monshi, p. 284.

possibly by Pari herself: Birjandifar, p. 63.

"battle axes, swords, and daggers": Monshi, pp. 288–289.

"riffraff and unruly elements": Monshi, p. 291.

"bazaar was reopened": Ibid.

"it was Pari Khan Kanom who gave the orders": Ibid.

"pressing administrative and financial problems": Monshi, p. 292.

"Not one of them": Ibid.

Pari Khan Kanom's servants and stewards: Monshi, p. 298.

"Have you not understood": Ibid.

"was a hard-hearted man": Monshi, p. 309.

"[i]f you treat me lovingly and justly": Monshi, p. 298.

"in his heart he planned": Ibid.

"with the result that he saw enemies everywhere": David Blow, *Shah Abbas: The Ruthless King Who Became an Iranian Legend* (London: I.B. Tauris, 2009), p. 21.

also had put to death all the chief governors: *A Chronicle Of The Carmelites In Persia and the Papal Mission of the XVIIth and XVIIIth Centuries*, vol. 1 (London: Eyre & Spottiswodde, 1939); p. 57, archive.org/details/in.ernet.dli.2015.173539/page/n11/mode/2up?q=A+Chronicle+Of+The+Carmelites+In+Persia+vol+I.

"a reign of terror in which nobody felt safe.": Quoted in Gholsorkhi, "Pari Khan Khanum," p. 151.

survived the purge: It is believed that Ismail—in a rare display of mercy—spared Khundabanda and his children because the otherwise ruthless shah and his elder brother shared the same mother, who doted on her grandchildren. "[T]his," according to Munshi, "induced some slight feeling of shame in the Shah and made him hesitate to take action against them. Nevertheless, he pondered their fate night and day." See Monshi, p. 312.

her assets and properties: Said to be between 10,000 to 15,000 tomans, approximately $2.4 and $3.25 million in today's dollars. See Szuppe, p. 152.

"slander of our cuckoldry": Quoted in Birjandifar, p. 102.

Another issue: Quoted in Birjandifar, p. 103.

I have studied the books of jurisprudence: Quoted in Birjandifar, p. 104.

"Truly, it is not possible to rule through murder": Ibid.

"conspired with the maidservants": Monshi, p. 327.

"shrewd and prudent": etc., *Chronicle Of The Carmelites*, p. 57.

"she should be the real ruler": Monshi, p. 328.

"upon her own shoulders": Monshi, p. 333.

"emirs obeyed her orders": Ibid.

"hell for leather to Shiraz": Monshi, p. 334.

Looking to his own interests: Ibid.

"[W]ell cultivated": Szuppe, p. 158.

[Mizra Salman] made it clear: Monshi, pp. 334–335.

"jealousy [Mahde] bore [Pari]": *Chronicle of the Carmelites*, p. 59.

"was tossed to and fro": Monshi, p. 337.

"no affair was conducted without her advice": Quoted in Szuppe, p. 159.

"known for her severe criticism of amirs": Szuppe, p. 159.

"Your Majesty well knows": Monshi, p. 370.

"a pious, ascetic, and gentle soul": Ibid.

"being of an aggressive temperament": Ibid.

"declared that she had no intention": Monshi, p. 371.

"idea of a woman openly active on the political scene": Szuppe, p. 161.

a double standard: See Emily T. Amanatullah, Catherine H. Tinsley, "Punishing female negotiators for asserting too much . . .or not enough: Exploring why advocacy moderates backlash against assertive female negotiators," *Organizational Behavior and Human Decision Processes*, 120, no. 1 (January 2013), pp. 110–122, www.sciencedirect.com/science/article/abs/pii/S0749597812000416. Last accessed October 10, 2024.

Later historians: Gholsorkhi, "Pari Khan Khanum," p. 156.

"[i]t seems clear": Ahmadi, p. 317.

CHAPTER 8

both male and female: David E. Jones, *Women Warriors: A History*, (Washington: Brassey's, 1997), p. 84.

"Amina conquered all the towns": H.R. Palmer, tr., "The Kano Chronicle," *The Journal of the Royal Anthropological Institute of Great Britain and Ireland*, 38 (1908), p. 75.

a luxury trade good: Paul E. Lovejoy, "Kola in the History of West Africa (La Kola Dans l'histoire de l'Afrique Occidentale)," *Cahiers d'Études Africaines* 20, no. 77/78 (1980), pp. 115–116 www.jstor.org/stable/4391682. Last accessed October 10, 2024.

prized as an alternative to coffee: Ibid., p. 98.

no monarch had before: Marilyn French, *From Dawn to Eve: A History of Women, Volume 2: The Masculine Mystique*, (City University of New York, 2008), p. 172.

"[T]he most extensive among the kingdoms of Hausa": Muhammad Bello, "On the Land of Hausa, Its Regions and Those Who Reside There," *Infaq'l-Maysuur*, Muhammad Shareef bin Farid, tr. (Sennar: Institute of Islamic-African Studies International, 2008), siiasi.org/digital-archive/sultan-muhammad-bello/infaql-maysuur/. Last accessed October 10, 2024.

"to the sea in the south and the west": Quoted in French, p. 173. The "sea" was likely the confluence of the Niger and Benue Rivers; see LaRay Denzer, "Amina," in Emmanuel Kwaku Akyeampong, Henry Louis Gates, Jr., eds., *Dictionary of African Biography*, vol. 1 (Oxford University Press, 2012), p. 219.

Hausa legend: Samuel Aja Brown Onwuka, "Evolution of Maga'ajiya n Military Barracks Of Nigeria," pp. 1–2, online resource, www.academia.edu/50818515/ARTICLE_WRITTEN_BY_SAMUEL_AJA_BROWN_ONWUKA_EVOLUTION_OF_MAGAAJIYA_IN_MILITARY_BARRACKS_OF_NIGERIA. Last accessed October 10, 2024.

before the ninth century CE: Saad Abubakr, "Queen Amina of Zaria," in Bolanle Awe, ed., *Nigerian Women: A Historical Perspective* (Sankore: Bookcraft Ltd., 2001), p.14.

a "Black Moses": Joyce A. Ladner, "Racism and Tradition: Black Womanhood in Historical Perspective," in Berenice A. Carroll, ed., *Liberating Women's History: Theoretical and Critical Essays* (Urbana: University of Illinois Press, 1976), p. 182. Ladner cites Marie Perinbaum in a lecture given at Spelman College in Atlanta, Georgia, in 1969, for her description of the Magajiyya legend.

According to Hausa legend: Jones, p. 84; see also French, p. 171; Catherine Coquery-Vidrovitch, *African Women: A Modern History*, Beth Gillian Raps, tr., (Boulder: Westview Press, 1997), p. 42.

"in olden times": S.J. Hogben and A.H.M. Kirk-Greene, *The Emirates of Northern Nigeria: A Preliminary Survey of their Historical Traditions* (London: Oxford University Press, 1966), p. 147.

Studies have shown: Niara Sudarkasa, "The 'Status of Women' in Indigenous African Societies," in Andrea Cornwall, ed., *Readings in Gender in Africa* (Bloomington: Indiana University Press, 2005), p. 142.

If men proved to be ineffective or incompetant: Tsitsi Mhike Musingafi, "The Matriarchs of Africa," in Maxwell Constantine Chando Musingafi, Chipo Hungwe, eds., *Women Empowerment and the Feminist Agenda in Africa* (IGI Global, 2023) p. 66.

Beyond the halls of the palace: Sudarkasa, p. 95.

"active in business": Coquery-Vidrovitch, p. 38.

"the female stranger": Hogben, p. 216.

"Around the time of her ascension": Ibid.

The mythology of the Magajiyya: Hogben, pp. 145–146; see also, Dierk Lange, *Ancient Kingdoms of West Africa: African-centred and Canaanite-Israelite Perspectives* (Germany: J.H. Röll, Dettelbach, 2004). pp. 287–296; Abba Gana Wakil Mahamadou, "Bayajidda Hausa Historical Legend or Myth," CSAN, January 10, 2020, www.csan-niger.com/bayajidda-hausa-historical-legend-myth-or-reality.php#Abba_Gana_Wakil_Mahamadou. Last accessed October 10, 2024.

sister or another female relative: W. K. R. Hallam, "The Bayajida Legend in Hausa Folklore," *The Journal of African History* 7, no. 1 (1966), p. 4, n 6, www.jstor.org/stable/179458. Last accessed October 10, 2024. See also Lange, p. 290, n. 302.

"marched southwards into the desert": Hallam, p. 50.

"seems possible": Ibid.

"Abu Yazid's defeated army": Ibid.

a symbol of Bornu's economic and political dominance: Lange, p. 286.

the defeat of Sarki: Hallam, p. 58.

The marriage of Bayajidda and Daura: Malcom J. Lamb, "THE HAUSA TANNERS OF NORTHERN NIGERIA And The Production Of Sokoto Tanned Goatskins," web.archive.org/web/20061021231513/http://www.harmatan.co.uk/news/articles.php.

"[s]ome part of this kingdome is plaine": al Wazzan, vol. 3, p. 831.

From the late fifteenth century: Detlef Gronenborn, "Polities and Trade in Medieval Northern Nigeria," in Kathleen Bickford Berzock, ed., *Caravans of Gold. Fragments in Time: Art, Culture, and Exchange Across Medieval Saharan Africa* (Evanston, IL: Northwestern University, 2019), p. 169.

"resulting for individuals in sets of beliefs and practices": Abdullahi Smith, "Some notes on the history of Zazzau under the Hausa kings," in M.J. Mortimore, ed., *Zaria and its Region: A Nigerian Savanna City and its Environs* (Zaria:Ahmadu Bello University Department of Geography Occasional Publication no. 4, 1970), p. 95.

grown fabulously wealthy: Musingafi, p. 66.

the influence of Arab/Muslim culture: Warda Abbas, "The Importance of Documenting Muslim Women in History and Now: Honouring the Leadership Legacy of Queen Amina of Zaria," Amaliah, April 20, 2021, www.amaliah.com/post/60307/muslim-women-in-islam-and-history-honouring-leadership-legacy-queen-amina-zaria. Last accessed October 10, 2024.

On one occasion: Ibid.

swordsmanship and horseback riding: Fongot Kini-Yen Kinni, *Pan-Africanism: Political Philosophy and Socio-Economic Anthropology for African Liberation and Governance: Caribbean and African American Contributions* (Langaa RPCIG, 2015), p. 736.

Among her mentors: Abubakr, p. 18; see also Abbas.

heir apparent: Abubakr, p. 18.

eldest daughter: Denzer, p. 219.

***Zazzau's* Makaman:** Hogben, p. 217.

what is today the Emir of Zaria's palace: Hogben, p. 216.

young women of the palace sang: Abubakr, p. 18.

stories were told: Abubakr, p. 20.

warrior who was never happier: Hogben, p. 217.

from the fifteenth century on: Basil Davidson, *West Africa Before the Colonial Era: A History to 1850* (London: Routledge, 1998), p. 7; cf. Ira Lapidus, *A History of Islamic Societies*, 2nd ed., (Cambridge University Press, 2002), p. 408.

"was always among the first to arrive": Denzer, p. 219.

"was a foregone conclusion": Abubakr, p. 20.

Lingering Hausa animist beliefs: "Mail armour from Nigeria, Africa," Arms and Armour, Pitt Rivers Museum, University of Oxford, web.prm.ox.ac.uk/weapons/index.php/tour-by-region/oceania/africa/arms-and-armour-africa-8/index.html. Last accessed October 10, 2024.

the first to encircle Zaria with a city wall: Davidson, p. 110.

Archaeologists who have studied the ruins: Denzer, p. 219.

an enduring, complimentary saying in Hausa culture: Abubakr, p. 24.

from Ghana: Elena Lourie, "Black Women Warriors in The Muslim Army Besieging Valencia and The Cid's Victory: A Problem of Interpretation." *Traditio* 55 (2000), p. 199, www.jstor.org/stable/27831993. Last accessed October 10, 2024.

"a wonder to behold": Quoted in Lourie, p. 183.

"always takes with him into the field": Mansel Longworth Dames, tr., *The Book of Duarte Barbosa* (London: Printed for the Hakluyt Society, 1918), p. 12.

"those most renowned for their bravery": Duarte Lopez, *A Report of the Kingdom of Congo: And of the Surrounding Countries*, Margarite Hutchinson, tr., (London: John Murray, 1881), pp.118-119.

luxury items found in the burial sites: Gronenborn, pp. 167–168; see also Gronenborn, "States and Trade in the Central Sahal," in Peter Mitchell, Paul Lane, eds., *The Oxford Handbook of African Archaeology* (Oxford University Press, 2013), pp. 852–853.

chain mail sulke (shirts) and armor: Mail armour.

cowerie shell cap: Gronenborn, "Polities and Trade," pp. 167–168. Also discovered in the royal Katsina tombs.

"She waged war in the Hausa lands": Quoted in Hogben, p. 217.

Historians question: Smith, pp. 86–86.

well into the eighteenth century: Smith, p. 86.

"to the kingdoms of Yirwu": Shareef bin Farid. The kingdoms named here are all to the south and south east of Zaria.

the primary source of slaves: Micheal Crowder, *The Story of Nigeria*, 3rd ed. (London: Faber and Faber, 1973), p. 45.

"marked the beginning of the process": Abubakr, p. 23.

increased industrialization and commerce: Paul E. Lovejoy, "The Role of the Wangara in the Economic Transformation of the Central Sudan in the Fifteenth and Sixteenth Centuries," *The Journal of African History* 19, no. 2 (1978), p. 186, www.jstor.org/stable/181597. Last accessed October 10, 2024.

introduced into Hausaland's economy: Palmer, p. 75.

never spent more than three months: Abubakr, p. 23.

"never relied solely on information": Abubakr, pp. 25–26.

"the overriding authority of Zazzau": Smith, p. 87.

"she would never be subject to any man": Abubakr, p. 26.

she took a different lover in every town: Hogben, p. 218.

"in a place called Ataagar": Shareef bin Farid.

a source of brass rings and cowrie shells: Chinyere S. Ecoma, Lequome E. Ecoma, "History of Trading Currencies in the Upper Cross River Region of Nigeria Before the Nineteenth Century," *Canadian Social Science* Vol. 9, No. 5, (2013), pp. 192–197 www.researchgate.net/publication/356666552_History_of_Trading_Currencies_in_the_Upper_Cross_River_Region_of_Nigeria_before_the_Nineteenth_Century. Last accessed October 10, 2024.

"one of the last bastions": Kinni, p. 736.

"unparalled . . . historically strong, social rights and status": Shirin Edwin, "Connecting Vocabularies: A Grammar of Histories, Politics, and Priorities in African and Islamic Feminisms," in *Privately Empowered: Expressing Feminism in Islam in Northern Nigerian Fiction* (Northwestern University Press, 2016), pp. 68–69, www.jstor.org/stable/j.ctt22727xh.7. Last accessed October 10, 2024.

European explorers and traders: Lapidus, p. 204.

CHAPTER 9

around a thousand pounds of pressure: Dana Hucklebridge, *No Beast So Fierce: The Terrifying True Story of the Champawat Tiger, the Deadliest Animal in History* (New York: HarperCollins Publishers Limited, 2019), p. 17.

the district's bountiful fields: F.S. Growse, *Mathura: A District Memoir*, 3rd ed., (North-Western Provinces and Oudh Government Press, 1883), p. 71.

Snatching their targets in the open: Hucklebridge, p. 45.

shimmering, embroidered tents: "Mughal Shahi Lal Dera Tent," TRC (Textile Research Center) Leiden, trc-leiden.nl/trc-needles/com-k2/individual-textiles-and-textile-types/furnishings/tent-of-shah-jahan. Last accessed October 10, 2024. See also Beenish Tahir, Muhammad Asghar, and Sumera Jawad, "From Babar to Aurangzib: A Historical Review of Mughal's Textile Tent Tradition," *International Review of Social Sciences*, Volume 9, Issue 1, (January 2021): p. 81.

the Emperor and his royal huntsmen: Samyukta Ninan, "Mughal Emperors and the Imperial Hunt," Peepul Tree Stories, May 27, 2021, peepultree.world/livehistoryindia/story/people/mughal-hunt. Last accessed October 10, 2024.

From the age of twelve: Wheeler M. Thackston, ed. and tr., *The Jahangirnama: memoirs of Jahangir, emperor of India* (New York: Oxford University Press, 1999), p. 216.

"to give up hunting": Thackston, p. 276.

The gesture was a sacrificial one: Thackston, p. 281; see also Ellison B. Findly, "Jahāngīr's Vow of Non-Violence," *Journal of the American Oriental Society*, Vol. 107, No. 2 (Apr–Jun, 1987), p. 247.

his estimated nineteen wives: Ruby Lal, *Empress: The Astonishing Reign of Nur Jahan* (New York: W.W. Norton, 2018), p. 100.

Trained from an early age: Findly, *Nur Jahan: Empress of Mughal India* (New York: Oxford University Press, 1993), p. 116.

"set out with the ladies": Thackston, pp. 219, 313.

"two of them with one shot each": Thackston, p. 219.

"such marksmenship": Ibid.

"An elephant is not at ease": Alexander Rogers, tr. and Henry Beveridge, ed., *Tuzuk-i Jahangari or Memoirs of Jahangir*, 2 vols., vol 2 (London: Royal Asiatic Society, 1968), p. 105, catalog.hathitrust.org/Record/012155312. Last accessed October 10, 2024. An earlier translation of *The Jahangirnama.*

"so well on the first shot": Thackston, p. 313.

Though Nur Jahan be in the form of a woman: Rogers and Beveridge, vol. 1, p. 375, n. 1.

an empire that at its height: J. C. Sharman, *Empires of the Weak: The Real Story of European Expansion and the Creation of the New World Order* (Princeton University Press, 2020), p. 3.

"effects would not be felt": Dowson, *The History of India as Told by its Own Historians*, vol. 5, (Frankfurt: Anatiposi, 2023), p. 407.

"great troubles arose in Persia": Ibid.

By the time Ghiyas and his family left Herat: Lal, p. 18.

"Followers of various religions": Thackston, p. 40.

Babur sought peace: Kamaly, p. 108.

ordered a minaret to be constructed: Lal, p. 12.

a story with which Indians: Lal, p. 26.

"He [Ghiyas] brought with him his wife": Niccolao Manucci, *Storia do Mogor or Mogul India 1653–1708*, William Irvine, tr., vol. 1 (London: John Murray, 1907), 164, books.google.com/books?id=1VEtAAAAMAAJ&source=gbs_navlinks_s.

the earliest to include: Findly, *Nur Jahan*, p. 9.

When they had advanced: Alexander Dow, *The History of Hindostan*, 3 vols. (London: John Murray, 1792), vol. 3, p. 23, archive.org/details/in.ernet.dli.2015.116935/page/n3/mode/2up

"later fame and renown": Mohammad Shujauddin & Razia Shujauddin, *The Life and Times of Noor Jahan*, (Lahore: The Caravan Book House, 1967), p. 3.

"said to have been known to Akbar": Abul Fazl Allami, *The Ain-i Akbari*, H. Blochmann, tr., vol.1 (Calcutta: The Asiatic Society of Bengal, 1873), 509. Quoted Findly, p. 10.

"both in writing and in transacting business": E&D, *The History of India, as Told by Its Own Historians*, vol. 6 (London: Trübner and Co., 1875), p. 404, books.google.com/books?id=WNUNAAAAIAAJ&newbks=1&newbks_redir=0&printsec=frontcover&source=gbs_ge_summary_r&cad=0#v=onepage&q&f=false. Herafter E&D (1875). Mutamad Khan was a contemporary biographer of Jahangir.

"with the utmost care and attention": B.S. Dahiya, ed., *The history of Hindustan : originally translated from Persian by Alexander Dow 1770–72 A.D*, 2nd ed., vol. 3 (Delhi: Motilal Banarsidass, 2003), p. 12. This is a modernized translation of Dow.

Her history lessons: Lal, p. 56.

"Her disposition was volatile": Dahiya, p. 12.

"a very large city": Joannes de Laet, *The Empire of the Great Mogol*, J.S. Hoyland, tr., 2nd ed., (New Delhi: Oriental Books Reprint Corporation, 1974), p. 11.

"mere village": de Laet, pp. 37–38.

"a remarkable beauty": Findly, *Nur Jahan*, p. 36.

"all the ladies of the East": Dahiya, p. 12.

"a tall, attractive woman": Shujauddin, p. 132.

contemporary images: Findly, *Nur Jahan*, pp. 36–37.

In Mughal society: Shadab Bano and Shadaba Bano, "Age of Marriage in Pre-Colonial India," *Proceedings of the Indian History Congress* 64 (2003), p. 597, www.jstor.org/stable/44145494. Last accessed October 10, 2024.

"promoted to a rank befitting his station": Thackston, p. 79.

While eldest sons were often preferred: Lisa Balabanlilar, *The Emperor Jahangir: Power and Kingship in Mughal India* (London: I.B. Tauris, 2020), p. 182.

At the age of eighteen: Thackston, p. 184.

I started drinking wine: Thackston, p. 185.

"loved grandchildren more than sons": Quoted in Munis D. Faruqui, *The Princes of the Mughal Empire, 1504–1719* (Cambridge University Press, 2012), p. 31.

"from drunkenness and bad companionship": Quoted in Balabanlilar, p. 29.

"evil-minded persons": Ibid.

kept a watchful eye: Lal, pp. 79–80.

"After my accesion": Thackston, p. 79.

"If I offend": Quoted in Balabanlilar, p. 53.

"it was not proper": Thackston, p. 79.

"chopped him to pieces": Ibid.

It was Mughal tradition: Findly, *Nur Jahan*, p. 32.

when Haidar Malik Chadurah: Chandra Pant, *Nur Jahan and Her Family*, (Allahabad: Dan Dewal, 1978), p. 45.

"did not spare any moment": Lal, p. 92.

"a certain dervish": de Laet, p. 180. de Laet included Van den Broeke's *Fragment of Indian History* in his own *De Imperio Magni Moguls (Empire of the Great Mogol)* published in Antwerp in 1631. Van den Broeke, in turn, drew much of his material for the *Fragment* from the *Remonstrantie* (Report) of Francisco Pelsaert, a Dutch East India spice merchant who was based in Agra from 1618 to 1625. Multilingual, Pelsaert gathered his material from local sources and by studying the history of the country.

"always came to pass": Pieter Van den Broeke, *A Contemporary Dutch Chronicle of Mughal India*, Brij Narin and Sri Ram Sharma, trs. and eds., (Calcutta: Susil Gupta, 1957), p. 41.

"that the king": de Laet, p. 180.

"conceived a great affection for [Mihr]": Van den Broeke, p. 41.

"an immense staff": Lal, p. 97.

writing poetry: Lal, pp. 97–98.

***boldly drew back her* chaddar:** Van den Broeke, p. 41.

"he was in raptures": Dahiya, p. 13.

"he could hardly be restrained": Ibid.

Her stature, her shape, her gait: Ibid.

"fell so violently in love with her": Manucci, p. 161.

"nor would she would hear a word": Ibid.

"that as soon as Sher Afghan should arrive": Ibid.

"unsupported by contemporary testimony": K.S. Lal, *The Mughal Harem* (New Delhi: Aditya Prakashan, 1988), p. 71.

"[H]er appearance": E&D (1875), pp. 404–405.

"Day by day her influence": E&D (1875), p. 405.

"all her connexions": Ibid.

"[t]here was nothing new in this": K.S. Lal, p. 80.

"was primarily a family affair": Ibid.

as historians have labeled it: E.g. Renuka Nath, *Notable Mughal and Hindu Women* (New Delhi: Inter-India, 1990), p. 73; see also Findly, (*Nur Jahan*), who devotes an entire chapter to the political shift, pp 43–61.

"is King in name only": Francisco Pelsaert *Jahangir's India: The Remonstrantie of Francisco Pelsaert*, W.H. Moreland and P. Geyl, eds., (Cambridge: W. Heffer & Sons, 1925), p. 50.

"If anyone with a request": Pelsaert, pp. 50–51.

"sat at the* jharoká*": E&D (1875), p. 398.

Prior to this: Kamaly, p. 112.

"a profound and public affirmation": Balabanlilar, p. 66.

"In short, by degrees": E&D (1875), p. 398.

"Sorceries practis'd by her": Edward Gray, ed., *The Travels of Pietro Della Valle in India*, vol.1 (London: Hakluyt Society, 1892), p. 54.

"prejudice against Nur Juhan": Satish Chandra, *Medieval India: From Sultanat to the Mughals Part Two Mughal Empire (1526–1748)*, rev. ed. (2006; reprint ed., New Delhi: Har-anand, 1999), p. 245.

"were relatively free": Gregory C. Kozlowski, "Private Lives and Public Piety: Women and the Practice of Islam in Mughal India," in Hambly, p. 470.

"authors readily acknowledged": Ibid.

"vulgar report[s]": Sir Richard Carnac Temple, ed., *The Travels of Peter Mundy, in Europe and Asia, 1608–1667*, vol. 2, Travels in Asia 1628–1634 (London: Hakluyt Society, 1914), p. 206, catalog.hathitrust.org/Record/002811172. Last accessed October 10, 2024.

"a woman of great judgement": Manucci, p. 162.

"wholly gouerneth": William Foster, ed. *The Embassy of Sir Thomas Roe to the Court of the Great Mogul, 1615–1619, As Narrated in His Journal and Correspondence*, 2 vols., vol 1 (London: hakluyt Society, 1899), p. 111.

added opium: Foster, ed. *Early Travels in India, 1583–1619* (Oxford University Press, 1921), p. 116.

"used to say": E&D (1875), p. 399.

"a bottle of wine": Ibid.

"skill and experience": Rogers and Beveridge, 2, pp. 213–214.

"It is impossible to describe": E&D (1875), p. 405.

"grain, butter, and other provisions": Pelsaert, p. 4.

"In Asia, the great are never approached": Francois Bernier, *Travels in the Mogul Empire, A.D. 1656–1668*, Archibald Constable, ed., 2nd ed., (Oxford: Humphrey Milford, 1916), p. 200.

not "to be surprised at this": Pelsaert, p. 58.

"bears in every part": Wolsey Haig, plan., and Richard Burn, ed., *The Cambridge History of India*, vol. 4, *The Mughal Period* (Cambridge, 1937), p. 552.

"very expensive buildings": Pelsaert, p. 50.

"innumerable lamps": Bernier, p. 413.

recounted Khafi Khan: Quoted in Findly, *Nur Jahan*, p. 110.

considered the most sophisticated: Findly, *Nur Jahan*, p. 231.

may have come to India: Findly, *Nur Jahan*, pp. 231–232; see also Nath, p. 100.

Architectural historians believe: Ibid.

"of one mind": Findly, *Nur Jahan*, p. 241.

"down to the details": Kamaly, p. 115.

"She was an asylum for all sufferers": E&D (1875), p. 399.

the queen "herself pulled it out": E&D (1875), p. 427.

"spend lavishly on the needy and the poor": Shujauddin, p. 124.

CHAPTER 10

Many of the extravagant sultan's personal items: Sher Banu A.L. Khan, *Sovereign Women in a Muslim Kingdom: The Sultanahs of Aceh, 1641–1699* (Ithaca: Southeast Asia Program Publications, Columbia University Press, 2017), p. 68.

"no more than pebbles": Quoted in Khan, p. 79.

"Doubtless mortified": Khan, pp. 87–88.

"western gate of the Indonesian Archipelago": Drs. Rusdi Sufi, "Laksamana Keumalahayati", in *Wanita utama Nusantara Dalam Lintasan Sejarah = Prominent Women in the Glimpse of History*, Ismail Sofyan, M. Hasan Basry, T. Ibrahim Alfian, eds., (Jakarta: Jayakarta Agung Offset, printer), p. 28.

later geographers: Kamaly, p. 125.

"commercial emporium": Anthony Reid, "Trade and the Problem of Royal Power in Aceh c. 1550–1700," in Anthony Reid and Lance Castles, eds., *Pre-Colonial State Systems in Southeast Asia* (Kuala Lumpur: MBRAS, 1979), p. 46.

"first truly global commodity": Roger Crowley, *Spice: The 16th Century Contest That Shaped the Modern World* (New Haven: Yale University Press, 2024), p. 3.

"the still greater potential richness": C. R. Boxer, "A Note on Portuguese Reactions to the Revival of the Red Sea Spice Trade and the Rise of Atjeh, 1540–1600," *Journal of Southeast Asian History* 10, no. 3 (1969), p. 424, www.jstor.org/stable/27651719. Last accessed October 10, 2024.

"great quantities of gold": Ibid.

In Roman times: John O'Connell, *The Book of Spice: From Anise to Zedoary* (New York: Pegasus Books, 2016), p. 47.

When spice merchants formed a guild: Ibid., p. 46.

"rents, taxes and dowries": Ibid., p. 45.

"an essential element": John Villiers, "Aceh, Melaka and the 'Hystoria Dos Cercos de Malaca' of Jorge de Lemos," *Portuguese Studies* 17 (2001), p. 76, www.jstor.org/stable/41105160. Last accessed October 10, 2024.

"prosperous and powerful": Leonard Y. Andya, *Leaves of the Same Tree: Trade and Ethnicity in the Straits of Melaka* (Honolulu: University of Hawai'i Press, 2008), p. 70.

"entrepot of choice": Ibid.

"most of the Malay Peninsula": Ibid.

booming economy: Amirul Hadi, *Islam and State in Sumatra: A Study of Seventeenth-Century Aceh* (Leiden: Brill, 2004), p. 33.

"nullifying or reversing": Kamaly, p. 127.

"large stately Houses": Augustine de Beaulieu, "The Expedition of Commodore Beaulieu to the East Indies," in *Navigantium atque Itenerarium Bibliotecha. Or a Complete Collection of Voyages*, trans. M. Thevenot, ed. John Harris, in two vols., vol 1 (London: printed for T. Osborne, et. al., 1774), p. 746.

with sundry sorts off exquisite torments: Temple, *The Travels of Peter Mundy in Europe and Asia, 1608–1667*, five volumes, vol. 3, part 2 (London: The Hakluyt Society, 1907), p. 330.

"his short reign": Khan, p. 58.

"for each one": Quoted in Hadi, p. 72.

The arguments led to bloodshed: Khan, "Men of Prowess and Women of Piety: A Case Study of Aceh Dar al-Salam in the Seventeenth Century," *Journal of Southeast Asian Studies* 44, no. 2 (2013), p. 224, www.jstor.org/stable/43863025. Last accessed October 10, 2024.

"was not unusual": Hadi, p. 79.

"Chiefest Counsellers": A.H. Markham, ed., *The Voyages and Works of John Davis the Navigator* (London: The Hakluyt Society, 1880), p. 150.

including the head: Sufi, p. 31.

"for hee will trust no men": Markham, p. 150.

composed of 3000 women: de Beaulieu, p. 744.

on Foote with bowes and arrowes: Temple, p. 131.

"the diamond-exporting centre": Reid, "Female Roles in Pre-Colonial Southeast Asia," *Modern Asian Studies*, 1988, Vol. 22, No. 3, Special Issue, Asian Studies in Honour of Professor Charles Boxer (1988), p. 640, www.jstor.org/stable/312601. Last accessed October 10, 2024.

"conducted trade and diplomatic ties": Cheah Boon Kheng, "Power Behind the Throne: The Role of Queens and Court Ladies in Malay History," *Journal of the Malaysian Branch of the Royal Asiatic Society* 66, no. 1 (264) (1993), p. 8, www.jstor.org/stable/41486187. Last accessed October 10, 2024.

"accidents of succession": Reid, "Female Roles," p. 640.

"understand market forces": Reid, "Female Roles," pp. 641–642.

"as the widow": Khan, "Men of Prowess," 225.

"an ethical guide for rulers": Rosalind Noor, "Tāj al-salāṭīn: An Instruction Manual for Kings," Medium, December 5, 2021, rosalindnoor.medium.com/t%C4%81j-al-sal%C4%81%E1%B9%AD%C4%ABn-an-instruction-manual-for-kings-670a299cd431. Last accessed October 10, 2024.

"during turbulent times": Quoted in Hadi, p. 81.

"our Lord's orders": Quoted in Hadi, p. 159.

"equality between men and women": Hadi, p. 85.

***the position of* hakim:** Ibid.

"make the state safe": Reid, "Female Roles," p. 641.

"religious enemies": Kamaly, p. 128.

"accursed" Dutch: Khan, *Sovereign Women*, p. 155.

"drawn into a brawl": Ibid.

some historians: E.g. J. Kathirithamby-Wells, "Achehnese Control over West Sumatra up to the Treaty of Painan, 1663," *Journal of Southeast Asian History*, Dec., 1969, Vol. 10, No. 3, International Trade and Politics in Southeast Asia 1500–1800 (Dec., 1969), pp. 435–479.

Expanded trade concessions: Kathirithamby-Wells, p. 466.

"How could I accept a condition": Quoted in Khan, *Sovereign Women*, p. 147.

"the very name of a Kinge": Thomas Bowery, *A Geographical Account of Countries Round the Bay of Bengal, 1669 to 1679*, R.C. Temple, ed., (Cambridge: Printed for the Hakluyt Society, 1905), p. 296. Bowery was an English merchant and mariner who traveled in the East from 1669 to 1688.

"[s]hold cause noe act": Bowery, p. 299.

"male-dominated political factions": Khan, *Sovereign Women*, 235.

"the orangkaya found they could govern": Reid, "Female Roles," p. 641.

"a more decentralized system": Hadi, p. 103.

"was extremely prosperous": Quoted in Reid, "Female Roles," p. 641.

"she was fair in all matters": Quoted in Sufi, "Sultanah Safiatuddin Shah," in *Wanita utama Nusantara*, p. 54.

"gold mines were discovered": Sufi, "Sultanah Safiatuddin Shah," p. 53.

[T]he royal elephants: William Marsden, *The History of Sumatra*, 3rd edition (London: Printed for the Author, 1811), p. 402, https://books.google.com/books?id=Yx5MAAAAcAAJ&newbks=1&newbks_redir=0&printsec=frontcover&source=gbs_ge_summary_r&cad=0#v=onepage&q&f=false.

"a female ruler": Hadi, p. 108.

"a curtain of gauze": Marsden, p. 402.

she expanded the production of pepper: Andaya, p. 144.

"immense cultural significance": Sake Sentema, "History and Importance of Rice in Indonesia." NOW! Jakarta. March 11, 2024. www.nowjakarta.co.id/history-and-importance-of-rice-in-indonesia/. Last accessed October 10, 2024.

"by many Indonesians": Justus M. van der Kroef, "Rice Legends of Indonesia," *The Journal of American Folklore* 65, no. 255 (1952), p. 49, doi.org/10.2307/536286. Last accessed October 10, 2024.

"God says since antiquity": Quoted in Khan, "Men of Prowess," p. 216.

"she feared Allah": Quoted in Sufi, "Sultanah Safiatuddin Shah,", p. 45.

"a very gracious": Quoted in Khan, "Men of Prowess," p. 220.

"became the most productive center": Andaya, p. 125.

first translated into Malay: Mohamad Hussin and Muhammad Hakim Kamal, "Translation of al-Quran into the Malay Language in the Malay World," IJISH (International Journal of Islamic Studies and Humanities), 4, no. 1 (April 2021), p. 33, media.neliti.com/media/publications/411642-translation-of-al-quran-into-malay-langu-3956e390.pdf. Last accessed October 10, 2024.

whose syntax and poetic genres: Andaya, p. 125.

"the major center of transmission": Ibid.

"after reigning, with a degree of tranquility": Marsden, p. 449.

"her death was not accompanied": Khan, *Sovereign Women*, 248.

"The people being now accustomed": Marsden, p. 449.

"became somewhat of a template": Khan, "Men of Prowess," p. 225.

"political and commercial autonomy": Khan, *Sovereign Women*, p. 268.

"ensured that customs duties": Ibid.

"wasteful and dangerous wars": Ibid.

"male by default": Khan, *Sovereign Women*, p. 259.

Epilogue

restricted women's rights: As reported by Amnesty International, Human Rights Watch, and others. Since the early 2000s, the Kingdom has enacted reforms to its policies on women in society. But local activists and rights groups say there is much left to be done.
See, www.hrw.org/news/2021/02/25/saudi-arabia-proposed-reforms-neglect-basic-rights; www.amnesty.org/en/latest/press-release/2019/08/saudi-arabia-womens-rights-reforms-must-be-followed-by-release-of-detained-activists/. Last accessed October 10, 2024.

"to justify discrimination": Tamara Kharroub, "Five things you need to know about women in Islam: Implications for advancing women's rights in the Middle East." Arab Center Washington DC. October 4, 2015. arabcenterdc.org/resource/five-things-you-need-to-know-about-women-in-islam-implications-for-advancing-womens-rights-in-the-middle-east/#:~:text=While%20family%20law%20and%20personal,of%20the%20Qur'an%20dispute.

issued a ban: "The Taliban publish vice laws that ban women's voices and bare faces in public," Associated Press, August 23, 2024, apnews.com/article/afghanistan-taliban-vice-virtue-laws-women-9626c24d8d5450d52d36356ebff20c83?user_email=220804442f1d34cccc937ccd96b4df69065f79a3a2468b3fea27543d079f48fc&utm_medium=Morning_Wire&utm_source=Sailthru_AP&utm_campaign=Morning%20Wire_26/August/2024&utm_term=Morning%20Wire%20Subscribers. Last accessed October 10, 2024. One women's-rights activist in Kabul told a Western journalist that Afghanistan "has turned into a graveyard for women's dreams." Rick Noack, "Taliban begins enforcing new draconian laws, and Afghan women despair," Washington Post, September 15, 2024, www.washingtonpost.com/world/2024/09/15/taliban-afghanistan-laws-women-rights/.

"the rights of women and girls": United Nations Economic and Social Council. "Removal of the Islamic Republic of Iran from membership in the Commission on the Status of Women for the remainder of its 2022–2026 term." United States of America: draft resolution. 2023 session. 25 July 2022–26 July 2023. Agenda item 19 (a) Social and human rights questions: advancement of women. documents.un.org/doc/undoc/ltd/n22/710/64/pdf/n2271064.pdf?OpenElement&_gl=1*1cg6vn4*_ga*MzU4MTQ4OTU3LjE3MjQ4NTI1MzM.*_ga_S5EKZKSB78*MTcyNDg1MjUzMi4xLjEuMTcyNDg1MjU4OS4zLjAuMA..*_ga_TK9BQL5X7Z*MTcyNDg1MjUzMi4xLjEuMTcyNDg1MjU4OS4wLjAuMA. Last accessed October 10, 2024.

Married Women's Property Act: www.legislation.gov.uk/ukpga/Vict/45-46/75. Last accessed October 10, 2024.

"enjoyed property rights": Bishin, Benjamin G., and Feryal M. Cherif, "Women, Property Rights, and Islam." *Comparative Politics* 49, no. 4 (2017), p. 501. www.jstor.org/stable/26330985. Last accessed October 10, 2024.

"feminism much before it gained prominence": Priya Mirza, "The remarkable Begums who defied patriarchal norms to rule Bhopal for more than a century," PRISM, June 3, 2019, www.dawn.com/news/1486294/the-remarkable-begums-who-defied-patriarchal-norms-to-rule-bhopal-for-more-than-a-century. Last accessed October 10, 2024.

"women have continued": Egypt's Dar al-Ifta, "Women as Heads of State," www.dar-alifta.org/en/article/details/142/women-as-heads-of-state. Last accessed October 10, 2024.

"a majority of all Muslims": Noor Mohammad Osmani, Mohmmad Omar Farooq, and Abu Umar Faruq Ahmad, "Women Empowerment and Leadership in Islam between Myth and Reality," in Toseef Azid and Jennifer Ward-Batts, (eds.), *Economic Empowerment of Women in the Islamic World: Theory and Practice* (London: World Scientific, 2020), p. 62.

"[c]onversion was aimed": Deborah Gaitskill, "Devout Domesticity? A Century of African Women's Christianity in South Africa," in Andrea Cornwall, ed., *Readings in Gender in Africa* (Bloomington: Indiana University Press, 2005), p. 179.

"appropriate gender roles": Barbara Bush, "Gender and Empire: The Twentieth Century," in *Gender and Empire*, Philippa Levine, ed. (Oxford University Press, 2004), p. 85.

"patrimonial colonial domination": Anne M. Price, "Colonial History, Muslim Presence, and Gender Equity Ideology: A Cross-National Analysis." *International Journal of Sociology* 38, no. 1 (2008), p. 83, www.jstor.org/stable/20628320. Last accessed October 10, 2024.

especially the U.S.: Jasmine Mithani, "Why the 2022 election was historic for Muslim women's representation," December 12, 2022, The 19th. 19thnews.org/2022/12/muslim-women-made-history-midterm-elections/. Last accessed October 10, 2024.

are becoming increasingly accepted: Asma Manzoor et. al., "Economic and Political Leadership Role of Muslim Women In Global Context," *Journal of Positive School Psychology*, 2023, Vol. 7, No. 6, p. 1224.

as their numbers continue to grow: Rabi'ah Aminudin, "The Evolution of Muslim Women's Political Participation," September 24, 2023, IslamiCity. www.islamicity.org/88970/the-evolution-of-muslim-womens-political-participation. Last accessed October 10, 2024.

"It is clear that women's engagement": Manzoor et. al., p. 1217.

Bibliography

Primary Sources

Ahmed Ibn Mohammed Al Makkari, *The History of the Mohammedan Dynasties in Spain*. Translated by Pascual de Gayangos. 2 Vols., Vol. 2. Delhi: Idarah-I Adabiyat-I, reprint, 1984.

Al Hasan Muhammad al Wazzan. *The History and Description of Africa*. Translated by John Pory. Robert Brown, ed., 3 Vols., Vol. 2. London: Printed for the Hakluyt Society, 1896.

Al Maqrizi. "Extracts From An Arabian Manuscript." Appendix to John de Joinville, *Chronicles of the Crusades: Contemporary Narratives of the Crusade Of Richard Cœur De Lion by Richard Of Devizes and Geoffrey De Vinsauf and of the Crusade of Saint Louis by Lord John De Joinville*. London: George Bell and Sons, 1888.

Al Masudi, *Meadows of Gold and Mines of Gems*. Translated by Tarif Khalidi. vol. 1. Online edition: www.khalidilibrary.org//public/files/server/1615293155.pdf. Last accessed October 10, 2024.

Al Muqaddasi. *The Best Divisions For Knowledge Of The Region*. Translated by Basil Collins. Calcutta: Asiatic Society of Bengal, 1897.

Al Tabari. *The History of al-Tabari*. Translated by C.E. Bosworth. The Abbasid Caliphate in Equilibrium, Volume XXX of XXXVIII volumes. Albany: State University of New York, 1989.

--- *The History of al-Tabari*. Translated by Hugh Kennedy. Al Mansur and Al Mahdi, Volume XXIX. Albany: State University of New York, 1990.

Al Zubayr. *Book of Gifts and Rarities*. Translated by Ghada al-Hijjawi al-Qaddumi. Harvard University Press, 1996.

Bar Hebraeus. *The Chronography of Bar Hebraeus*, Book X, "Concerning the enthronement of Ghoyuk [Guyuk] Khan in the place of the Khan his brother." Translated by Earnest A. Wallis Budge. vol. 1. London: Oxford Univerity Press, 1932. rbedrosian.com/BH/bh60.htm Last accessed on September 5, 2024.

Begam Gulbadam. *The History of Humayun*. Translated by Annette S. Beveridge. London: Royal Asiatic Society, 1902.

Bello, Muhammad. "On the Land of Hausa, Its Regions and Those Who Reside There." *Infaq'l-Maysuur*. Translated by Muhammad Shareef bin Farid. Sennar: Institute of Islamic-African Studies International, 2008. siiasi.org/digital-archive/sultan-muhammad-bello/infaql-maysuur/. Last accessed October 10, 2024.

Bernier, Francois. *Travels in the Mogul Empire, A.D. 1656–1668*. Edited by Archibald Constable. 2nd ed. Oxford: Humphrey Milford, 1916.

Bowery, Thomas. *A Geographical Account of Countries Round the Bay of Bengal, 1669 to 1679*, edited by R.C. Temple. Cambridge: Printed for the Hakluyt Society, 1905.

A Chronicle Of The Carmelites In Persia and the Papal Mission of the XVIIth and XVIIIth Centuries. Vol. 1. London: Eyre & Spottiswodde, 1939.

Dahiya, B.S. ed. *The history of Hindustan : originally translated from Persian by Alexander Dow 1770–72 A.D.* 2nd ed., vol. 3. Delhi: Motilal Banarsidass, 2003.

D'Alessandri, Vincentio. "Narrative of the Most Notable Vincentio D'Alessandri." In *A Narrative of Italian Travels in Persia, in the Fifteenth and Sixteenth Centuries.* Translated and edited by Charles Grey, 209–229. London, Printed for the Hakluyt Society, 1873. archive.org/search?query=external-identifier%3A%22urn%3Aoclc%3Arecord%3A263034296%22. Last accessed October 26, 2024.

Dames, Mansel Longworth tr. *The Book of Duarte Barbosa.* London: Printed for the Hakluyt Society, 1918.

Davis, William Stearns. *Readings in Ancient History: Illustrative Extracts from the Sources, Volume II: Rome and the West.* Boston: Allyn and Bacon, 1913.

Davey, Richard. *The Sultan and His Subjects* 2 vols., vol. 1. London: Chapman and Hall, 1897.

de Beaulieu, Augustine. "The Expedition of Commodore Beaulieu to the East Indies." In *Navigantium atque Itenerarium Bibliotecha. Or a Complete Collection of Voyages.* M. Thevenot, tr., John Harris, ed. in two vols., vol 1, 717-749. London: printed for T. Osborne, et. al. 1774.

de Busbecq, Ogier Ghiselin. *The Turkish Letters of Ogier Ghiselin de Busbecq.* Translated by Edward Seymour Forster. Baton Rouge: Louisiana State University, 1927.

De Castries, H., ed. *Les Sources Inedites de Les Histoire du Maroc.* vol. 1. Paris: Ernest Leroux, 1921.

de Clavijo, Gonzalez. *Embassy to Tamerlane, 1403–1406.* Translated by Guy Le Strange. London: George Routledge & Sons, 1928.

de Laet, Joannes. *The Empire of the Great Mogol*, J.S. Hoyland, tr., 2nd ed., New Delhi: Oriental Books Reprint Corporation, 1974

Dow, Alexander. *The History of Hindostan*, 3 vols. vol 3. London: John Murray, 1792.

Dowson, John tr. *The History of India as Told by its Own Historians.* Vol. 5. Reprint of original 1873 edition. Frankfurt: Anatiposi, 2023.

Elliott, Miers & Dowson, John editors. *The History of India, as Told by Its Own Historians.* 3 vols., vol. 2. London: Trubner & Co., 1869.

--- *The History of India, as Told by Its Own Historians.* vol. 6. London: Trübner and Co., 1875.

Foster, William ed. *The Embassy of Sir Thomas Roe to the Court of the Great Mogul, 1615–1619, As Narrated in His Journal and Correspondence.* 2 Vols., Vol 1. London: Hakluyt Society, 1899.

--- *Early Travels in India, 1583–1619.* Oxford University Press, 1921.

Gray, Edward ed. *The Travels of Pietro Della Valle in India.* Vol.1. London: Hakluyt Society, 1892.

Ibn Khallikan. *Ibn Khallikan's Biographical Dictionary.* Translated by Baron MacGuckin de Slane. 4 Vols, v. 1. Paris: Printed for the Oriental Translation Fund of Great Britain and Ireland, 1843.

Ibn Battuta, *The Travels of Ibn Battuta, A.D. 1325–1354.* Translated by H.A.R. Gibb. Vol. III. Cambridge University Press, 1971.

Ibn Wasil, "Saint Louis' Crusade." In *Arab Historians of the Crusades.* Selected and translated from the Arabic sources by Franceso Gabrieli. Translated from the Italian by E. J. Costello. University of California Press, 1984.

Bibliography

Idris Imad al Din's *Uyun al akhbar*. In *The Fatimids and their Successors in Yaman: The History of an Islamic Community* edited by Ayman Fuad Sayyid, Paul E. Walker, and Maurice A. Pomerantz. London: I.B. Tauris, 2003.

Abdul Malik Isami, *Futuh-us-Salatin*. Edited by Agha Mahdi Husain. 3 Vols., Vol 2. London: Asia Publishing House, 1977.

Herodotus. *The History of Herodotus*. Translated by David Grene. University of Chicago Press, 1987.

Lassner, Jacob. *The Topography of Baghdad in the Early Middle Ages: Text and Studies*. Detroit: Wayne State University Press, 1979.

Le Strange, Guy. *Baghdad During the Abbasid Caliphate from Contemporary Arabic and Persian Sources*. Elibron Classics, reprint of 1900 edition by Clarendon Press, Oxford.

Lewis, Geoffrey, tr. *The Book Of Dede Korkut*. London: Penguin Books, 1974.

Lopez, Duarte. *A Report of the Kingdom of Congo: And of the Surrounding Countries*. Translated by Margarite Hutchinson. London: John Murray, 1881.

Markham, A.H. ed. *The Voyages and Works of John Davis the Navigator*. London: The Hakluyt Society, 1880.

Marsden, William. *The History of Sumatra*. 3rd edition. London: Printed for the Author, 1811.

Manucci, Niccolao. *Storia do Mogor or Mogul India 1653–1708*. Translated by William Irvine. Vol. 1. London: John Murray, 1907.

Membre, Michele. *Mission to the Lord Sophy of Persia (1539–1542)*. Translated by A. H. Morton. London: SOAS, 1993.

Minhaj al Din Siraj Juzjani. *Tabaqat-I Nasiri*. Translated by Maj. H. G. Raverty. Vol 1. London: Gilbert & Rivington, 1881.

Mohamed Kasim Ferishta. *History of the Rise of the Mahomedan Power in India Till the Year A.D. 1612*. Translated by John Briggs. 4 Vols., Vol. 1. Calcutta: R. Cambray & Co., 1908.

Eskander Beg Monshi [Munshi], *History of Shah Abbas the Great*. Translated by Roger M. Savoy. 2 vols., vol. 1. Boulder, CO: Westview Press, 1978.

Palmer, H.R., tr. "The Kano Chronicle." *The Journal of the Royal Anthropological Institute of Great Britain and Ireland*, 38, (1908): 58–98.

Pelsaert, Francisco. *Jahangir's India: The Remonstrantie of Francisco Pelsaert* edited by W.H. Moreland and P. Geyl. Cambridge: W. Heffer & Sons, 1925.

Rogers, Alexander, tr. and Beveridge, Henry, ed. *Tuzuk-i Jahangari or Memoirs of Jahangir*. 2 vols., vol 2. London: Royal Asiatic Society, 1968.

Sadeque, Syedah Fatima. *Baybers I of Egypt*. Oxford University Press, 1956.

Snir, Reuvin. Translator and editor. *Baghdad: The City in Verse*. Harvard University Press, 2013.

Temple, Sir Richard Carnac ed. *The Travels of Peter Mundy, in Europe and Asia, 1608–1667*. Vol. 2, Travels in Asia 1628–1634. London: Hakluyt Society, 1914.

Thackston, Wheeler M. ed. and tr. *The Jahangirnama: memoirs of Jahangir, emperor of India*. New York: Oxford University Press, 1999.

Umarah ibn Ali al Hakami, *Yaman: Its Early Medieval History*. Translated by Henry Cassels Kay. London: Edward Arnold, 1892.

Van den Broeke, Pieter. *A Contemporary Dutch Chronicle of Mughal India*. Translated and edited by Brij Narin and Sri Ram Sharma. Calcutta: Susil Gupta, 1957.

Yuzyil, Muhtesem. "Historical Letter from Hurrem Sultan to Kanuni Sultan Suleyman." Muhtesem Yuzyil English Translations. muhtesemyuzyilenglish.blogspot.com/2014/06/historical-letter-from-hurrem-sultan.html. Last accessed September 6, 2024.

Secondary Sources

Abbas, Warda. "The Importance of Documenting Muslim Women in History and Now: Honouring the Leadership Legacy of Queen Amina of Zaria." Amaliah, April 20, 2021. www.amaliah.com/post/60307/muslim-women-in-islam-and-history-honouring-leadership-legacy-queen-amina-zaria. Last accessed October 10, 2024.

Abbott, Nabia. *Two Queens of Baghdad: Mother and Wife of Harun al Rashid*. University of Chicago Press, 1946.

Ahmadi, Nozhat. "The Status of Women in Safavid Iran." In *The Safavid World,* edited by Rudi Matthee, 310–324. London: Routledge, 2022.

Abubakr, Saad. "Queen Amina of Zaria." In *Nigerian Women: A Historical Perspective* edited by Bolanle Awe, 12–26. Sankore: Bookcraft Ltd., 2001.

Al-Hamdani, Husain F. "The Life and Times of Queen Saiyidah Arwa the Sulaihid of the Yemen." *Journal of The Royal Central Asian Society* 18, no. 4 (1931): 505–17. doi:10.1080/03068373108725173.

Ali, Adam. "Slave, Queen, and Mother of Caliphs: The Story of Khayzuran," Medievalists.net. www.medievalists.net/2019/04/slave-queen-and-mother-of-caliphs-the-story-of-khayzuran/. Last accessed October 10, 2024.

--- "Sultana Raziya of Delhi: Pillar of Women and Queen of the Eras," Medievalists.net. www.medievalists.net/2018/11/sultana-raziya-delhi/ Last accessed on September 4, 2024.

Al Imad, Leila. "Women and Religion in the Fatimid Caliphate: The Case of al-Sayyidah al-Hurrah, Queen of Yemem." In *Intellectual Studies in Islam: Essays Written in Honor of Martin B. Dickson,* edited by Micel M. Mazzaoui and Vera B. Moreen, 137–144. Salt Lake City: University of Utah Press, 1990.

Al Sayyad, Nezar. *Cairo: Histories of a City*. Cambridge: Belknap Press, 2011.

Amanatullah, Emily T. and Tinsley, Catherine H. "Punishing female negotiators for asserting too much...or not enough: Exploring why advocacy moderates backlash against assertive female negotiators." *Organizational Behavior and Human Decision Processes* 120, no. 1 (January 2013): 110–122. www.sciencedirect.com/science/article/abs/pii/S0749597812000416. Last accessed October 10, 2024.

Aminudin, Rabi'ah. "The Evolution of Muslim Women's Political Participation," September 24, 2023, IslamiCity. www.islamicity.org/88970/the-evolution-of-muslim-womens-political-participation. Last accessed October 10, 2024.

Andya, Leonard Y. *Leaves of the Same Tree: Trade and Ethnicity in the Straits of Melaka*. Honolulu: University of Hawai'i Press, 2008.

Asimov, M. S. and Bosworth, C. E., eds. *History of Civilizations of Central Asia, Vol IV, Part One; The historical, social and economic setting*. Paris: UNESCO Publishing, 1998.

Babayan, Kathryn. "The 'Aqaid al Nisa': A Glimpse at Safavid Women in Local Isfahani Culture." In *Women in the Medieval Islamic World* edited by Gavin R. G. Hambly, 349–381. New York: St. Martin's Press, 1999.

Baer, Marc David. *The Ottomans: Khans, Caesars and Caliphs*. London: Basic Books, 2021.

Balabanlilar, Lisa. *The Emperor Jahangir: Power and Kingship in Mughal India*. London: I.B. Tauris, 2020.

Bibliography

Bano, Shadab, and Shadaba Bano. "AGE OF MARRIAGE IN PRE-COLONIAL INDIA." *Proceedings of the Indian History Congress* 64 (2003): 596–602. www.jstor.org/stable/44145494. Last accessed October 10, 2024.

Baron, Beth. *The Women's Awakening in Egypt: Culture, Society, and the Press*. Yale University Press, 1994.

Behrens-Abouseif, Doris. *Islamic Architecture in Cairo*. Leiden: E. J. Brill, 1992.

Birjandifar, Nazak. "Royal Women and Politics in Safavid Iran." Master's Thesis, Institute of Islamic Studies McGill University, December 2005. escholarship.mcgill.ca/concern/theses/6682x4295. escholarship.mcgill.ca/concern/theses/6682x4295. Last accessed October 10, 2024.

Bishin, Benjamin G., and Feryal M. Cherif. "Women, Property Rights, and Islam." *Comparative Politics* 49, no. 4 (2017): 501–19. www.jstor.org/stable/26330985. Last accessed October 25, 2024.

Blow, David. *Shah Abbas: The Ruthless King Who Became an Iranian Legend*. London: I.B. Tauris, 2009.

Bobrick, Benson. *The Caliph's Splendor: Islam and the West in the Golden Age of Baghdad*. New York: Simon and Schuster, 2012.

Bosworth, C.E. "Tabaqat-e Naseri." In *Encyclopædia Iranica*, online edition, 2010, available at iranicaonline.org/articles/tabaqat-naseri. Last accessed October 10, 2024.

Boxer, C. R. "A Note on Portuguese Reactions to the Revival of the Red Sea Spice Trade and the Rise of Atjeh, 1540–1600." *Journal of Southeast Asian History* 10, no. 3 (1969): 415–28. www.jstor.org/stable/27651719.

Bridge, Antony. *Suleiman the Magnificent: Scourge of Heaven*. New York: Franklin Watts, 1983.

Brijbhushan, Jamila. *Sultan Raziya Her Life and Times: A Reappraisal*. New Delhi: Manohar, 2016.

Brotton, Jerry. *This Orient Isle: Elizabethan England and the Islamic World*. London: Allen Lane, 2016.

Bush, Barbara. "Gender and Empire: The Twentieth Century." In *Gender and Empire* edited by Philippa Levine, 77–111. Oxford University Press, 2004.

Carr, Matthew. *Blood and Faith: The Purging of Muslim Spain*. New York: The New Press, 2009.

Chamorro, German Vasquez. *Mujeres Piratas*. Madrid: Algaba Ediciones, 2004.

Chandra, Satish. *Medieval India: From Sultanat to the Mughals Part Two Mughal Empire (1526–1748)*. Rev. ed. (2006) New Delhi: Har-anand, 1999.

Clot, André. *Harun al-Rashid and the World of the One Thousand and One Nights*. Translated by John Howe. London: Saqi Books, 2005.

Coquery-Vidrovitch, Catherine. *African Women: A Modern History*. Translated by Beth Gillian Raps. Boulder: Westview Press, 1997.

Cortese, Della and Calderini, Simonetta. *Women and the Fatimids in the World of Islam*. Edinburgh University Press, 2006.

Crowder, Micheal. *The Story of Nigeria*. 3rd ed. London: Faber and Faber, 1973.

Crowley, Roger. *Spice: The 16th Century Contest That Shaped the Modern World*. New Haven: Yale University Press, 2024.

Daftary, Farhad. "Sayidda Hurra: The Isma'ili Sulayhid Queen of Yemen." In *Women in the Medieval Islamic World* edited by Gavin R. G. Hambly, 117–130. New York: St. Martin's Press, 1999.

Davidson, Basil. *West Africa Before the Colonial Era: A History to 1850*. London: Routledge, 1998.

Davis-Kimball, Jeannine and Behan, Mona. *Warrior Women: An Archaeologist's Search for History's Hidden Heroines*. New York: Grand Central Publishing, 2003.

de Bellaigue, Christopher. *The Lion House: The Coming of a King*. New York: Farrar, Straus and Giroux, 2022.

Denzer, LaRay. "Amina." In *Dictionary of African Biography*. Edited by Emmanuel Kwaku Akyeampong and Henry Louis Gates Jr. Vol. 1, 219–220. Oxford University Press, 2012.

Dunn, Ross E. *The Adventures of Ibn Battuta: A Muslim Traveler of the Fourteenth Century*. University of California Press, 2012.

Dyson, Tim. *A Population History of India From the First Modern People to the Present Day*. Oxford University Press, 2018.

Ecoma, Chinyere S. and Ecoma, Lequome E. "History of Trading Currencies in the Upper Cross River Region of Nigeria Before the Nineteenth Century." *Canadian Social Science* vol. 9, no. 5, (2013):192–197. www.researchgate.net/publication/356666552_History_of_Trading_Currencies_in_the_Upper_Cross_River_Region_of_Nigeria_before_the_Nineteenth_Century. Last accessed October 10, 2024.

Edwin, Shirin. "Connecting Vocabularies: A Grammar of Histories, Politics, and Priorities in African and Islamic Feminisms." In *Privately Empowered: Expressing Feminism in Islam in Northern Nigerian Fiction*, 35–76. Northwestern University Press, 2016. www.jstor.org/stable/j.ctt22727xh.7. Last accessed October 10, 2024.

El Azhari, Taef. *Queens, Eunuchs and Concubines in Islamic History, 661–1257*. Edinburgh University Press, 2019.

Eraly, Abraham. *The Age of Wrath: A History of the Delhi Sultanate*. New York: Penguin/Viking, 2014.

Faruqui, Munis D. *The Princes of the Mughal Empire, 1504–1719*. Cambridge University Press, 2012.

Findly, Ellison B. "Jahāngīr's Vow of Non-Violence." *Journal of the American Oriental Society* 107, no. 2 (1987): 245–56. doi.org/10.2307/602833. Last accessed October 10, 2024.

--- *Nur Jahan: Empress of Mughal India*. New York: Oxford University Press, 1993.

French, Marilyn. *From Dawn to Eve: A History of Women, Volume 2: The Masculine Mystique*. City University of New York, 2008.

Gaitskill, Deborah. "Devout Domesticity? A Century of African Women's Christianity in South Africa." In *Readings in Gender in Africa* edited by Andrea Cornwall. Bloomington: Indiana University Press, 2005.

Garnett, Lucy M. J. "Famous Sultanas." *The Scottish Review* 34 (July and October 1899): 110–124.

Ghereghlou, Kioumars. "ESMAIL II," *Encyclopædia Iranica*, online edition, 2016 www.iranicaonline.org/articles/esmail-02. Last accessed on September 7, 2024.

Gholsorkhi, Shohreh. "Ismail II and Mirza Makhdum Sharifi: An Interlude in Safavid History." *International Journal of Middle East Studies* 26, no. 3 (1994): 477–88. www.jstor.org/stable/163700. Last accessed October 10, 2024.

--- "Pari Khan Khanum: A Masterful Safavid Princess." *Iranian Studies* 28, no. 3/4 (1995): 143–56. www.jstor.org/stable/4310940. Last accessed October 10, 2024.

Goodwin, Godfrey. *The Private World of Ottoman Women*. London: Saqi Essentials, 2006.

Gossip, Robert. *Turkey and Russia: Their Races, History, and Wars*. Vol 1. Edinburgh: Thomas C. Jack, Grange Publishing Works, 1878.

Granqvist, Hilma Natalia. *Marriage Conditions in a Palestinian Village*. New York: AMS Press, 1975.

Gronenborn, Detlef. "States and Trade in the Central Sahal." In *The Oxford Handbook of African Archaeology* edited by Peter Mitchell and Paul Lane, 845–858. Oxford University Press, 2013.

--- "Polities and Trade in Medieval Northern Nigeria." In *Caravans of Gold. Fragments in Time: Art, Culture, and Exchange Across Medieval Saharan Africa* edited by Kathleen Bickford Berzock, 161–171. Evanston, IL: Northwestern University, 2019.

Growse, F.S. *Mathura: A District Memoir*, 3rd ed. North-Western Provinces and Oudh Government Press, 1883.

Haag, Michael. *Guide to Egypt*. London: Travelaid, 1981.

Habibullah, A.B.M. "Sultanah Raziah." *The Indian Historical Quarterly*, vol. 16 (1940): 750–772.

--- *The Foundation of Muslim Rule in India*. 3rd rev. ed. Allahabad: Central Book Depot, 1976.

Hadi, Amirul. *Islam and State in Sumatra: A Study of Seventeenth-Century Aceh*. Leiden: Brill, 2004.

Haeri, Shahla. *The Unforgettable Queens of Islam: Succession, Authority, Gender*. Cambridge University Press, 2020.

Haig, Wolseley plan. and Burn, Richard ed. *The Cambridge History of India*. Vol. 4 The Mughal Period. Cambridge University, 1937.

Hain, Kathryn A. "Avenues to Social Mobility Available to Courtesans and Concubines." In *Concubines and Courtesans: Women and Slavery in Islamic History*, edited by Matthew S. Gordon and Kathryn A. Hain, 324–338. Oxford University Press, 2017.

Hallam, W.K.R. "The Bayajida Legend in Hausa Folklore." *The Journal of African History* 7, no. 1 (1966): 47–60. www.jstor.org/stable/179458. Last accessed October 10, 2024.

Halm, Heinz. *The Fatimids and Their Traditions of Learning*. London: I.B. Tauris, 1997.

Hassam, Sadru K. "The Socio-Economic Aspects of the Fatimid Caliphate," Simerg—Insights From Around the World. simerg.com/literary-readings/the-socio-economic-aspects-of-the-fatimid%C2%A0caliphate/. Last accessed October 10, 2024.

Hogben, S.J. and Kirk-Greene, A.H.M. *The Emirates of Northern Nigeria: A Preliminary Survey of their Historical Traditions*. London: Oxford University Press, 1966.

Holmes, Winifred. *She Was Queen of Egypt*. London: G. Bell & Sons Ltd., 1959.

Hourani, George. *Arab Seafaring in the Indian Ocean in Ancient and Early Medieval Times*. 3rd edition, revised and expanded by John Carswell. Princeton University Press, 1995.

Hucklebridge, Dane. *No Beast So Fierce: The Terrifying True Story of the Champawat Tiger, the Deadliest Animal in History*. New York: HarperCollins Publishers Limited, 2019.

Humphreys, R. Stephen. *From Saladin to the Mongols: The Ayyubids of Damascus, 1193–1260*. Albany: State University of New York Press, 1977.

Hussin, Mohamad and Kamal, Muhammad Hakim. "Translation of al-Quran into the Malay Language in the Malay World," IJISH (International Journal of Islamic Studies and Humanities) 4 no. 1 (April 2021): 32–50. media.neliti.com/media/publications/411642-translation-of-al-quran-into-malay-langu-3956e390.pdf. Last accessed October 10, 2024.

Ingrams, H. *The Yemen: Imams, Rulers and Revolutions*. London: John Murray, 1963.

Irwin, Robert. *The Middle East in the Middle Ages*. Carbondale and Edwardsville: Southern Illinois University Press, 1986.

Jackson, Peter. "Sultan Radiyya Bint Iltutmish." In *Women in the Medieval Islamic World* edited by Gavin R. G. Hambly, 181–197. New York: St. Martin's Press, 1999.

Jones, David E. *Women Warriors: A History*. Washington: Brassey's, 1997.

Kamaly, Hossain. *A History of Islam in 21 Women*. London: One World, 2019.

Kathirithamby-Wells, J. "Achehnese Control over West Sumatra up to the Treaty of Painan, 1663." *Journal of Southeast Asian History* 10, no. 3 (1969): 453–79. www.jstor.org/stable/27651721. Last accessed October 10, 2024.

Kennedy, Hugh. *When Baghdad Ruled the Muslim World: The Rise and Fall of Islam's Greatest Dynasty*. Boston: De Capo, 2005.

Khamakar News Agency, "A Morisco Appeal to the Ottoman Sultan," September 7, 2015. altahrir.wordpress.com/2015/09/07/a-morisco-appeal-to-the-ottoman-sultan/. Last accessed October 10, 2024.

Khan, Sher Banu A.L. "Men of Prowess and Women of Piety: A Case Study of Aceh Dar al-Salam in the Seventeenth Century." *Journal of Southeast Asian Studies* 44, no. 2 (2013): 204–25. www.jstor.org/stable/43863025. Last accessed October 10, 2024.

--- *Sovereign Women in a Muslim Kingdom: The Sultanahs of Aceh, 1641–1699.* Ithaca: Southeast Asia Program Publications, Columbia University Press, 2017.

Kharroub, Tamara. "Five things you need to know about women in Islam: Implications for advancing women's rights in the Middle East." Arab Center Washington DC. October 4, 2015. arabcenterdc.org/resource/five-things-you-need-to-know-about-women-in-islam-implications-for-advancing-womens-rights-in-the-middle-east/#:~:text=While%20family%20law%20and%20personal,of%20the%20Qur'an%20dispute. Last accessed October 10, 2024.

Kheng, Cheah Boon. "Power Behind the Throne: The Role of Queens and Court Ladies in Malay History." *Journal of the Malaysian Branch of the Royal Asiatic Society* 66, no. 1 (264) (1993): 1–21. www.jstor.org/stable/41486187. Last accessed October 10, 2024.

Kimber, Richard. "The Succession to the Caliph Mūsā Al-Hādī." *Journal of the American Oriental Society* 121, no. 3 (2001): 428–48. doi.org/10.2307/606671. Last accessed October 10, 2024.

Kinni, Fongot Kini-Yen. *Pan-Africanism: Political Philosophy and Socio-Economic Anthropology for African Liberation and Governance: Caribbean and African American Contributions.* Langaa RPCIG, 2015.

King, Laura. "Lviv was once a safe haven for Ukrainians fleeing the war. Now it's suffering too." Los Angeles Times, November 26, 2022, www.latimes.com/world-nation/story/2022-11-26/ukraine-lviv-refugees-face-hardships-russian-attacks. Last accessed October 10, 2024.

Kozlowski, Gregory C. "Private Lives and Public Piety: Women and the Practice of Islam in Mughal India." In *Women in the Medieval Islamic World* edited by Gavin R. G. Hambly, 469–488. New York: St. Martin's Press, 1999.

Kroef, Justus M. van der. "Rice Legends of Indonesia." *The Journal of American Folklore* 65, no. 255 (1952): 49–55. doi.org/10.2307/536286. Last accessed October 10, 2024.

Ladner, Joyce A. "Racism and Tradition: Black Womanhood in Historical Perspective." In *Liberating Women's History: Theoretical and Critical Essays* edited by Berenice A. Carroll, 179–193. Urbana: University of Illinois Press, 1976.

La Verrone, Chantal de. "Sidda El-Horra, La Noble Dame." In *Hesperis*, Annee 1956, Tome XLIII. 221–225.

Lal, K.S. *The Mughal Harem.* New Delhi: Aditya Prakashan, 1988.

Lal, Ruby. *Empress: The Astonishing Reign of Nur Jahan.* New York: W.W. Norton, 2018.

Lamb, Harold. *Suleiman the Magnificent: Sultan of the East.* Garden City, NY: Doubleday, 1951.

Lamb, Malcom J. "THE HAUSA TANNERS OF NORTHERN NIGERIA and the production of Sokoto tanned oatskins." harmatan.co.uk/about/Hausa%20Tanners.pdf. Last accessed October 10, 2024.

Lane-Poole, Stanley. *The Barbary Corsairs.* 4th ed. London: T. Fisher Unwin, 1890.

Lange, Dierk. *Ancient Kingdoms of West Africa: African-centred and Canaanite-Israelite Perspectives.* Germany: J.H. Röll, Dettelbach, 2004.

Lapidus, Ira. *A History of Islamic Societies.* 2nd ed. Cambridge University Press, 2002.

Lebbady, Hasna. *Feminist Traditions in Andalusi-Moroccan Oral Narratives.* New York: Palgrave Macmillan, 2009.

Lebbady, Hasna, and اللبادي حسناء. "Women in Northern Morocco: Between the Documentary and the Imaginary / النساء في شمال المغرب: بين التسجيلي والتخييلي." *Alif: Journal of Comparative Poetics*, no. 32 (2012): 127–50. www.jstor.org/stable/41850741. Last accessed October 10, 2024.

Levanoni, Amalia. "Shajar al-Durr: A Case of Female Sultanate in Medieval Islam." In *Egypt and Syria in the Fatimid, Ayyubid and Mamluk Eras*. U. Vermeulen and J. Van Steenbergen editors. Proceedings of the 6th, 7th and 8th International Colloquium organized at the Katholieke Universiteit Leuven in May 1997, 1998 and 1999. Uitgeverij Peeters Leuven 2001.

Lone, Mahlia. "Suleyman The Magnificent & Hurrem Sultan." Good Times (August 16, 2017). www.goodtimes.com.pk/2017/08/16/suleyman-the-magnificent-hurrem-sultan-2/. Last accessed October 10, 2024.

Lourie, Elena. "Black Women Warriors in The Muslim Army Besieging Valencia and The Cid's Victory: A Problem of Interpretation." *Traditio* 55 (2000): 181–209. www.jstor.org/stable/27831993. Last accessed October 10, 2024.

Lovejoy, Paul E. "The Role of the Wangara in the Economic Transformation of the Central Sudan in the Fifteenth and Sixteenth Centuries." *The Journal of African History* 19, no. 2 (1978): 173–93. www.jstor.org/stable/181597.

--- "Kola in the History of West Africa (La Kola Dans l'histoire de l'Afrique Occidentale)." *Cahiers d'Études Africaines* 20, no. 77/78 (1980): 97–134. www.jstor.org/stable/4391682. Last accessed October 10, 2024.

Maalouf, Amin. *The Crusades Through Arab Eyes*. Translated by Jon Rothschild. New York: Schoken Books, 1984.

Mackintosh Smith, Tim. *Yemen: Travels in Dictionary Land*. Woodstock, NY: The Overlook Press, 1999.

Mahamadou, Abba Gana Wakil. "Bayajidda Hausa Historical Legend or Myth." CSAN, January 10, 2020, www.csan-niger.com/bayajidda-hausa-historical-legend-myth-or-reality.php#Abba_Gana_Wakil_Mahamadou. Last accessed October 10, 2024.

Mahmood, Zainah. "Mongol Illustrated Manuscripts: The Jami al 'Tawarikh and the Shahnama," Asia Society. asiasociety.org/mongol-illustrated-manuscripts. Last accessed on September 7, 2024.

Mansel, Philip. *Constantinople: City of World's Desire 1453–1924*. New York: St. Martin's Press, 2006.

Margariti, Roxani Eleni. *Aden and the Indian Ocean Trade: 150 Years in the Life of a Medieval Arabian Port*. Chapel Hill: University of North Carolina Press, 2007.

Mark, Joshua J. "Women in Ancient Persia." World History Encyclopedia. January 30, 2020. www.worldhistory.org/article/1492/women-in-ancient-persia/. Last accessed October 10, 2024.

Marozzi, Justin. *Baghdad: City of Peace, City of Blood–A History in Thirteen Centuries*. Boston: De Capo Press, 2014.

Manzoor, Asma et al. "Economic and Political Leadership Role of Muslim Women in Global Context." *Journal of Positive School Psychology*, 2023, Vol. 7, No. 6, 1217–1226.

Mayor, Adrienne. *The Amazons: Lives and Legends of Warrior Women across the Ancient World*. Princeton University Press, 2014.

Menges, Karl Heinrich. "The Oriental Elements in the Vocabulary of the Oldest Russian Epos, The Igor' Tale." *Word: The Journal of the Linguistic Circle of New York*. Vol. 7, December 1951: 1–79.

Mernissi, Fatima. *The Forgotten Queens of Islam*. Translated by Mary Jo Lakeland. Minneapolis: University of Minnesota Press, 1993.

Miller, Barnette. *Beyond the Sublime Porte: The Grand Seraglio of Stanbul*. Yale University Press, 1931.

Mirza, Priya. "The remarkable Begums who defied patriarchal norms to rule Bhopal for more than a century." PRISM, June 3, 2019, www.dawn.com/news/1486294/the-remarkable-begums-who-defied-patriarchal-norms-to-rule-bhopal-for-more-than-a-century. Last accessed October 10, 2024.

Mithani, Jasmine. "Why the 2022 election was historic for Muslim women's representation." The 19th. December 12, 2022, 19thnews.org/2022/12/muslim-women-made-history-midterm-elections/. Last accessed October 10, 2024.

Mohammad, Sabah. "Baghdad and the Silk Road: A study on the commercial function of Baghdad in the middle ages." UNESCO. en.unesco.org/silkroad/sites/default/files/knowledge-bank-article/baghdad_and_silk_route.pdf. Last accessed September 3, 2024.

Mourtada-Sabbah, Nada, and Adrian Gully. "'I Am, by God, Fit for High Positions': On the Political Role of Women in al-Andalus." *British Journal of Middle Eastern Studies* 30, no. 2 (2003): 183–209. www.jstor.org/stable/3593222. Last accessed October 10, 2024.

Musingafi, Tsitsi Mhike. "The Matriarchs of Africa." In *Women Empowerment and the Feminist Agenda in Africa,* edited by Maxwell Constantine Chando Musingafi and Chipo Hungwe, 58–75. IGI Global, 2023.

Nanji, Azim. "Ismaili Philosophy." In *The Internet Encyclopedia of Philosophy*. iep.utm.edu/ismaili/. Last accessed on September 4, 2024.

Nasr, Jamil M. Abun. *A History of the Maghrib in the Islamic Period.* Cambridge University Press, 1993.

Nath, Renuka. *Notable Mughal and Hindu Women*. New Delhi: Inter-India, 1990.

Necipoglu, Gulru. *Architecture, Ceremonial, and Power: The Topkapi Palace in the Fifteenth and Sixteenth Centuries*. Cambridge, MA: MIT Press, 1991.

Newman, Andrew J. *Twelver Shiism: Unity and Diversity in the Life of Islam, 632 to 1722*. University of Edinburgh Press, 2013.

Ninan, Samyukta. "Mughal Emperors and the Imperial Hunt." Peepul Tree Stories. May 27, 2021. www.peepultree.world/livehistoryindia/story/people/mughal-hunt. Last accessed October 10, 2024.

Nizami, K.A. "The Early Turkish Sultans of Delhi." In *A Comprehensive History of India*. Edited by Mohammad Habib and Khaliq Ahmad Nazami. 12 vols., vol. 5, 191–208. Delhi: People's Publishing House, 1970.

Noor, Rosalind "Tāj al-salāṭīn: An Instruction Manual for Kings," Medium, December 5, 2021, rosalindnoor.medium.com/t%C4%81j-al-sal%C4%81%E1%B9%AD%C4%ABn-an-instruction-manual-for-kings-670a299cd431. Last accessed October 10, 2024.

O'Connell, John. *The Book of Spice: From Anise to Zedoary*. New York: Pegasus Books, 2016.

Onwuka, Samuel Aja Brown. "Evolution Of Maga'ajiya In Military Barracks Of Nigeria." Available online at www.academia.edu/50818515/ARTICLE_WRITTEN_BY_SAMUEL_AJA_BROWN_ONWUKA_EVOLUTION_OF_MAGAAJIYA_IN_MILITARY_BARRACKS_OF_NIGERIA. Last accessed October 10, 2024.

Osmani, Noor Mohammad; Farooq, Mohmmad Omar; and Ahmad, Abu Umar Faruq. "Women Empowerment and Leadership in Islam between Myth and Reality." In *Economic Empowerment of Women in the Islamic World: Theory and Practice* edited by Toseef Azid and Jennifer Ward-Batts, 39–70. London: World Scientific, 2020.

Pant, Chandra. *Nur Jahan and Her Family*. Allahabad: Dan Dewal, 1978.

Peters, F.E. *Mecca: A Literary History of the Muslim Holy Land.* Princeton University Press, 1994.

Pierce, Leslie. *The Imperial Harem: Women and Sovereignty in the Ottoman Empire*. New York: Oxford University Press, 1993.

--- *Empress of the East: How a European Slave Girl Became Queen of the Ottoman Empire*. New York: Basic Books, 2017.

Prasad, Ishwari. *A Short History of Muslim Rule in India*. Rev. ed. Allahabad: The Indian Press, 1965.

Presnel, Anna. "Political Women: A Double Standard." UAB Institute for Human Rights Blog. (January 21, 2021). sites.uab.edu/humanrights/2021/01/21/political-women-a-double-standard/. Last accessed October 10, 2024.

Price, Anne M. "Colonial History, Muslim Presence, and Gender Equity Ideology: A Cross-National Analysis." *International Journal of Sociology* 38, no. 1 (2008): 81–103. www.jstor.org/stable/20628320. Last accessed October 10, 2024.

Reid, Anthony. "Trade and the Problem of Royal Power in Aceh c. 1550–1700." In *Pre-Colonial State Systems in Southeast Asia* edited by Anthony Reid and Lance Castles. Kuala Lumpur: MBRAS, 1979.

--- "Female Roles in Pre-Colonial Southeast Asia." *Modern Asian Studies* 22, no. 3 (1988): 629–45. www.jstor.org/stable/312601. Last accessed October 10, 2024.

Rizvi, Kishwar. "Gendered Patronage: Women and Benevolence During the Early Safavid Empire." In *Women, Patronage, and Self-Representation in Islamic Societies*, edited by D. Fairchild Ruggles, 123–154. Albany: State University of New York Press, 2000.

Rodenbeck, Max. *Cairo: The City Victorious*. New York: Knopf, 1999.

Sattin, Anthony. *Nomads: The Wanderers Who Shaped Our World*. New York: W.W. Norton, 2022.

Schregle, Gotz. *Die Sultanin von Ägypten:Šağarat ad-Durr in der arabischen Geschichtsschreibung und Literatur*. Wiesbaden: Otto Harrassowitz, 1961.

Salas-Betsch, Isabela & Kelly, Kate. "What Comes Next for the Equal Rights Amendment?" The Center for American Progress (CAP20). August 26, 2024 www.americanprogress.org/article/what-comes-next-for-the-equal-rights-amendment/. Last accessed October 10, 2024.

Sentema, Sake. "History and Importance of Rice in Indonesia." NOW! Jakarta. March 11, 2024. www.nowjakarta.co.id/history-and-importance-of-rice-in-indonesia/. Last accessed October 10, 2024.

Setton, Kenneth M. ed. *A History of the Crusades*, vol. 2, Madison: University of Wisconsin Press, 1969.

Sharma, L. P. *History of Medieval India (1000–1740 A.D.)*. 3rd edition. Delhi: Konark Publishers, 1997.

Sharman, J. C. *Empires of the Weak: The Real Story of European Expansion and the Creation of the New World Order*. Princeton University Press, 2020.

Sharma, Sudha. *The Status of Muslim Women in Medieval India*. Los Angeles: Sage Publications, 2016.

Shujauddin, Mohammad Shujauddin, Razia. *The Life and Times of Noor Jahan*. Lahore: The Caravan Book House, 1967.

Smith, Abdullahi. "Some notes on the history of Zazzau under the Hausa kings." In *Zaria and its Region: A Nigerian Savanna City and its Environs* edited by M.J. Mortimore, 82–101. Zaria: Ahmadu Bello University Department of Geography Occasional Publication no. 4, 1970.

Smith, David G.; Rosenstein, Judith E.; and Nikolov, Margaret C. "The Different Words We Use to Describe Male and Female Leaders." Harvard Business Review. (May 25, 2018). hbr.org/2018/05/the-different-words-we-use-to-describe-male-and-female-leaders. Last accessed October 10, 2024.

Smith, G.R. "Sulyahids." In *The Encyclopedia of Islam*, New Edition. Edited by C.E. Bosworth et.al. Vol. 9, 815–817. Leiden: Brill, 1997.

Soudavar, Abolala. "The Age of Muhammadi." *Muqarnas* 17 (2000): 53–72. doi.org/10.2307/1523290. Last accessed October 10, 2024.

Staffa, Susan Jane. "Dimensions of Women's Power in Historic Cairo." In *Islamic and Middle Eastern Societies*. Robert Olson, ed. Brattleboro, VT: Amana Books, 1987.

Stern, S. M. "The Succession to the Fatimid Imam Al-Āmir, the Claims of the Later Fatimids to the Imamate, and the Rise of Ṭayyibī Ismailism." *Oriens* 4, no. 2 (1951): 193–255. doi.org/10.2307/1579511. Last accessed October 10, 2024.

Stewart, Desmond. *Cairo: 5500 Years*. New York: Thomas Y. Crowell Company, 1968.

Stookey, Robert W. *Yemen: The Politics of the Yemen Arab Republic*. Boulder, Colorado: Westview Press, 1978.

Sudarkasa, Niara "The 'Status of Women' in Indigenous African Societies." In *Readings in Gender in Africa* edited by Andrea Cornwall, 25–31. Bloomington: Indiana University Press, 2005.

Sufi, Drs. Rusdi "Laksamana Keumalahayati." In *Wanita utama Nusantara Dalam Lintasan Sejarah = Prominent Women in the Glimpse of History*, edited by Ismail Sofyan; M. Hasan Basry; and T. Ibrahim Alfian. Jakarta: Jayakarta Agung Offset, printer.

Szuppe, Maria. "Status, Knowledge, and Politics: Women in Sixteenth-Century Safavid Iran." In *Women in Iran from the Rise of Islam*, edited by Guity Nashat and Lois Beck, 140–169. Urbana: University of Illinois Press, 2003.

Tahir, Beenish; Asghar, Muhammad; and Jawad, Sumera. "From Babar to Aurangzib: A Historical Review of Mughal's Textile Tent Tradition." *International Review of Social Sciences* Volume 9 Issue 1 (January 2021): 80–93.

Thorau, Peter. *The Lion of Egypt: Sultan Baybars I and the Near East in the Thirteenth Century*. Translated by P.M. Holt. London: Longman, 1992.

Traboulsi, Samer. "The Queen Was Actually a Man: Arwā Bint Aḥmad and the Politics of Religion." *Arabica* 50, no. 1 (2003): 96–108. www.jstor.org/stable/4057749. Last accessed October 10, 2024.

Villiers, John. "Aceh, Melaka and the 'Hystoria Dos Cerços de Malaca' of Jorge de Lemos." *Portuguese Studies* 17 (2001): 75–85. www.jstor.org/stable/41105160. Last accessed October 10, 2024.

Vinograd, Cassandra and Kim,Victoria. "Russia Targets Kyiv and Lviv With Attack Drones." The New York Times, June 20, 2023. www.nytimes.com/2023/06/20/world/europe/russia-drones-kyiv-lviv-ukraine-war.html. Last accessed October 10, 2024.

Walther, Wiebke. *Women in Islam*. Princeton: Markus Wiener Publishing, 1993.

Yermolenko, Galina. "Roxolana: 'The Greatest Empresse of the East.'" *The Muslim World* 95 (April 2005). 231–248.

--- ed. *Roxolana in European Literature, History and Culture*. Farnham: Ashgate, 2010.

Zakaria, Rafiq. *Razia: Queen of India*. Oxford University Press, 1999.

Index

Index